D1083122

AMERICAN
LEGAL
INJUSTICE

AMERICAN LEGAL INJUSTICE

BEHIND THE SCENES WITH AN EXPERT WITNESS

Emanuel Tanay, MD

Foreword by
Robert I. Simon, MD

JASON ARONSON
Lanham • Boulder • New York • Toronto • Plymouth, UK

Published by Jason Aronson
An imprint of Rowman & Littlefield Publishers, Inc.
A wholly owned subsidary of The Rowman & Littlefield Publishing Group, Inc.
4501 Forbes Boulevard, Suite 200, Lanham, Maryland 20706
http://www.rowmanlittlefield.com

Estover Road, Plymouth PL6 7PY, United Kingdom

British Library Cataloguing in Publication Information Available

Library of Congress Cataloging-in-Publication Data

Tanay, Emanuel.
  American legal injustice : behind the scenes with an expert witness /
Emanuel Tanay ; foreword by Robert I. Simon.
     p. cm.
  Includes bibliographical references and index.
  ISBN 978-0-7657-0775-8 (cloth : alk. paper) — ISBN 978-0-7657-0777-2
(electronic)
  1. Criminal justice, Administration of--United States. 2. Forensic
psychiatry—United States. 3. Forensic psychiatrists—United States. I. Title.
  KF9223.T36 2010
  345.73'05—dc22
                                                            2010010073

∞™ The paper used in this publication meets the minimum requirements of
American National Standard for Information Sciences—Permanence of Paper
for Printed Library Materials, ANSI/NISO Z39.48-1992.

Printed in the United States of America

CONTENTS

FOREWORD

I feel like the midwife to Dr. Tanay's book. I was assisted by his lovely wife, Sandra, and others who encouraged Dr. Tanay to write this magnificent book. It is true that I importuned Dr. Tanay to write about his extensive experience as a forensic psychiatrist. He has testified in many notorious cases, including those of Jack Ruby, Sam Sheppard, and Theodore "Ted" Bundy. I also unabashedly resorted to employing guilt and appealing to his sense of duty to share the immense knowledge and perspective of forensic psychiatry, accrued over fifty years.

I have known Dr. Tanay (Emek to his friends) for more than twenty-five years as both a friend and esteemed colleague. I know of no other psychiatrist or forensic psychiatrist who possesses Dr. Tanay's depth and scope of knowledge and experience in psychiatry and the law.

Dr. Tanay has a highly individual, distinct style of testifying. At his presentations on the role of the forensic psychiatric expert, given at the American Academy of Psychiatry and Law, I have admonished attendees that, while the content of Dr. Tanay's presentations is extraordinarily informative, his style of testimony is entirely unique. There is only one Dr. Tanay. He can only be imitated at ones' peril. Dr. Tanay will not shrink from confrontation or suffer any shenanigans from opposing counsel. He is a strong advocate for his expert opinion; otherwise he would not be in court. An adage of Dr. Tanay's is often quoted by forensic colleagues: "I may be wrong but I am not in doubt." Psychiatrists and forensic psychiatrists are taught that engaging opposing counsel in an assertive or aggressive manner will diminish their credibility. Not so with Dr. Tanay, whose testimonial style has proven riveting and highly credible to judges and juries alike.

Dr. Tanay's aphorisms are classic. For example, "One has no friends when going to court." This statement is true on many levels. It resonates with my experience that being an expert witness can be quite lonely and anxiety provoking. When I shared these feelings with an attorney acquaintance, he responded, "Don't worry, you are only a spoke on the wheel or hood ornament on the litigation vehicle that the attorney drives into court." While this has proven helpful in reducing my unease, I am sure Dr. Tanay would strongly disagree with this advice. He would likely say, "You are the engine."

I recall another aphorism: "You can't be paranoid enough in litigation." Dr. Tanay does not mean clinical paranoia but rather vigilance. One learns through hard-won experience that litigation is a foreign landscape, full of traps and unexpected twists and turns for the unwary. As experts soon learn, there is an imperfect fit between psychiatry and the law.

Dr. Tanay emphasizes that the direct examination in court is the most important part of expert testimony. The expert must be able to give a coherent, reasonably complete, convincing presentation of his or her opinion to the judge or jury. In contrast, Dr. Tanay considers the cross-examination to be much easier to handle. This is contrary to the belief of fledgling forensic experts, who fret about the cross-examination.

As the reader will discover, true to form, Dr. Tanay holds strong opinions on the legal fictions that confront psychiatrists. For example, at depositions, the expert is often asked about how much time he or she spends treating patients versus acting as a forensic expert. Dr. Tanay emphatically insists that forensic psychiatry is clinical psychiatry. This false dichotomy between forensic and clinical psychiatry is used by opposing counsel to attack the credibility of the psychiatric expert who sees few or no patients. The same professional skills and knowledge that the psychiatrist possesses can be applied to a variety of clinical and forensic roles.

Dr. Tanay is a superb strategist. Lawyers frequently seek his opinions about tactics and strategy. Even so, Dr. Tanay is first and foremost a caring physician. This quality is clearly present in all his forensic cases and especially visible in the discussion of the Andrea Yates case.

Dr. Tanay is passionate about the injustice of justice. He does not shy away from expressing his thoughts and feelings about controversial issues. The law can be a cruel and blunt instrument when dealing with the mentally ill. Readers may strongly agree or disagree with Dr. Tanay's views, but they will be richly rewarded in encountering the heart and the mind of a great forensic psychiatrist.

Robert I. Simon, M.D.,
Clinical Professor of Psychiatry
and Director of the Program in Psychiatry and Law
at Georgetown University School of Medicine
and former President of the
American Academy of Psychiatry and the Law

PREFACE

"True patriotism hates injustice in its own land more than anywhere else."

—Clarence Darrow

I have been a forensic psychiatrist for almost fifty years, working against injustice within the American system of justice. Being a forensic psychiatrist has been more than an occupation, more than a profession; it has been a calling for me. Fighting injustice is rooted in my life history, and giving testimony in hundreds of cases fulfilled my need to do meaningful work. My goal in writing this book is not only to share my experiences but to demonstrate the ways in which our legal system is rife with injustice.

Many of the cases I describe in this book sound like fiction, but they did happen—often to ordinary, law-abiding citizens. Similarly, the incompetence, deception, and misguided zeal of the prosecutors, police officers, and judges whose behavior I describe in these pages may also strike you as astonishing, yet such behavior is far from rare in the politicized American legal system. In fifty years of experience with the system, I have taken part in thousands of criminal and civil cases. It took two trucks to transport my case files and notes dealing with countless forensic cases to the Wayne State University Archives.

The average American sees the nation's justice system as an efficient and benevolent social institution. However it is a sad fact that innocent people are often accused, convicted, and incarcerated, allowing the real perpetrators of the crime to remain free. It is also troubling that people who do commit crimes often have their offenses mischaracterized, their motives misapprehended, and their pathologies undiagnosed or misdiagnosed, resulting in unnecessarily harsh, lengthy sentences or death verdicts. Most Americans have images of the justice system based upon news media stories that pander to common prejudices. Lawyer bashing is highly popular. Trial lawyers are blamed for everything from the high cost of medical care to the rising crime rate. I believe that lawyers and the law made America the great country that it is. Alexis de Tocqueville had this to say about lawyers: "Lawyers form a society of minds. They are less afraid of tyranny than of arbitrary power. They have authority over the government and derive authority from the government. Lawyers are the American aristocracy. Lawyers and judges are interpreters of the law. When the American people are intoxicated by passion, or carried away by the impetuosity of its ideas, it is checked and stopped by the almost invisible influence of its legal counselors."[1]

An expert witness is not only an observer of a real-life drama but also a participant. He or she deals not only with the past but also the future. The homicide, the life-endangering mishap, took place in the past; however, the verdict will take place in the future and will be just or unjust. A trial is not like a television play or a novel—it has an impact on living human beings.

A professional qualifies to be an expert witness if he or she has the requisite knowledge of the subject matter in dispute. A forensic expert has the technical knowledge, understanding of legal issues, and testimonial skills. Testimony is one of the primary functions of a forensic expert witness. Yet forensic experts have limited testimonial skills since they receive no formal training in the craft of testimony.

This book demonstrates the significance of expert testimony in the prevention of injustice and the importance of testimonial skills. However, most lawyers choose experts based upon credentials. Lawyers are suspicious of experts who devote a great deal of time to testifying. It is absurd to belittle a practitioner who frequently performs one of the functions of his profession. Realistically, the opposite should be the case, since proficiency is acquired by practice.

Let me repeat: most professionals have adequate knowledge to serve as experts, but few have the ability to give effective testimony. At times, style of presentation prevails against merit. This is, however, not an argument against persuasive expert testimony. According to Aristotle, rhetoric is a tool that can serve a good or bad purpose. He defined rhetoric as "the art of discovering the available means of persuasion in a given case." The style of testimony, more than any other factor, determines the impact which the expert makes upon the jury.

NOTE

1. Alexis de Tocqueville, *Democracy in America,* ed. Isaac Kramnick and Gerald Bevan (New York: Penguin, 2003).

ACKNOWLEDGMENTS

Robert Simon, MD, and John Chambers, JD, have encouraged me to write this book. Bob, a fellow forensic psychiatrist and author of many books on forensic psychiatry, has for years insisted that it is my duty as one of the most experienced forensic psychiatrists to tell other experts the "secrets" of my success as an expert witness. John, an outstanding trial lawyer, whom I first met as my cross-examiner and with whom I worked on many cases, urged me to write a book that would help lawyers to deal with experts. I am grateful to both of them.

My wife, Sandra, played a significant role by creating an environment in which I could work and consistently encouraged me to continue the project. She remembers my cases in great detail and has contributed valuable suggestions. My daughter Elaine spent many hours with me in a review of the final product. Eileen Pollack, professor at University of Michigan, helped me to revise the introduction, as did my daughter Anita. Katie Wilson, Jennifer Michaels, and Christine Carroll helped as editorial assistants. Tracey Payne and Nicole Root did most of the typing. David Karczynski contributed editorial assistance. My son-in-law, Steve Hersh, an advertising executive, made some valuable recommendations. Tom Gutheil, MD, professor of psychiatry at Harvard Medical School, made useful suggestions. This book would not have been possible without a great many lawyers who have worked with me and lawyers who have worked against me on countless cases. I am particularly grateful to Julie E. Kirsch, the editorial director of Jason Aronson, a division of Rowman & Littlefield Publishers, Inc., whose advice and careful review of the manuscript has been invaluable to me. She devoted countless hours to this project.

INTRODUCTION

Once, at a cocktail party, a lawyer's wife asked me what a forensic psychiatrist does. Before I could answer, her husband self-righteously replied that forensic psychiatrists are called upon to testify in cases of insanity defense and the effects of psychic trauma. I challenged the lawyer to name a single field of law in which I hadn't testified. He thought for a while and with a triumphant smile asked, "How about zoning?" When I cited zoning cases in which my testimony had been critical (in one, the plaintiffs charged the owners of a golf course bordering their property with causing them emotional distress by converting the golf course into a shopping center), he conceded that yes, I had testified in cases from A (airline disasters) to Z (zoning).

Lawyers often tell me that they remember my testimony "because without you we could have never gotten the verdict." Naturally, I am pleased when my testimony leads to a favorable outcome for the side I have supported, but this is not always the case. The following letter shows the impact a forensic psychiatrist can make even on cases that did not turn out favorably for the side he supported. It was written by Commander William Pawlyk, who was convicted of two homicides. Pawlyk served for five years aboard the nuclear submarine the *James K. Polk* and had commanded Submarine Group 9 at Bangor. At the time of the homicides, he was the head of a reserve unit in Portland, Oregon. Pawlyk was sentenced to life in prison in spite of my testimony that he was not criminally responsible for the two homicides that he committed. I received the following letter from him after the trial:

June 30, 1991
Dr. Emmanuel Tenay[sic],

Thank you sir, and bless you for your sterling efforts on my behalf. It's true that you are an "expert" witness, but this is especially so because you bring together very humane qualities, with medical-psychiatric expertise, and courtroom experience.

Many of the things you said I found disturbing and difficult to hear, but I recognize their validity. You answered many questions for me, and gave me much food for thought and analysis.

I realize the impracticality of further one-on-one analysis because of distance, access problems, and cost, but I offer my case for any use you see fit—in any way you desire. If you have need of more information that I can help provide in your future work please feel free to ask. That is the least I can do to show you my appreciation and gratitude.

I was amazed by your mastery of my case; in sharp contrast to the superficial, almost unprofessional basis used by Doctors Harris and Dunnet [the prosecution's experts]. With their strong, almost exclusive reliance on DSM-III criteria, neither one directly and rigorously pursued examining me for those indications. They based their opinions on "lack of evidence" which they sought indirectly and shallowly at best.

Their version of professionalism served only to elevate yours even more. There are very frightening aspects and consequences for others, if their approach is widespread. Indeed it's frightening that it exists at all where people's lives and treatment is at stake. . . . Yours is the most human and humane of the sciences. And you have shown me that you are among the most human and humane of its practitioners, as well as among the most knowledgeable and insightful. Again my most grateful thanks for your help at a time of utter desperation. No matter that the final legal outcome, you made possible the more important internal verdict within me. Thank you.

I have been a psychiatric expert witness in the trials of some famous defendants like Jack Ruby, Sam Sheppard, and Theodore Bundy; I was retained in the malpractice case against the psychiatrist who treated John Hinckley, Jr. Several of these high-profile cases are discussed in detail in the pages that follow. No less revealing, however, are the cases of defendants and plaintiffs whose names are not well known, such as Sterling Spann, an innocent man who spent years on death row whose case I describe later.

The story of how I became a psychiatrist and a full-time forensic expert is a long one, but I'll give you the short version here. My experiences as a Holocaust survivor from Poland implanted in me a commitment to the principles of justice. After the war I earned a medical degree from the University of Munich, and I later completed my psychiatric training in America. In 1958, I became an associate director of Detroit Receiving City Hospital Department of Psychiatry, which also served then as the hospital for the Wayne State University Medical School. I joined the faculty of Wayne State University as an assistant professor in the Department of Psychiatry and became clinical professor some years later.

I testified for the first time as a forensic expert in 1954 on behalf of Alice, a fourteen-year-old schizophrenic girl who was my patient at Elgin State Hospital in Illinois. Alice had drowned a four-year-old child and was charged with first-degree murder. Her homicidal behavior was an act of automatism that bypassed rational reasoning,[1] yet Alice was charged with first-degree murder. Her pro bono lawyer had to rely on the testimony of a psychiatric resident whose command of English at that time was rudimentary and who had no courtroom experience.

I studied the legal and forensic literature and wrote an extensive report in which I argued that this was a case of insanity. My report was admitted into evidence despite the prosecutor's objections, and to the surprise of all, my testimony led to the rare result of the judge directing the jury to find the defendant legally insane. One by one, other lawyers asked me to testify for their clients. A turning point in my career came when the attorneys defending Jack Ruby requested that I examine their client prior to his retrial for the murder of Lee Harvey Oswald (after Ruby had been sentenced to death following his conviction for Oswald's murder in March 1964).

I testified in nearly every state of the Union, from remote regions of Alaska to the courtrooms of Manhattan, including military court in Vietnam. In 1981 I testified in San Francisco in the trial of Rev. Jim Jones's disciple Larry Layton for killing Representative Leo Ryan in Guyana. By 1980, my travels had become so disruptive that I gave up a successful and rewarding practice in psychoanalytic therapy and became a full-time forensic psychiatrist, though I continued to teach psychiatry.

I have testified in hundreds of different trials. In addition to criminal trials, I have been called on as an expert witness in countless personal injury lawsuits and legal and medical malpractice cases. I testified on behalf of a professional hockey player whose brain injury, sustained when another player clobbered him with a stick, was the result of a tendency by the team's management to encourage violence among its players. I also testified on behalf of a University of Michigan football player who charged the university with negligence in allowing him to graduate without the education that might have allowed him to get a job and function in society. I have testified in various federal courts and a number of military courts as well. I was the expert witness in the case of the marine Robert Garwood who was in Vietcong captivity for fourteen years and upon release was charged with being a deserter and collaborator.

As my time in the courtroom increased, I quickly realized several things that the average citizen may find surprising (I certainly did). For one, I learned that a person who is a suspect in a crime will most likely become a defendant and that once he or she is a defendant the chances of being convicted of a major crime are high; in fact, I found that the bigger the crime, the greater the likelihood that the defendant will be convicted, even if innocent. The implications of this are chilling. Criminal justice scholars often say that the true number of innocent people convicted of crimes is unknown—in fact, unknowable—but a new University of Michigan study challenges that belief in one context, the death penalty. Among defendants sentenced to death in the United States since 1973, at least 2.3 percent of them—and possibly more—were falsely convicted, said University of Michigan law professor Samuel Gross in a study coauthored by Barbara O'Brien, a professor at Michigan State University College of Law.[2]

I quickly realized that "innocent until proven guilty" is a legal fiction; the reality is that a defendant is guilty unless proven innocent. Every law student is taught that a presumption of innocence relieves defendants of the need to prove their innocence, but a lawyer who relies on this noble principle is committing legal malpractice. The convergence of many factors makes it likely that a defendant, unless proven innocent, will be convicted. Time and again I have encountered cases where people were found guilty of murder in spite of overwhelming evidence that they were innocent. Many prosecutors tend to be overly zealous in turning suspects into defendants, especially in homicide cases. America is the only country where prosecutors and judges are elected. They live and die by publicity. Prosecutors know little if anything about the psychology of homicide, and they file criminal charges even though the evidence presented by the police is inconclusive. Eyewitness testimony has led to many convictions of innocent people. Quite often there is no malice involved; the eyewitness truly believes he or she has identified the perpetrator. Donald Thompson, an Australian forensic expert, was on a television show in which he discussed the unreliability of eyewitness testimony. In her book on memory Sue Halpern writes, "Not long afterward [Thompson] was summoned to a police precinct, put in a line-up, and identified by a woman as the man who had raped her. Though he had an incontrovertible alibi—he was on national television at the time of the attack and seen by hundreds of thousands of viewers—he was charged with the crime on the basis of her unwavering eye witness testimony." It was later discovered that during the assault the woman's television was on and she confused the face of Thompson with that of her rapist.[3]

Other injustices are the result not of legal principles and procedures but due to the relative skills of lawyers and expert witnesses. Obviously, some lawyers are smarter, more experienced, more eloquent, and more astute than others. Just as obviously, a defendant's ability to hire a lawyer with the strongest qualifications depends on his or her ability to pay that lawyer's fees. Less obviously, but just as significantly, the skills and knowledge of an expert witness will influence the outcome of a trial.

In this book I detail just how expert testimony can best serve justice. Conversely, I will examine several instances where poor performance by an expert witness resulted in injustice.

Many students and friends find it hard to believe my contention that innocent people are frequently charged with committing brutal rapes and gruesome murders, that eyewitness identification is unreliable, and that a basic ignorance of the psychology of homicide on the part of police officers, prosecutors, judges, jurors, and attorneys often results in wrongful convictions. But with so many falsely accused defendants now being exonerated because of DNA evidence, fewer people are doubting my claims. I recently entered "declared innocent" on Google and got 7,940,000 hits in less than a second. Obviously this covers the whole world and some of these hits are irrelevant to the issue at hand, but on further scrutiny I found accounts of countless wrongful convictions. When I entered "death row inmate declared innocent" I got 55,100 hits. The number of inmates on death rows across the nation is 3,309.

As a forensic psychiatrist, I have learned that trials always happen in two places at once—the courtroom and the living rooms of the defendant's home community—and that while one may be acquitted in a court of law, once accused one is always considered guilty in the court of public opinion. It has therefore become my practice to advise defendants acquitted of a crime, particularly murder, to leave town and change their name. Those who remain in their hometown will often sooner or later be arrested for some other reason, and they will be forever harassed; those who leave gain the possibility of a new life. A Kansas woman, Mrs. H., killed her husband and pled insanity; the insanity defense did not prevail but I succeed in helping her to get a commutation of the sentence after many years of imprisonment. Mrs. H. did not return to her hometown, where she was well known due to the prominence of her husband. She moved, instead, to another state, changed her name, and corresponded with me for thirty years until her death. I was the only person who knew who she was and where she lived. She became quite successful in the counseling profession and led a happy life. She died in her eighties.

The role of forensic psychiatry is especially significant in cases involving mentally ill defendants, yet experience has shown me that a major cause of injustice in our legal system is the prejudice against and misunderstanding of the insanity defense. The insanity defense still exists in theory, but as a practical matter it rarely succeeds, regardless of merit. Our legal system has been politicized to such an extent that the public, the news media, jurors, and judges tend to perceive the insanity defense as a ploy used by crafty lawyers to protect criminals. I gave up testifying in obvious cases of insanity because it was predictable that no matter how convincing the evidence, no matter how persuasive my testimony, the outcome would be a rejection of the insanity defense.

The reality is that most people with severe mental illnesses will eventually run afoul of the law if they live outside the protective environment of an institution. This is now the norm: in the past two or three decades, an unholy alliance of social liberals and fiscal conservatives has succeeded to eliminate most state mental hospitals. Even when mentally ill people are believed to have the potential to commit a crime, liberals and libertarians seek to protect them from being held in institutions against their will. With the abolition of the state hospital system, prisons are the default institutions for the care of the mentally ill.

The following is an example that literally gave me nightmares. One morning in February 2006, my wife came to the bathroom as I was shaving and said, "You must have had a rough night. You had bad dreams. You talked a lot." Since this was an unusual occurrence, Sandy had made notes of my disjointed words. As soon as she read them back to me, I knew that I'd had nightmares based on a *60 Minutes* segment I had seen the night before, a case that reminded me of many similar cases of which I had been a part. This episode depicted the death of a prison inmate named Timothy Souders who, like so many psychotic patients in this country, ended up in prison—and tried to kill himself three times while there. Convicted of resisting arrest and assault (for waving a pocketknife), Souders had been sent to the Southern Michigan Correctional Facility, a large complex of five thousand inmates known as Jackson Prison. There, as a punishment for showering without permission, Souders was taken to an isolation cell and strapped down by his ankles and wrists on a cement slab. After four days on the slab, he died of dehydration. According to a CBS website, if not for the efforts of a federal judge named Richard Alan Enslen, who had started monitoring Jackson Prison in the 1980s, "No one would have been the wiser, but a medical investigator working for Judge Enslen . . . caught wind of Souders' death."[4]

As part of my work, I have visited countless prisons and grown familiar with the negligence and inhumanity that characterize the incarceration of mentally ill people. Years ago, on a tour of the psychiatric section of the same prison in which Timothy Souders died, I was escorted through the ancient cells of that facility by a psychiatrist in charge of the inmates' treatment. I learned that my colleague had completed his residency at the famous Menninger Clinic located in Topeka, Kansas. I asked if he was working fulltime at Jackson Prison or whether he also maintained a private practice. "Oh, no," he said, "I'm an inmate." It turned out that he was serving time for bank robbery (a crime he claimed his chauffeur had committed). The "nurses" who tended to the mentally ill prisoners were also prisoners; the psychiatric section of the prison was being operated entirely by inmates, with a local psychiatrist serving as an occasional consultant.

Jack Ruby's trial is emblematic of the failed collaboration of psychiatry and law and the incompetence of defense lawyers when faced with mental illness. The original lawyer for Ruby's defense was Melvin Belli, an outstanding civil lawyer, but he had little understanding of forensic psychiatry. Belli rejected the advice of a leading forensic psychiatrist, Dr. Manfred Guttmacher (whose seminal textbook *Psychiatry and the*

Law I consulted repeatedly early in my career and whose lectures I attended whenever I could), in whose opinion Ruby was a chronically depressed man given to explosive rages and impulsive acts. Belli chose to argue that Ruby suffered epilepsy variant and was insane at the time he shot and killed Lee Harvey Oswald. The result was that Ruby was convicted of first-degree murder and sentenced to die.

Over the years, homicide cases have comprised a large portion of my work, including a number of serial killers, some of whom captured the public's fascination, such as Theodore "Ted" Bundy. Charged with murdering an unknown number of young women (Bundy confessed to killing at least thirty in the mid-1970s, although he might have killed as many as a hundred, their bodies having been discovered in California, Florida, and Colorado, often with bite marks on their breasts and other signs that they had been raped and tortured before being murdered), Bundy faced the death penalty. His defense lawyers retained me as their expert witness, hoping that I would testify that their client was not guilty by reason of insanity. After interviewing Bundy for three hours, I reached the conclusion that Ted Bundy's diagnosis was antisocial personality disorder and that he was not mentally ill, which was the prerequisite for asserting the insanity defense. I deal with the Bundy case in more detail in chapter 6.

The satisfaction I have derived from testifying in homicide cases has come not only from helping to prevent injustice but also from the unique ability of a forensic psychiatrist to help people involved in tragic crimes understand aberrant behavior. In a small Oklahoma town, a woman was charged with first-degree murder for killing her abusive husband; at the trial, I testified about her conflict-ridden life and how years of mistreatment by her husband had traumatized her to such an extent that she entered a state of dissociated rage and shot him. As soon as I got off the witness stand, a man with tears running down his cheeks came up to me, reached for his belt buckle, removed it from his belt, and handed it to me. "This is my favorite possession," he said. "I want you to have it." The defendant was his daughter. I was a court-appointed expert, which meant that the family must be indigent, and the father's belt buckle was all he could give me to show his appreciation. I tried to resist accepting this man's one treasure, but he insisted. "No matter what happens in the trial, you helped us understand why she did it. Thank you." (As a result of my testimony, his daughter was convicted of manslaughter and not first-degree murder, as the prosecutor had charged.)

Of course, not all my experiences have been so inspiring. Some have involved threats on my life. In the 1960s, a series of young female students at the University of Michigan were found murdered, and a man who had been taken into custody for impulsively killing his girlfriend was suspected of being the "Coed Killer" of Ann Arbor. Not only did I testify that, given this young man's personality, he could not possibly be a serial killer, but I also testified that he had killed his girlfriend in a moment of rage precipitated by her sexual escapades. In my opinion, his was a case of diminished responsibility, and he was found guilty of manslaughter rather than first-degree murder. This verdict outraged some people and led to my receiving a number of death threats. These were neither the first nor the last death threats I received.

No matter what the prosecution or others threw at me, I have never been shy or timid, especially in the cause of preventing injustice. As the case histories in this book illustrate, whether a trial received a great deal of attention from the media or was carried out in relative obscurity I always provided my expert opinion, even when I knew that my testimony would make me unpopular.

In this book, I am critical of the incompetence of police investigators, prosecutors, and a number of expert witnesses; I reproach criminal defense lawyers who are inexperienced and decry the judiciary for being biased and politicized; I sympathize with plaintiffs whose lawyers don't have the financial resources to represent their clients in contests with powerful insurance companies; I rail against appellate courts and legislators who pander to corporations; I expose the myth of frivolous civil lawsuits as propaganda; and I advocate the censure of unethical experts and call attention to the racial biases of white and black jurors that result in injustice.

Whenever I become downhearted about the incompetence of a defense attorney or the overzealous behavior of a prosecutor or political prejudices of a judge, I remind myself that thirty-five of the founding fathers of this country were lawyers and that judges elevated to appellate courts (including the Supreme Court of the United States) often act in ways that run counter to the political beliefs of the presidents who appointed them, as when President Eisenhower appointed Governor Earl Warren to the Supreme Court, never anticipating that under Warren's leadership the Court would become a liberal institution, or when President George W. Bush appointed to a federal judgeship John Jones III who, in a strongly worded decision, prohibited the teaching of creationism under the cover of "intelligent design."

Although the focus of this book is the process that leads to injustice within our justice system, a positive feeling for the law and lawyers is essential for any forensic expert. In a democracy such as ours, even a single juror has the power over life and death; without giving any reason, such a juror can frustrate the prosecution's determination to convict an innocent defendant or the efforts by the defense to declare a guilty person innocent. Juries, like anything else created by human beings, are not a perfect instrument, but the jury system has served us well and it is our duty as citizens to make our courts work as well as is humanly possible.

This book is divided into two parts. In the first, I introduce the origins of injustice in our legal system, and I discuss the main players in the courtroom and explain the rules according to which a trial unfolds. In the second part, which is the majority of the book, I shift my focus from concepts to cases. Throughout both sections, I have tried to strike a balance between the technical aspects of law and psychiatry and their often dramatic real-life antecedents. It is my hope that the reader of this book walks away with a more realistic idea of how the American legal system functions, and how—and why—it sometimes fails.

NOTES

1. For a recent reference see *Automatism, Insanity, and the Psychology of Criminal Responsibility: A Philosophical Inquiry* by Robert F. Schopp (Cambridge, UK: Cambridge University Press, 1991).

2. Personal communication from Dr. Samuel Gross.

3. *Can't Remember What I Forgot: The Good News from the Front Lines of Memory Research* by Sue Halpern (New York: Harmony Books, 2008).

4. CBS *60 Minutes*, February 7, 2009.

I

LAW UNDER SCRUTINY

1

THE ROOTS
OF INJUSTICE

ABSOLUTE INJUSTICE

"If you are neutral in situations of injustice, you have chosen the side of the oppressor."

—Bishop Desmond Tutu

"Let no one unacquainted with geometry enter here" was the motto on the door to Plato's Academy. "Let no one unacquainted with injustice enter here" should be the inscription on every law school's entry doorway. A sense of justice is one of the fundamental features of a society; however, its meaning varies greatly from society to society, and even among individuals in a particular society. We are a country of law, but elected prosecutors and judges determine what the law is. Readers of newspapers encounter, with increasing frequency, cases of individuals convicted of crimes they did not commit. The following is an example of one such person.

On January 24, 1984, in the city of Detroit, sixteen-year-old Michelle Jackson was raped and strangled while walking to her high school. Ten months later, Eddy Joe Lloyd, a patient at the state-run Detroit Psychiatric Institute, sent a Freedom of Information Request to the Detroit Police Department regarding Jackson's case. He had been civilly committed to this institution, of which I had been the associate director.

Detroit police interpreted Lloyd's curiosity about the case as evidence that he was the perpetrator of the crime. Based on this speculation, the police arrested Lloyd, placed him in jail, and used deception to induce him to "confess" on tape to the rape and murder of Jackson. His confession, the police promised him, would smoke out the real perpetrator. The Innocence Project, an organization that would later bring about the setting aside of Loyd's conviction, describes the police scheme as follows: "They [the police] fed him details that he could not have known, including the location of the body, the type of jeans the victim was wearing, a description of earrings the victim wore, and other details from the crime scene. Lloyd signed a written confession and gave a tape-recorded statement as well."[1]

The use of deception to gain confessions is widespread in police work. A popular and authoritative textbook, *Criminal Interrogation and Confessions* by Fred E. Inbau, John E. Reid, Joseph P. Buckley, and Brian C Susane, states:

> In criminal investigations, even the most efficient type, there are many instances where physical clues are entirely absent, and the only approach to possible solution of the crime is the interrogation of the criminal suspect himself, as well as others who may possess significant information. . . . They also frequently require the use of psychological tactics and techniques that could well be classified as "unethical," if evaluated in terms of ordinary, everyday social behavior. We are opposed, to force, to the use of force, threats of force or promises of leniency. We do approve, however, of psychological tactics and techniques that may involve trickery and deceit; they are not only helpful but frequently indispensable in order to secure incriminating information from the guilty or obtain investigative leads from otherwise uncooperative witnesses or informants.[2]

When Lloyd insisted that he was "tricked" to confess as a maneuver to "smoke out the real killer," no one believed the incredible but true story. Significantly, the police file was (and still is) missing. Even those who support coercive techniques to gain information from suspects, I would hope, would reject the use of trickery.[3]

Even Lloyd's lawyer believed that his client was the perpetrator of this terrible crime. I was contacted by the lawyer, who was considering the insanity defense. He hoped that with a psychiatric plea Lloyd might have a chance to get a lesser verdict than first-degree murder. Lloyd rejected an insanity defense because he was innocent and believed that he would be acquitted once he told his story in the courtroom. He trusted the justice system. This proved to be a mistake.

At trial, the prosecution played the audiotape of the "confession" to the jury and claimed that Lloyd had killed Jackson in order to get away with rape. The forensic evidence consisted of a nonspecific semen stain on long johns used as a ligature to strangle the victim, a bottle that had been forced into her vagina, and a piece of paper with a semen stain that was stuck to the bottle. The only testing presented at trial consisted of confirming the presence of semen and other biological matter. This evidence proved that a rape took place, but it did not identify the perpetrator. The jury found Lloyd guilty after deliberating just thirty minutes, a speedy verdict of injustice. Lloyd did not testify because his lawyer believed that he was guilty and would tell the incredible story that police tricked him. Judge Leonard Townsend presided over the trial. At the time of Lloyd's sentencing in 1985, the judge declared on the record, "The sentence that the statute requires is inadequate. The justifiable sentence, I would say, would be termination by extreme constriction and on account of this case; a lot of people who had reservations about capital punishment have been convinced that they should jump over the fence and sign petitions. The sentence the statute requires is inadequate. I cannot impose the sentence that the facts call for in this matter."[4]

The victim of this miscarriage of justice was considerably more thoughtful than the self-righteous judge who used a euphemism for hanging. At the time of his sentencing in 1985, Lloyd said:

> Into each life tears must fall. That means on both sides. MJ [the victim] had a right to live, as we all do . . . she said goodbye . . . and disappeared in the darkness never to be seen again alive. One day later, she was found in a vacant garage. Cold, alone, and lifeless. . . . Eddie Lloyd was focused on as a suspect while he was a mental patient and somewhere along the line he was charged and convicted of the crime, a heinous crime, brutal. What I want to say to the court is that, to the family, MJ, to the city of Detroit, to everybody who was involved with the case, I did not kill MJ. I never killed anybody in my life and I wouldn't.[5]

After all legal appeals failed, Lloyd contacted the Innocence Project, a nonprofit clinic staffed primarily by students at the Benjamin N. Cardozo School of Law at Yeshiva University. The Innocence Project was created by Barry C. Scheck and Peter J. Neufeld in the early 1990s and was designed to help exonerate wrongfully convicted defendants.

Innocence Project students searched for the physical evidence of the rape of which Lloyd was convicted. Finally, a number of evidence items were found and the Forensic Science Associates (FSA) tested the green bottle that was found at the crime scene (which had been broken) as well as the piece of paper stuck to the bottle. The FSA painstakingly reconstructed the bottle and obtained a profile from the spermatozoa on the mouth of the bottle, as well as the spermatozoa on the piece of paper. The profiles matched each other as well as the sample of spermatozoa on the long johns found at the crime scene. The Michigan State Crime Lab replicated the FSA's work and got the same results. In addition, the state crime lab obtained a matching DNA profile from the anal slides containing semen taken from the victim's autopsy. These slides had previously been reported lost. Each profile from the items of evidence matched each other and all of them excluded Eddie Joe Lloyd. The website of the Innocence Project states:

> On Monday, August 26, 2002, Eddie Joe Lloyd was exonerated and re-leased from prison. Several rounds of DNA testing that took place over the last year have proven that Lloyd is innocent of the murder for which he served over 17 years. The Innocence Project at the Cardozo School of Law, the Wayne County Prosecuting Attorney's Office, and the Detroit Police Department joined in filing a motion to vacate Lloyd's conviction. Lloyd becomes the 110th person in the United States to be exonerated by post conviction DNA testing.[6]

Judge Townsend, who had presided at the 1985 trial in which Lloyd, an innocent, mentally ill man, was convicted of a brutal rape-murder, also presided over the exoneration hearing on August 26, 2002. He did not assume any responsibility for this miscarriage of justice, either on his own behalf or on the part of the criminal justice system. The judge declared, "Even though he [Lloyd] might have lied about what he did, the fault falls on him. The fault lies with no one else."[7] In the eyes of Judge Townsend, Lloyd is no longer guilty of murder, but he remains guilty of lying and the egregious injustice, including *seventeen* years in prison, is Lloyd's own fault. Michigan law deprived the judge of the ability to follow through with his desire to impose "termination by extreme constriction," but in forty states Lloyd would have been sentenced to death.

RELATIVE INJUSTICE

> *"He who knows only his own side of the case knows little of that."*
>
> —John Stuart Mill, "On Liberty"

Since the Magna Carta, proportionality has been part of the common-law tradition. In popular language, the punishment must fit the crime. However, there is no objective standard of what is considered "fitting." No matter which type of justice we are dealing with—divine revelation, natural law (human nature), or social contract—human interpretation is necessary. This interpretation varies between cultures, communities, and individuals. Relative injustice happens when the culture, community, or individual metes out punishment that does not proportionally correspond with the crime. The following case is an example of relative injustice.

In 2002 Arizona state police arrested Morton Berger, a high school teacher, for possession of twenty images depicting acts of child pornography. Prior to his arrest, Berger had never had a single conflict with the law. He was a husband, father, and award-winning teacher. No other live human being was affected by Berger's actions. A risk assessment conducted by a clinical and forensic psychologist concluded that Berger "posed no risk of repeating his conduct or of acting out toward children."[8] But none of this information mattered. As a result of having the nation's strictest child pornography laws, the state of Arizona sentenced Berger to 200 years in prison (the trial judge imposed the minimum; the maximum sentence was 340).

The state court justified its sentence by comparing it to sentences for committing twenty murders or twenty rapes. There is an enormous difference in terms of direct damage to society and to the victims between committing twenty murders or twenty rapes and possessing twenty pictures of child pornography, but the court did not choose to take this into account. Berger filed an appeal, but the Arizona Supreme Court upheld the original ruling and the U.S. Supreme Court refused to intervene.

We know what Thomas Jefferson would say about this injustice. In a letter to Edmund Pendleton (August 26, 1776) he wrote, "What is just in this sense, then, is what is proportional, and what is unjust is what violates the proportion. Aristotle, wrote in *The Nicomachean Ethics* 113 (350 B.C.E.) 'Punishments I know are necessary, and I would provide them, strict and inflexible, but proportioned to the crime.'"[9]

Berger, his children, his entire family, and his students are the victims of this injustice. The prestige of the United States worldwide has also suffered as a consequence of this irrational punishment. If we assume that this prisoner will live twenty years, the state of Arizona will spend at least $700,000 to keep a harmless man incarcerated.

THE JUDGE AND JUSTICE

The *Journal of the American Bar Association* informs its readers that practicing before a "good judge is a real pleasure," and "practicing before a bad judge is misery."[10] I have experienced both good and bad judges and agree completely.

In 1972, I testified in Monroe, Michigan, a small industrial town, before Judge William Weipert. A nineteen-year-old defendant was charged with first-degree murder after killing his father's girlfriend. The Monroe case was a "bench trial," meaning that the judge was the fact finder. The lawyer knew that Judge Weipert was devoted to justice. It was my opinion that the defendant was not criminally responsible and he was acquitted by reason of insanity.

At the conclusion of my testimony, Judge Weipert asked me into his chambers, and we talked for two hours on the relationship between psychiatry and law. Judge Weipert was an erudite and kind man. I looked forward to testifying in Monroe, knowing that he and I would have interesting conversations afterwards. Eighteen years later, in 1990, the defendant wrote me a lengthy letter of gratitude. By that time, he had two children and a steady job. This was in the days when the insanity defense, when well-founded and well-presented, had a chance of prevailing.

I have also met narrow-minded, even dull-witted judges. One judge excused the jury in the midst of my testimony and interrogated me on my "beliefs." He cautioned me that if I persisted in the "belief" that, according to a scientific study, 70 to 80 percent of murderers knew their victims before killing them, he would disqualify me from testifying in his courtroom. Apparently, this judge could not distinguish statistics from beliefs.

Some prejudiced judges interfere with the testimony of an expert by deliberately creating distractions. Once, in a small Michigan town, a lawyer was about to ask the first question of my testimony when the judge addressed the jury: "Which one of you people parked in my spot?" A juror sheepishly raised her hand. "Go and move the car." We dutifully waited until the juror found a new parking spot and returned. A few minutes later, as I answered my first question, the judged barked at me, "You should answer this question with a yes or a no."

I turned to him and said loudly, "I respectfully suggest that you should not yell." He shouted back that he was not yelling. I replied, "Everyone in this courtroom can hear that you are shouting at me. There is no reason in the world for you to do that." From that point on, the judge did not interfere with my testimony. However the judge had the last word when he determined that my entire fee in this court-appointed case was $150.00. That barely paid for the mileage from my home to the court and back.

I recall a federal judge in Providence, Rhode Island, who acted as if he were a feudal lord. I was testifying for the plaintiff in a major malpractice lawsuit. The plaintiff was a brilliant naval intelligence officer who suffered from tardive dyskinesia, a drug-induced incapacitating movement disorder. Thorazine had been unnecessarily prescribed for him. The judge prohibited the plaintiff's lawyer from inquiring about my qualifications. The lawyer then asked the judge to stipulate to my qualifications.

"I will do no such thing," the judge said angrily. "I do not know this man, I do not know this man's qualifications."

"Judge," I introjected, "I am not a man."

"Who are you?" the judge asked.

"I am a doctor and a professor of psychiatry," I said.

My purpose was to expose the judge's bias against the plaintiff and his expert. The lawyer then proceeded to ask questions about the case, but the judge tolerated only yes-or-no answers. I later learned that the judge and the defense lawyer were friends. The stringent evidentiary restrictions enforced during the direct examination were absent during the cross-examination. I succeeded in putting most of the significant details on the record during the cross-examination. The case was settled for a million dollars before the jury started its deliberation. My cross-examination benefited the plaintiff.

I recall with pleasure a trial that took place in Boston with U.S. District Court Judge Joseph Tauro presiding. A much-decorated Vietnam helicopter pilot and a few of his buddies took a one-week sailing course, bought a Gulf Star 50 sailboat, and sailed to Morocco to buy hashish. When they arrived in the port of Boston, customs agents welcomed them with an arrest warrant. The essence of my testimony was that risk-taking had become a defensive psychic mechanism that helped them to cope with posttraumatic stress disorder.

During my cross-examination, I questioned the Gulf Star 50 sailboat's suitability for crossing the Atlantic. The prosecutor objected, stating that I was not qualified as an expert on sailboats. I pointed out that I had more than twenty years' sailing experience at that point. The judge ruled in the prosecutor's favor and instructed the jury to disregard my comment about the Gulf Star sailboat as irrelevant.

At the recess, Judge Tauro asked me to approach the bench. Everyone assumed that I would be chastised for my forceful behavior vis-à-vis the prosecutor. Instead, Judge Tauro commented, "Doctor, you have sailed for 20 years. I have sailed for 40. I don't know about your psychiatric opinions, but I fully agree with you that the Gulf Star 50 was not a good choice for crossing the Atlantic."

Years later, I attended a party in a beautiful Traverse City home overlooking Lake Michigan. To my surprise, one of the guests was the lead man in the Morocco sailing adventure. Had this man been sentenced to a prolonged imprisonment, he might have come out of prison a seasoned criminal. Instead, he was a successful businessman. This is one case where assisting the court in understanding the motivation and personality of the perpetrators resulted in a lenient verdict, including a short prison term that did not destroy the men involved.

Electing judges is a unique American tradition, going back to colonial times. In a common-law system, judges exercise enormous influence. Some elected judges are ill-suited for this responsibility. Some judges are better politicians than they are jurists. For many of them these positions are only a first step to higher elected offices. A great deal of injustice is the consequence of this trend.

People who vote for American judges and prosecutors are rarely making informed choices. As a practical matter, most judges are "elected" by special interest groups who financially support their campaigns. A recent *New York Times* editorial entitled "Honest Justice" stated in part,

The right to a fair hearing before an impartial judge, untainted by money or special interests, is at the heart of the nation's justice system and the rule of law. That right is more secure following a 5-to-4 ruling on Monday by the United States Supreme Court. The case involved some egregious ethical myopia on the part of Justice Brent Benjamin of the West Virginia Supreme Court. Justice Benjamin, who is now the state's chief justice, twice cast the deciding vote to throw out a $50 million verdict against Massey Energy, one of the country's biggest coal companies. He sat in judgment on the case even though Massey's chief executive, Don Blankenship, spent an extraordinary $3 million to help Justice Benjamin get elected to the state's top court. . . . "Not every campaign contribution by a litigant or attorney creates a probability of bias that requires a judge's recusal, but this is an exceptional case," wrote Justice Anthony Kennedy in the majority opinion, which was joined by Justices John Paul Stevens, David Souter, Ruth Bader Ginsburg and Stephen Breyer.[11]

If a citizen offers an official money in an attempt to influence a legal decision, that is considered bribery. Both the citizen and the official are likely to be charged with a crime. It is, however, perfectly legal to contribute to the electoral campaigns of prosecutors and judges. This system for selecting judges and prosecutors and the huge costs of elections result in legalized corruption. The ultimate consequence of this is that many people are elected to judicial positions as a result of their fame and finances, rather than their relevant skills or judicial temperament.

The American Bar Association defines the term judicial temperament as "compassion, decisiveness, open-mindedness, sensitivity, courtesy, patience, freedom from bias and commitment to equal justice."[12] Judge Warfield Moore of the Detroit criminal court known as Recorders Court would not meet these criteria, but he was repeatedly elected. In 1993, I was the sole defense expert witness in the first-degree murder trial of Harry Ransom. The defense was diminished capacity in an impulsive homicide. As I waited to take the stand, Judge Moore asked if there was anything either lawyer wanted to take up with the court. At this point, Demetria Brue, an assistant prosecuting attorney, embarked upon a lengthy denunciation of me. She wanted a motion *in limine* prohibiting me from using unprofessional language, such as saying that the defendant "went bananas."[13] She was not claiming that I ever used such language; she was just citing a case that prohibited such language.

Judge Moore declared on the record that in a previous trial before him, I had used the term "irrelevant." Judge Moore admonished me not to use such language and not to think of myself as a lawyer and judge rolled into one. I did not know that "irrelevant" was limited in its usage to lawyers and judges.

"I know Dr. Tanay is hired a lot by the defense," said Judge Moore. "In fact, he was in court yesterday working for the defense." Working for the defense evidently diminished my credibility in the eyes of this jurist. Prosecutor Brue made a number of derogatory comments about "hired witnesses"—despite the fact that the rebuttal witnesses were employees of the State Center of Forensic Psychiatry, which testifies almost exclusively for prosecution. Throughout the proceedings Judge Moore's behavior was unfavorable to the defense. He responded to prosecutor Brue's request to disqualify me with a left-handed compliment. "Dr. Tanay is world famous," he said. "He does not need to give testimony just to please whoever hired him. If he did, he would be prostituting himself."

The courtroom audience could hear all these comments; more significantly, the jurors were in a nearby room that was not soundproofed and no doubt heard these denunciations of an expert who had not yet taken the witness stand. The prosecutor then argued that the diminished-capacity defense requires an opinion that the person is mentally ill "as defined in the statute." She claimed that I was laughing about her legal argument while sitting in the audience. My disagreement may have shown in my face, but her claim that I was laughing was absolutely untrue. I was seated in the back row of the large courtroom full of spectators; she could barely see me. Nevertheless, the judge went into a lengthy comment about how one should not laugh because that shows lack of respect and "we all should be respectful of others regardless of our religion, whether we are Jews or blacks." He then mentioned a newspaper headline that spoke of Israelis and Arabs reaching some understanding, implying that if Arabs and Israelis can get along, Jews and blacks should—an obvious reference to my being a Jew and implying racial bias in relation to the African American prosecutor.

When I finally took the witness stand, prosecutor Brue interrupted my direct testimony every few minutes. She jumped up, screamed, and threw her hands in the air, and the judge tolerated her outrageous behavior. When I asked her to lower her voice, the judge intervened: "She only has a naturally high-pitched voice." I said that she was obviously screaming at me. "You are in Detroit, Doctor," the judge said, implying that I did not appreciate cultural differences between blacks and whites. This was one of the many innuendos the judge and the prosecutor made to a black jury sitting in judgment of a white defendant and his white expert witness.

Throughout the trial Judge Moore sided with the prosecution. When at one point I referred to Ransom's mental state, Brue interrupted me in mid-sentence, screaming that there was no reference in my report to brain damage. Evidently, for her "mental state" was synonymous with "brain damage." The judge picked up from there and went on discussing brain damage at length. He eventually ruled that because I did not say in my report that the defendant suffered from a brain disease, the experts for the prosecution could now sit in the courtroom so that they could listen to my testimony and properly address this issue on rebuttal.

I later discovered that Dr. Robert Mogy, a psychologist from the State Center of Forensic Psychiatry, and his colleague had been listening to my testimony from their adjoining room, even though the judge ruled that experts were to be sequestered. They were not visible in the courtroom, but they were able to hear every word spoken. Thus, the prosecution had circumvented sequestration of witnesses.

During my testimony, the prosecutor argued that diminished capacity required compliance with the statutory definition of mental illness—which was legally incorrect. The opposite was the case. Judge Moore added the requirement that the defendant should be unable to adhere to the law or to appreciate the wrongfulness of his conduct. He made these comments in the presence of the jury. Thus, the judge ruled that a defendant had to be declared insane by the defense expert in order to allow the expert to testify that a defendant acted under diminished capacity. This was not even remotely in keeping with the law as it existed at the time. The very essence of the diminished capacity defense was that there was no insanity claimed.

Since I did not testify that Ransom suffered from mental disease, the judge ruled that my testimony was to be stricken. The prosecutor was shouting that the jury should treat me as if I had never entered the courtroom. At this point, the judge and the prosecutor were talking over each other. Ransom was convicted of two counts of first-degree murder and two counts of felony-firearms.

My most memorable moment in Judge Moore's courtroom had nothing to do with the trial. It came when Prosecutor Brue argued that I should be disqualified from being an expert. Judge Moore said, "I cannot do that. He is an old-timer."

"You have it right, Judge," I said. "I will be sixty-five years old tomorrow."

After I took the witness chair next day, Judge Moore said to the jury and the courtroom audience, "Ladies and gentlemen, today is Dr. Tanay's birthday. Let's sing 'Happy Birthday.'"

Everyone joined the judge in singing "Happy Birthday." Woody Allen could not improve upon this episode. This, however, was not a comedy but a trial that resulted in a first-degree murder conviction of a man who committed manslaughter. It was not a happy birthday for me, and it certainly was not a happy day for the defendant, who became a victim of relative injustice.

THE PROSECUTOR AND JUSTICE

The prevention of injustice is a responsibility entrusted to prosecutors and judges. However, far too often in the United States, the decision of whether to prosecute is dominated by political considerations.

Rudolph W. Giuliani became the U.S. Attorney for New York in 1983. He said years later, "If you had offered me one job in government, I would not have said mayor, I would not have said president, I would have said prosecutor. . . . It's really an ideal job for an idealistic man; you never have to do the wrong thing."[14] Contrary to Giuliani's claim, however, prosecutors quite often do many wrong things. Michael Powell wrote in the *New York Times*:

> There was, however, another side to the young prosecutor, a moralistic and carnivorously ambitious man who desired public office. Mr. Giuliani, who was 38 when he became United States Attorney in 1983, threatened his targets with long prison sentences, and he infuriated judges with leaks of grand jury testimony to the press. His agents handcuffed Wall Street arbitrageurs before prosecutors investigated them. Apology was weakness; skeptics were "jerks."
>
> Like a medieval crusader, he rarely flinched at hard tactics in pursuit of exalted goals. . . . Mr. Giuliani married aggressiveness to moral absolutes, reflecting his steeping, he said, in the Catholic catechism.[15]

To me, Giuliani is the prototypical American prosecutor: dogmatic, fanatical, and often a promoter of injustice under the auspices of justice. If you embrace the principle that the end justifies the means, then Giuliani is your man.

The so-called Duke Lacrosse Team Rape Case demonstrated how publicity and money consume elected prosecutors in the United States. Duke University's lacrosse team came to national attention after a Durham go-go dancer claimed that she was raped at a March 2006 team party. Three team members were charged with rape. Prosecutor Michael B. Nifong needed the black vote to be elected and arranged for the three young white men from the lacrosse team to be arrested on the Duke campus in front of television cameras. The lacrosse team's season was cancelled and the coach was forced to resign. When this story first became public, I was giving a series of lectures in Sarasota, Florida. I commented that this sounded like the prosecutorial publicity stunts that I have encountered so many times in my forensic practice. Most of my audience did not share my skepticism.

It was no surprise to me when the December 24, 2006, issue of the *New York Times* reported that Brian W. Meehan, director of a private laboratory that performed DNA testing, informed Nifong that "none of the DNA material [gathered from the crime scene] was from the three players or any of their teammates."[16] The summary report that Meehan made available to the defense did not include this critical fact. The *Times* reported that on the witness stand, "A defense lawyer asked Mr. Meehan if the decision to omit the test results was 'an intentional limitation' arrived at between him and Mr. Nifong.' Meehan replied, 'Yes.'"[17] Thus, the prosecutor induced the expert witness to introduce false testimony as evidence.

Finally, a headline in the *New York Times* on April 12, 2007, proclaimed, "All Charges Dropped in Duke Case." Durham County District Attorney Mike Nifong was subsequently disbarred for breaking more than two dozen rules of professional conduct in his handling of the case. The players' families spent millions of dollars on legal bills in their sons' defense, but even after acquittal, the defendants will labor under the presumption of guilt and the legacy of their negative publicity for the rest of their lives. One of the wrongfully accused members of the Duke lacrosse team astutely observed that his being accused of rape will probably be part of his obituary.

American prosecutors are among the most powerful of public officials. "With a stroke of my pen, I can make your lives disappear," Reed Walters, a district attorney, reportedly told high school students in Jena, Louisiana, after an incident of racial antagonism.[18] Since every prosecutor has that power, the personality of some prosecutors must be considered to determine whether he or she is acting in a way that best serves justice. One classic example of the vindictive prosecutor is Nancy Grace, formerly of Court TV and now host of a CNN show described by the network as "television's only justice themed interview/debate show, designed for those interested in the justice stories of the day."[19]

Nancy Grace originally wanted to be an English teacher and a mother, but her fiancé was murdered during a robbery. This tragedy motivated her to enter law school, and she became an avenging prosecutor in Atlanta. Her ruthless demeanor appealed to many Court TV viewers. Some describe her as an advocate of mob justice; she saw herself as a voice for victims. In an interview with *Psychology Today*, she describes her transformation.

Q: When did you start to feel comfortable as an avenger?

A: It took years. Seven years after Keith's murder, I was walking into the courthouse, and I knew at that moment that I could do something—something that could make it better. The first time I stood before a jury, I felt like a bird that had been let out of a cage to fly. [Note that she does not object to being described as an avenger.]

Q: What else changed?

A: I grew up in a world where in the distance, the chimes in the Methodist church would ring us home at 6 o'clock from riding our bikes. It was like: God will take care of you. There are times I still think I should have a family and live in Colorado, as Keith and I were going to do. Sometimes I'm getting ready to be on [CNN] *Headline News*, and I think: I could be somewhere whipping up dinner, or taking kids to soccer practice. That would really be wonderful. But that is not the way it turned out. . . .

Q: Your public image is tough, even mean. Is that who you are?

A: I see myself as trying to protect innocent people from those who are more powerful, more cunning, more evil. You win a battle by raising your sword and your shield. I don't care about politics. I think I'm extremely tolerant, except when it comes to violent crime. When it comes to that—what's there to be tolerant of? [Ms. Grace was on a personal vendetta that should have disqualified her for a professional position.][20]

USA Today reported on June 26, 2003, about a study by the Center for Public Integrity on prosecutorial misconduct.[21] Steve Weinberg headed a team that spent three years researching 11,458 appellate court decisions in all 2,341 state prosecutor jurisdictions in the country (the team did not examine federal prosecutors' conduct). In the cases the team studied, judges cited 223 prosecutors for two or more instances of misconduct. Two prosecutors were disbarred for mishandling cases. In another *USA Today* article, Weinberg says, "Prosecutors are the last sacred cow. They are unaccountable. Who is the boss of the prosecutor? You could say the voters, but in most jurisdictions, most voters can't name the prosecutor."[22]

Overzealous prosecutors are often guilty of willful omission of the facts that contradict the indictment. The Innocence Project, which uses DNA testing to determine the validity of verdicts for convicted felons, has found that thirty-four of the first seventy defendants it had helped to exonerate had been subject to prosecutorial misconduct. Peter Neufeld, cofounder of the Innocence Project, says that DNA testing has provided a window through which prosecutors' conduct can be examined closely. "But I assure you, it hasn't just happened in these cases."[23]

Criminology and sociology professor Richard Moran of Mount Holyoke College conducted a study of 124 exonerations of death-row inmates from 1973 to 2007. In a *New York Times* op-ed piece, he writes that "80, or about two-thirds, of their so-called wrongful convictions resulted not from good-faith mistakes or errors but from intentional, willful, malicious prosecutions by criminal justice personnel." (There were four cases in which a determination could not be made one way or another.) Moran also addresses "relative injustice": "In the interest of fairness, it is important to note that those who are exonerated are not necessarily innocent of the crimes that sent them to death row. They have simply had their death sentences set aside because of errors that led to convictions, usually involving the intentional violation of their constitutional right to a fair and impartial trial. Very seldom does the court go the next step and actually declare them innocent."[24]

A *New York Times* headline on October 22, 2008, states "Prosecutor Misconduct, at a Cost of $3.5 Million." The article describes a prisoner named Shih-Wei Su who spent thirteen years in prison for a conviction for attempted murder based upon barefaced lies "tolerated" by the prosecutor's office. He was sent to prison at the age of seventeen; at the age of thirty his conviction was vacated and the prosecutor's office "sent my legal aid lawyer to tell me that they would nail me to the wall unless I made a deal." The prosecutor demanded that he plead guilty, after which he would walk out free. When he refused he was put in Riker's Prison and kept there for another ninety days. The *New York Times* points out that there has been a pattern in practice at the Queen's District Attorney's office when the prosecutors commit misconduct. "In 80 convictions from Queen's that were overturned between 1989 and 2003 by Appeals Court for prosecutorial misconduct, Mr. Rudin said, Senior officials took no disciplinary action." Mr. Su, who is a financial consultant, filed a complaint against the prosecutor who handled the case, Linda Rosero. "The grievance committee decided that Ms. Rosero did not know the details of the deal with Mr. Shih-Wei Su and said she had been 'naive, inexperienced and possibly stupid.'"

The extent of the punishment was a written admonition to Ms. Rosero. Mr. Su wrote to the committee, "With all due respect, the message that this committee is sending out is loud and clear: don't worry about using false evidence; you'll only get an admonition if you are stupid enough to admit it."[25]

Electoral politics should not dominate professional conduct. We do not elect our physicians or engineers, so why should we elect our prosecutors?

NOTES

1. "The Innocence Project—Know the Cases: Browse Profiles: Eddie Joe Lloyd," http://www.innocenceproject.org/Content/201.php.

2. Fred E. Inbau, John E. Reid, Joseph P. Buckley, and Brian C. Susane, eds., *Criminal Interrogation and Confessions*, 4th ed. (Sudbury, MA: Jones & Bartlett Publishers, 2004).

3. See J.G. Grano, *Confessions, Truth and the Law* (Ann Arbor: University of Michigan Press, 1993).

4. "The Innocence Project."

5. "The Innocence Project."

6. "The Innocence Project."

7. "The Innocence Project."

8. Petition for a writ of certiorari to the Arizona Supreme Court.

9. Letter from Thomas Jefferson, in 1 The Papers of Thomas Jefferson, 1760-1776, at 505 (quoted by Berger's lawyers).

10. "Good Trial Judges," *Litigation* 9, no. 3 (1983): 8.

11. *New York Times*, June 9, 2009.

12. American Bar Association, *Standing Committee on Federal Judiciary: What It Is and How It Works* (American Bar Association, 1991), 4.

13. A motion *in limine* is a pretrial motion whose purpose is to give the trial judge notice that the witness is likely to introduce evidence which may irretrievably infect the fairness of the trial.

14. Michael Powell, "His Past as Prosecutor Shapes the Candidate Giuliani," *International Herald Tribune*, December 10, 2007, http://www.iht.com/articles/2007/12/10/news/giuliani.php.

15. Michael Powell, "The Long Run: Crime Buster with Eye on the Future," *New York Times*, December 10, 2007, http://www.nytimes.com/2007/12/10/us/politics/10prosecutor.html.

16. David Barstow and Duff Wilson, "DNA Witness Jolted Dynamic of Duke Case," *New York Times*, National Desk Late Edition, December 24, 2006, 1.

17. Barstow and Wilson, "DNA Witness Jolted."

18. Steve Coll, "Disparities," *The New Yorker*, October 8, 2007, 31.

19. I heard this comment made by Nancy Grace on CNN and made note of it.

20. Kathleen McGowan, "Nancy Grace on Endurance," *Psychology Today* (March/April 2006).

21. Associated Press, "Dozens Falsely Imprisoned amid Thousands of Cases of Misconduct by Local Prosecutors," *USA Today*, June 26, 2003.

22. Laura Parker, "Court Cases Raise Concerns," *USA Today*, June 25, 2003.

23. Parker, "Court Cases Raise Concerns."

24. Richard Moran, "The Presence of Malice," *New York Times*, August 2, 2007.

25. *New York Times*, October 22, 2008.

Emanuel Tanay is profiled as a "supershrink" by Michigan: The Magazine of the Detroit News. *1983.*

2

SCIENCE AND
THE LAW

Since Roman times, we have called on expert witnesses to assist judges and jurors in dealing with issues that go beyond common understanding. Let me use the involuntary hospitalization of the mentally ill—which requires a court's civil commitment—as an example of how law, public opinion, and science interact.

Until the 1970s, civil commitment of the mentally ill was considered a humanitarian approach. Psychiatry and the public considered state hospitals to be the best way to manage chronic psychotic illness. In the 1950s and the 1960s, I worked in state hospitals and observed the beneficial function of these institutions in the care of the mentally ill. However, in the 1970s, idealistic civil rights lawyers declared the civil commitment system a deprivation of liberty. With the support of fiscal conservatives, who considered state hospitals a form of socialized medicine, these civil rights advocates virtually eliminated this time-tested system for the care of the mentally ill.

Today, most psychotic Americans are either homeless or live with relatives who are often unable to provide the medical care that they need. Due to managed care restrictions, even those with health insurance often have their hospital stays limited to days or weeks. As a practical matter, long-term hospital care of the grossly psychotic has been abolished in the United States. To initiate civil commitment proceedings in most states, one has to prove not only severe psychosis but also an overt act that makes the person dangerous. Many such "overt acts" violate criminal law, and therefore psychotics quite often end up in jails instead of being committed to institutions for the mentally ill. Our "correctional institutions" hold thousands of psychotics.

After the Virginia Tech tragedy of 2007, in which a psychotic student named Seung-Hui Cho killed thirty-two of his fellow students and professors, I wrote an editorial in the *Journal of the American Academy of Psychiatry and the Law* on the "pseudo-liberation" of the mentally ill from state hospitals into the streets.[1] Most commentary today neglects the social issue of the criminalization of mental illness. Our jails have become the default institutions for the care of psychotics. The criminal justice system intervenes after a crime has been committed, as it should, but in the past provisions for the care of the psychotics were preventive in nature. Those who showed psychotic illness were committed, without the requirement of an actual dangerous act.

Since as yet there are no means of primary prevention of schizophrenia, our only possibility of treatment involves reducing the suffering that this illness inflicts upon the patients, their families, and the society. Let us take as an example the above-mentioned case of the psychotic Virginia Tech student. We know that Cho was driven to become a "mass murderer" by his psychosis. He told us as much when he stated in his second video sent to NBC the day of the tragedy, "Do you think I want to do this? Do you think I ever dreamed of dying like this in a million years? I didn't want to do this." Cho's cry for help, demonstrated by bizarre behavior and writings both during this tragedy and for years before, went unheeded. Thirty-two people paid with their lives for the failure of our society to respond.

The euphemism "mental health system" bespeaks the reluctance of our society to recognize that there are thousands of citizens suffering from the incurable illness called schizophrenia. The needs of people whose problems are treatable by psychotherapy and medication are different from the needs of those who suffer from a lifelong psychosis that, in most cases, is schizophrenia. In the 1960s a myth that schizophrenics are not dangerous was popularized. In my fifty years of forensic psychiatric practice, I have encountered countless homicides committed by schizophrenics whose behavioral pleas for help produced Band-Aid-type responses of a few days' hospitalization.

The reality is that many schizophrenics' delusional ideas include homicidal impulses, which, depending on the setting, may result in a homicide. When I worked in state hospitals, I had many homicidal patients who were potentially dangerous, but in the institutional setting were unlikely to act upon their urges. The same individual in the community, by contrast, may implement his delusions. In the recent past, it has been quite common for schizophrenics who kill someone to be treated as if they were not afflicted by psychosis and charged with capital murder, which leads to a sentence of death or life in prison. Our prison system is ill-suited for long-term care of psychotics; the mentally ill are often abused and the other prisoners suffer from exposure to disturbed inmates.

This brings us back to Cho. For a few years prior to this tragedy, Cho showed symptoms of severe psychosis, most likely schizophrenia. In all of the discussions about Cho's "mental health," only counseling was considered. His brief hospital stay presumably was voluntary, since it did not appear on his gun-purchase screening. His case represents yet another consequence of the failure of psychiatry, the government, and the law to meaningfully interact with each other. We will now discuss the role of the forensic expert in this interaction.

THE FORENSIC EXPERT

An expert witness is anyone who has greater knowledge about the subject at issue than the average juror. An expert has acquired this knowledge by virtue of training, education, or experience. From the perspective of the law, the function of an expert witness in the court-room is to assist the jury to deal with technical aspects of the case at hand.[2] A forensic expert is at first an advisor to the retaining lawyer or agency. The next step is the collection of data that may support or negate the claim made by the lawyer. Once the expert has reached an opinion that is supportive of the position of the lawyer and takes the witness stand, the expert's function is to inform and persuade the legal decision makers.

A professional takes the witness stand by choice, and he or she should have testimonial skills. Being knowledgeable in a field of science that is relevant to the lawsuit at hand is not sufficient. A lawyer's choice of an expert determines the fate of his client. The British diplomat Harold Nicholson said, "The first essential is to know what one wishes to say, the second is to decide to whom one wishes to say it."[3] It is equally im-portant to decide who should say it. A forensic expert is a professional who combines knowledge of a specific field of science with a familiarity with the law and the skill of testimony. The world's greatest expert on a given subject is of little value to the moving party if he or she is unable to function effectively in the courtroom setting. Thus, a plaintiff claiming damages by producing a treating doctor of high competence as his or her primary expert witness is not likely to prevail. The same is true for a defendant who claims the insanity defense and produces as his expert witness an outstanding psychiatrist who has never been in the courtroom. Insurance companies and prosecutors rarely make such erroneous choices of experts.

Unlike the material witness, a professional who testifies did not just "happen to observe a relevant fact" and is not compelled to give testimony. An expert is retained to interpret data available to both sides. The expert witness is a proponent of an opinion that he or she has reached after a great deal of work before entering the courtroom. When I testify that a defendant is not criminally responsible, I am giving my opinion, which is a counterclaim to the prosecutor's argument that the defendant was of sound mind and perpetrated the homicide with premeditation. The prosecutor has presented evidence to justify his claim. I have also presented in my testimony evidence that justifies my opinion.

The opposite of opinion testimony is not a falsehood but another opinion. The divergence of appellate judges' opinions is rarely the result of bias or corruption. Opinions are not "the truth" in a dogmatic sense. David Hume (1711-1776), the Scottish philosopher, recognized that when he said, "It may further be said, that, though men be much governed by interest; yet even interest itself, and all human affairs are entirely governed by opinion."[4]

The diagnostic function of the expert cannot be separated from the expert's role as a forensic consultant on strategy. For example, I was once the expert for the defense in a civil case of a police inspector who had severely beaten a car-wash attendant. The officer suspected that the attendant stole his gun and walkie-talkie and was trying to beat a confession out of the man. It turned out that the policeman had misplaced both items in his car. The injured plaintiff claimed posttraumatic stress disorder and chronic organic brain syndrome as a result of the beating. When I examined the plaintiff, it was obvious to me that he was mentally retarded and not a victim of traumatic brain injury. On my advice, an investigator traveled to the plaintiff's hometown in Alabama, where he was known to be mentally retarded. We had a great deal of evidence to back my diagnosis. The jury was offended by the plaintiff's lawyers' exaggerated claims and awarded the plaintiff no damages. I was distressed by the extent of "our victory," as the plaintiff was entitled to some compensation for the psychic trauma caused by the beating. I often tell lawyers that a plaintiff loses by exaggeration, but the defense loses by denying obvious responsibility. In this case, the jury punished the plaintiff for excessive claims.

An expert's consultative role presumes that the lawyer has contacted the expert witness shortly after he has been retained. Unfortunately, many lawyers postpone contacting an expert. Here is an example of a lawyer's failure to contact an expert in a timely manner.

A young woman in Texas was about to be married to a young man from Michigan. There was conflict about the degree of religious commitment of the bride. The bridegroom terminated the engagment and the young woman committed suicide. Her father, a distinguished scientist, became profoundly depressed. He blamed the young man's father, a Michigan physician, for causing the breakup. The bereaved father made death threats against the groom's father for an extensive period of time, resulting in felony charges. Shortly before the trial, the lawyer representing the defendant came to see me seeking my testimony on behalf of his client. In my opinion, the case was indefensible. The lengthy written and recorded death threats by the defendant left no doubt in my mind that a guilty verdict would result. Almost inadvertently, I discovered that the prosecutor had offered the defendant the choice to plead guilty to a misdemeanor. I advised the lawyer in very strong terms that he would be committing malpractice if he exposed his client to the risk of being found guilty of a felony. When my opinion was communicated to the defendant, he agreed to plead guilty to a misdemeanor.

Testimony does not take place in a vacuum; it is given in the context of adversary proceedings. "In US, Expert Witnesses are Partisan," proclaimed a *New York Times* headline on August 12, 2008. Judge Denver D. Dillard in Johnson County, Iowa, had to decide whether an Iowa man was competent to stand trial. Judge Dillard was troubled that the opinions of the two psychologists consulted in the case were "polar opposites." The expert for the defendant testified that Timothy M. Wilkins was mentally retarded; he had an IQ of 58, and therefore could not understand the proceedings. The expert for the prosecution testified that Wilkins's verbal IQ was 88—above the cut-off for mental retardation—and therefore was competent to stand trial. Judge Dillard concluded that the experts were biased "in favor of the parties who employed them" and that they had "given predictable testimony." In his opinion, the judge wrote that the "two sides had cancelled each other out." Nevertheless, Judge Dillard found Wilkins not competent to stand trial, a decision that the appellate court reversed. Was the trial judge biased? Were the appellate judges less than impartial? They gave their opinions, just like the experts who expressed their considered judgment on the issue of competence. If judges can disagree on matters of law, why should we expect experts to be unanimous? Whether Wilkins was able to understand the proceeding depends upon the interpretation of the legal criteria. The notion of a single impartial expert witness is an illusion.

Let us imagine a more concrete situation than the ability to stand trial. Assume that there is a controversy about the collapse of a bridge. The plaintiff claims that faulty bridge construction led to the disaster. The defense argues that poor maintenance was the reason for the collapse of the bridge. An impartial expert would give an opinion that favors one side or the other. In that case, the expert would not be giving expert testimony, but making an adjudication: he or she would not be an expert witness but an arbitrator. Every expert witness is asked: "What is your opinion?" The expert responds: "It is my opinion that. . . ." The use of the possessive adjective *my* identifies that the opinion is subjective; to speak of an objective opinion is contradictory.

One has to distinguish between the merits of the testimony of a given expert, the persuasiveness of the presentation, and the impact of the personality of the witness. (I describe later how a meritorious case supported by the world's leading scientists was lost because the experts were "courtroom virgins.") The expert's testimony is not the only variable that determines the outcome of a case. This fact does not diminish the significance of expert testimony, which, in some cases, is critical to the result.

A forensic chemist can focus on the concrete data in his testimony; his function is to report findings. A forensic psychiatric expert, in contrast, deals with a defendant's state of mind. The torment of Andrea Yates, a psychotic mother driven by delusions to drown her five children, cannot and should not be told without compassion. Effectiveness in the courtroom requires reliance upon reason and emotion. Juries do not render verdicts based upon logic or law alone. A forensic expert who has agreed to evaluate a case and has an opinion based upon data favorable to one party in a dispute has taken sides. He or she is a witness for or against the plaintiff. Neither ethics nor a sense of fairness demand that the expert witness walk down the middle in a legal dispute. On the contrary, it is the expert's contractual agreement that upon taking the witness stand, he or she will effectively testify in support of one side. In some disputes there is no other side from a scientific perspective. It would be unethical for a physician to testify that asbestos inhalation in a workplace or exposure to second-hand cigarette smoke of a bartender is harmless.

A forensic expert would be self-destructive if he or she interpreted the data in order to arrive at a tailor-made opinion to help the lawyer who has retained him. This would not be partisanship—it would be deception. Unethical professionals would be ill-advised to go into forensic work, as it is much easier to be unethical outside the scrutiny of adversary proceedings. Success in forensic work depends upon rigorous adherence to ethical standards.

The most challenging and productive contribution of an expert is to advise a lawyer that he has no case. In the 1960s, I was consulted by Joseph Louisell, who was Michigan's foremost criminal lawyer. The client, whom I will call Mr. Jones, had killed his wife. Louisell expected that I would testify in support of the insanity defense and filed an insanity notice. However, the insanity defense was not likely to prevail, and if it failed Jones would be found guilty of first-degree murder and sentenced to life in prison without the possibility of parole. Louisell's goal was to gain the best possible result for his client. After hearing the details of the case, I convinced him that, based upon my experience, a diminished-capacity defense was more promising. Louisell accepted my advice and withdrew the insanity defense. The result was a manslaughter verdict instead of first-degree murder. Under the circumstances, it was a victory for the defense and justice.

When a lawyer comes to see me before he or she has filed a lawsuit, I know that we will have an effective collaboration. This lawyer recognizes the importance of an experienced forensic expert. However, when the lawyer comes to see me after filing a lawsuit and is locked into a strategy—despite having no idea of the scientific realities of the case—I know that he has not understood the value of an experienced forensic expert. Some lawyers view the expert in the pre-trial phase not as a consultant but as a prospective mouthpiece. The maxim, "A man who is his own lawyer has a fool for a client" is just as true for a lawyer who sees himself as his own expert. It is essential for lawyers to recognize that a professional who is knowledgeable in a given science is not necessarily a forensic expert. Forensic experts have scientific knowledge and courtroom experience.

Because forensic experts are involved in many cases, they acquire a sense of litigation strategy and can be valuable consultants for lawyers. A lawyer's competence is honed by deep involvement in a relatively small number of cases, but a forensic expert's skills are sharpened by countless courtroom appearances. I once asked my friend Jack Chambers, one of the most active and successful trial lawyers in Michigan, with whom I have worked on many cases, how he could remember every case on which we had collaborated. "That's simple," he said. "I never tried more than four cases a year and you worked on more than that in a month." A surgeon is defined by his ability to operate. An expert witness is defined by his ability to testify.

Lawyers file and argue lawsuits but do not give testimony. Most lawyers know little about testimonial skills and most perform poorly on the witness stand. I have observed outstanding lawyers do a poor job testifying. This is not surprising; we gain proficiency by practice. Acquisition of a skill is dependent upon neuroplasticity, which is a slow process. Long intervals between performances lead to a return to the "baseline." An attorney's scrutiny of an expert should focus upon the expert's capacity to function in the courtroom.

I enter the courtroom with the anticipation of contributing to a good cause. Most of the time, I leave the courtroom feeling that I have done my part. I have never testified in a case in which I doubted the merit of my position. I am aware, of course, that others may dispute my statement. The guilt or innocence of a defendant in a criminal or civil case is, after all, usually a matter of opinion. There is always some merit on both sides in a case that proceeded to trial; most of the time it is the interpretation of the facts that gives rise to differences of opinions. For instance, the defendant may have committed homicide, but the issue may be whether it was first-degree murder or manslaughter.

An attorney's failure to seek advice from a psychiatrist or qualified psychologist can be a violation of a defendant's Sixth Amendment right to effective assistance of counsel. This certainly applies to all homicide cases.[5] In a murder trial, the judge and jury need to understand the psychology of homicide, which requires the testimony of an expert. In this country, psychological testimony is admissible only when the defense of insanity is asserted. In most European countries every homicide perpetrator must undergo psychiatric examination.

THE TRIAL

In a trial both sides believe that the controversy should be resolved in their favor. It is rare for lawyers to argue cases purely for symbolic reasons without the hope of a victory. The primary vehicle of persuasion in the courtroom is testimony, which is an exchange of messages in an interactive manner. Testimony has intellectual content and the feelings that come with it. Emotions, facial expressions, body movements, are all part of the rich human communication system. Whoever tries to limit communication to the spoken or written word is giving up millions of years of evolutionary contributions to human communication. Dr. Paul MacLean, a research scientist at the National Institute of Mental Health, has stressed that our brain is the result of neuro-evolutionary changes, which have created a triune brain with three distinct brains: the reptilian brain, the limbic brain, and the neocortical brain.[6]

Testimony is an exchange that involves a number of participants. The testifier and the interrogator are the central figures. However, the opposing attorney participates through legal objections. The judge participates through rulings and other interventions. The whole process is governed by complex conventions, which are well known to the legal participants and are a mystery to most witnesses. This asymmetry of knowledge of the rules of the game and skills produce at times paradoxical results. A classic example is depicted in an excellent book called *A Civil Action* by Jonathan Harr,[7] which details a case in which the world's greatest geologist offered valid, accurate testimony, but a skillful cross-examination made him appear to be poorly informed and less than forthright.

Like surgeons, trial lawyers and forensic expert witnesses must acquire the skills of their profession through practice. For some strange reason if a forensic expert testifies often, he risks being held in disdain by lawyers who think of him as a "hired gun"— someone who plies his testimony for personal gain. Some lawyers prefer to hire experts who are "courtroom virgins." It has been my experience, in and out of the courtroom, that virginity is overrated.

In his most recent book, *Outliers: The Story of Success,* best-selling author Malcolm Gladwell explores research that shows that one needs 10,000 hours of deliberate practice to be an expert. Gladwell goes on to show that this applies not just to classical musicians, the group studied in the research he cites, but also to many other fields. Gladwell uses such diverse examples as the classical composer Mozart, chess grandmaster Bobby Fischer, the Beatles, and programmer Bill Gates.[8]

Plaintiffs in civil litigation are often represented by inexperienced trial lawyers with limited financial resources; they are usually unable to pursue lengthy lawsuits. On the other side are insurance companies, which are represented by experienced lawyers with unlimited resources. *Jones v. Smith* is usually *Jones v. Insurance Corpration*, although the jury is forbidden to know that. It is the law that if the word "insurance" passes anyone's lips, a mistrial is declared, supposedly to protect defendants from jurors' propensity to award outrageous amounts of money to plaintiffs with insurance companies to back them up. To make matters worse, the insurance industry's propaganda machine has created the myth that most civil lawsuits are frivolous, prejudicing the jury against the plaintiff from the start. The plaintiff in a civil case and the defendant in a criminal case are at a great disadvantage. Competent legal representation, a fair-minded judge, and robust expert testimony are essential to ensure some level of fairness.

Still, when the plaintiffs in civil lawsuits are treated unjustly, they lose only their compensation. When innocent defendants in criminal cases are convicted, they give up years of their lives in prison or, in some cases, they give up their very lives. For every innocent person convicted of a crime, the police investigator and the prosecutor are guilty of pursuing a charge that wasn't true, whether through malice or incompetence, yet few investigators or prosecutors are ever punished.

For every innocent person convicted of a crime, a guilty person goes free and is likely to commit a crime again. I testified in the case of Dr. Sam Sheppard (the television show and movie *The Fugitive* were loosely based on this case), who in 1954 was convicted of murdering his wife while the actual killer, Richard Eberling, was free to go on killing women for more than a decade. Similarly, Sterling Spann, a young African American resident of Clover, South Carolina, was convicted of the rape, torture, and murder of an elderly woman—a crime that was later proved to have been committed by a man named Johnny Hullett who had a well-established history of sadism. I will discuss the Spann-Hullet case in greater detail in a later chapter.

THE SCOPE OF EXPERT TESTIMONY

In civil and criminal cases the testimony of witnesses is limited to observation, knowledge, and recollection. Opinion testimony is divided into two categories, lay opinion and expert opinion. The scope of opinion testimony of a lay witness is very limited. An expert witness or professional witness has, as the result of education, training, skill, or experience, knowledge in a particular subject beyond that of the average person. American courts are concerned that experts will have too much influence upon the jury. Therefore, court rules prevent experts from "usurping the province of the jury." In real life, the expert's testimonial skills play a critical role in the degree of influence the expert will have upon the jury. In a courtroom a Nobel prizewinner in physics may be less persuasive than a high school teacher. Many an eminent scientist subjected to a forceful cross-examination was perceived by the jury to be contradictory and even foolish.

According to the Federal Rules of Evidence, experts may base their testimony on a variety of sources: "The facts or data in the particular case upon which an expert bases an opinion or inference may be those perceived by or made known to the expert at or before the hearing. If of a type reasonably relied upon by experts in the particular field in forming opinions or inferences upon the subject, the facts or data need not be admissible in evidence."[9]

The expert and the direct examiner have to keep a sharp eye on the opposing lawyers and the judge who may disturb the testimony by verbal and nonverbal means. I once testified in Detroit's Recorders Court on behalf of a defendant who was charged with first-degree murder of his wife. During my testimony, the judge was making a variety of gestures of disbelief. I turned to him and said, "Your Honor, if you have comments to make about my testimony, please put it in words and not in your body language." The judge excused the jury and chastised me for making this comment. I said to him, "Your Honor, I respectfully submit that everyone in this courtroom saw you making gestures of disbelief." The jury was returned and the judge no longer acted in this manner.

When a qualified expert gives opinions that are well-justified by the reasons provided, the expert is difficult to cross-examine. In these situations lawyers often resort to accusing the expert of being biased and a hired gun. These attacks are not likely to be of much value unless the expert is indeed biased, corrupt, or inexperienced. Courtroom-shy experts can be made to appear biased and corrupt even though they are competent and ethical. An effective expert witness rebuts every false accusation. Some biased judges try to prevent this by saying, "Doctor, you will have the chance to respond in detail on redirect by your lawyer." I often respond, "He is not my lawyer and I believe that I am entitled to explain why this statement is false." The judge frequently declares sternly, "My ruling stands," but the jury usually gets my message. It is foolish to antagonize a judge, but it is even more harmful to submit to an arbitrary or biased decision without protest.

AN EFFECTIVE EXPERT WITNESS

"Truth is what stands the test of experience."

—Albert Einstein

The American justice system is adversarial in nature, in contrast to the European system, which is inquisitorial. The decision makers in the inquisitorial system are experienced judges who have the power to assume investigative roles. In the adversarial system, the decision makers are the jury. Unlike inquisitorial judges, jury members are passive recipients of testimony. A jury is easier to manipulate than a panel of professional judges; therefore the relative skills of the participants play a more significant role in the American system.

All professionals are involved in a "community of practice." In medicine we call it clinical experience. I share Jean Lave and Etienne Wenger's view that learning as it normally occurs is a function of the practice, context, and culture in which it occurs.[10] Coaching and practice are the two common ways to become more skilled in an activity. This applies as much to playing tennis as to testifying in court. It is therefore astonishing that expert witnesses avoid these time-tested approaches. Only once in my whole career have I been retained by a law firm to coach a Colorado psychiatrist who was about to testify in a murder trial. The psychiatrist had never been in court, and the defense lawyer wanted me to advise the expert witness on the art of testimony.

The testimony of an expert is not a solo performance; it takes place as an interaction with lawyers. The expert's ability to function in this type of setting plays a major role in the outcome. The adversaries who have completely different objectives elicit the expert's testimony. However, direct and cross-examination are a unit. The true measure of an expert's effectiveness is the persuasiveness of his direct testimony and his ability to withstand a cross-examination. Effective testimony consists of valid and persuasive answers to appropriate questions asked by the direct examiner. An effective answer conveys a great deal of information and is emotionally gratifying to the fact finders.

The persuasive process is interactive; it is a relationship between the persuader and the audience. Through the mechanism of emotional identification, suffering is communicated to the jury by the witness. Most forensic experts are knowledgeable in their respective fields, but their ability to present their findings in the courtroom is understandably often inadequate. I say "understandably" because there is virtually no body of knowledge on the subject of giving testimony. Karl Popper, a philosopher of science, said that we are not students of subject matter but students of problems. If an expert has no trial experience, his or her ability to understand the problem is limited. Experts and lawyers make the erroneous assumption that the technical knowledge determines the value of the expert in a given case. I argue that a scientist without trial experience is not a forensic expert.

Scholarship without persuasiveness is a virtue in a research laboratory, but a flaw in the classroom and the courtroom. Good direct testimony frequently crumbles on cross-examination. Every witness is, or should be, committed to the truth of his testimony. However, no competent expert witness should be disinterested in (and therefore impartial to) the outcome. If I testify that Mr. Jones should be found legally insane instead of being found guilty of first-degree murder, I hope that the judge and jury will accept my opinion. If Mr. Jones is convicted, I will feel that the justice system failed and wonder whether my testimony was not sufficiently persuasive. The testifying expert's claim of impartiality is futile, counterproductive, and, above all, unnecessary. It is ethical to support one side in a controversy, if one is truthful and believes to be on the side of justice.

Persuasion is achieved by joining the forces of reason and emotion. To appreciate the significance of emotions in the litigation process, lawyers and experts need to ask themselves what kind of feeling the jury will have when they render a verdict in favor of or against this defendant. Will the jury feel proud of having found the defendant guilty or have a sense of shame for having imposed life in prison or a death sentence? Will they be pleased that they provided compensation for an injured plaintiff or will they feel gratified that they recognized a false claim?

For me, taking the witness stand is a magical experience. My usual distractibility gives way to concentration and synergy with the direct examiner. On cross-examination, I concentrate completely on the cross-examiner and try to put myself in his shoes. I testified in South Carolina before a trial judge who had to decide whether a new trial should be granted to a young black man who had spent half of his life on death row after having been wrongfully convicted of a sadistic sexual murder. I testified that he could not have been a sadistic sexual killer. The courtroom, which was in rural South Carolina, was full. On the right, the courtroom audience consisted of African Americans, primarily members of the church where the defendant's mother was an active member. On the left, the audience was mostly white members of the law-enforcement community and their supporters, who believed that the defendant was guilty.

At the end of my testimony, an elderly black man surrounded by a group of people approached me. "Doctor," he said in a booming voice, "you were almost as good as a preacher."

"Are you a preacher?" I asked.

"You better believe I am," he said.

The preacher was referring to my willingness to become emotional on the stand. He identified with my testimony. And while the trial judge did not agree that my opinions constituted "new evidence" that justified a new trial, the South Carolina Supreme Court found my testimony on behalf of the young man persuasive and reversed his conviction.

In Tulsa, Oklahoma, a mother abandoned by her husband carefully planned her suicide and the killing of her two small children. Mrs. Smith (not her real name) purchased a gun and took instructions on how to use it. She cancelled her mail delivery and took a vacation from her job as a nurse. Smith put her two children to sleep, laid down beside them, and shot them. She then placed the gun to the left of her sternum—the perfect location to hit the heart—and fired. She lay in a coma in her bed next to her two dead children for a week. A policeman who entered that bedroom never worked again after the shock of being exposed to this scene.

Smith lived and was charged with two counts of first-degree murder. The elected prosecutor cross-examined me. The defense was insanity. At one point the cross-examiner said, "Doctor, you said she committed suicide, but she is sitting here and looking at you." To this I replied in a slow but emotional voice, "A woman who killed her two children is dead." Suddenly there was complete silence in the courtroom and no more questions. The intense emotions of the case were crystalized in this single sentence. The jury returned an insanity verdict, the first one in anybody's memory in Tulsa. For years, I received a Christmas card from Smith and her mother.

If the expert's opinion does not support the view of the retaining lawyer, this does not mean that his or her work was not useful to the lawyer. The late Charles Simkins, a nationally known personal-injuries lawyer, repeatedly and publicly said that he found it useful when I advised him that some of the cases he referred to me were without merit. "It saved me from wasting time and money," he said.

An outstanding trial lawyer is a formidable opponent. I was the expert witness for plaintiffs whose four-year-old boy was electrocuted by a wire improperly repaired by a Detroit Edison Company electrical worker. The plaintiffs were represented by Michigan's most effective plaintiff's lawyers. Albert Miller, the defense lawyer, began his opening statement by saying something along the lines of, "We are guilty. Our negligence is responsible for the death of this beautiful child. The only question is, how much money should the parents receive, since no one can bring back their beloved youngster?" The jury found the electric company guilty—and returned a paltry $40,000 award. I called Miller, congratulating him on the outstanding outcome he had achieved for his client. Miller, on various occasions while giving speeches about trial technique, has said, "The plaintiff's expert, Dr. Tanay, congratulated me; however, my client was unhappy that I lost the case." The reality was that the plaintiff's lawyers were the losers, since the $40,000 did not cover the expenses associated with the case.

Miller's unconventional strategy produced an excellent result for the insurance company, and he was admired by members of his law firm.

What were the feelings of the parents of the dead child? Miller's arguments must have made them feel like money-hungry parents who were trying to enrich themselves by the death of their child. It is true that money could not have replaced the child, but it would have provided for treatment that both of these people desperately needed. They were also entitled to some compensation for the suffering they endured. The negligence of the electrical company was not punished. In the final analysis, this was a miscarriage of justice that would have produced widespread outrage if it had happened in a criminal case.

Most lawyers who come to my office "know in advance" what my opinion should be and how I should deliver it in the courtroom. Thus, my first task is to convert the lawyer from being my teacher into being my student. My next task is to reach an understanding with a lawyer as to what our goal is, that is, what will be considered a good result. When I testify in support of an insanity defense I hope to gain a lesser verdict than the first-degree murder sentence the prosecutor is seeking.

Often, my mentoring role becomes as significant for the case as my testimony. Some lawyers have been more receptive to my advice than others. Charles Simkins, the nationally known trial lawyer whom I have already mentioned, gave me a book, *The Sailing Doctor,* with this inscription: "December 4, 1992, Dr. Tanay: It is only fitting and proper that I should give you, the man who has guided my career, and navigated me so generously, this little book on sailing. I thank God daily for your presence in my life, I am very mindful of the fact that any success I may have achieved would not be possible without the benefit of having been under your protective wing. May God bless you. Always, most respectfully, Charles Simkins." The regard that Simkins had for me contributed to my effectiveness in testifying in his many cases. Somehow his respect for me was conveyed to the jury, who attached more weight to my testimony. The opposite occurs on cross-examination. The opposing lawyer often shows his contempt, and that, in turn, is communicated to the jury. That is one reason why I do not silently accept abuse, be it explicit or implicit, from a cross-examiner.

THE TRIAL LAWYER AND THE EXPERT

"A jury consists of 12 persons chosen to decide who has the better lawyer."

—Attributed to Robert Frost

A litigant looking for a trial lawyer who lets his fingers do the walking, as the *Yellow Pages* advertisement suggests, may end up with the equivalent of Clarence Darrow—or he may find a lawyer who has never tried a case before. A defendant or a plaintiff will not necessarily win because his lawyer is effective, but they are likely to lose, regardless of the merit of the case, if the lawyer is inexperienced.

The lawyer is the captain of the ship; the crew consists of a client, witnesses, and the lawyer's staff. The success of the voyage is the lawyer's responsibility, but not his sole achievement. A professional, whether a lawyer or expert witness, is judged not by intentions, but by performance. The word *performance* in this context is distasteful to many. A friend who is a forensic pathologist speaks of "performing an autopsy," but took umbrage when I complimented him on good performance in the courtroom. "I just told the truth," he said. The impact of an expert witness is based upon his or her entire image—personality, style of testimony, and ability to stand firm under attack. It takes a secure, assertive personality, along with courtroom experience, to cope effectively with a cross-examination.

A great deal of advice that lawyers get is based upon social science research, which, while valid statistically, is of little value when dealing with individuals. Statistics are useless when one deals with a population of one. There is a growing group of professionals known as "trial consultants"—professionals whom lawyers rely upon to help select juries and devise trial strategies. Trial consultants engage in witness preparation, but they do not qualify as expert witnesses themselves. They give advice on how to testify but they rarely, if ever, have given testimony. Most trial consultants are psychologists who rely on social psychology data to advise lawyers on trial strategy and tactics. An experienced forensic expert can be a good source of trial strategy advice in a specific case.

Most lawyers make assumptions about the biases of jurors. A plaintiff's lawyer may tell me, "The gray-haired juror in the first row is a conservative Republican; he will be against us," while a civil defense lawyer will say, "The juror to your right in the first row is a liberal Democrat; I couldn't get rid of him." These generalizations, even though possibly valid statistically, have little value when applied to one person.

Barry Waldman, one of the most effective trial lawyers I have ever known, went to great effort to get rid of a certain juror because she fell into a statistical category suggesting that she would be a bad juror for the plaintiff. She remained on the jury and became the foreperson. After the jury returned a large verdict in our favor, the woman asked Waldman, "Why were you so against me? I was on your side from the beginning."

My friend John Chambers, who is an outstanding trial lawyer, has a questionable rule that teachers make bad jurors. Some lawyers believe that Jews make good jurors for plaintiffs. These generalizations, like all generalizations, may be true in a large number of cases. A physician who treats an individual patient based upon epidemiological data rather than clinical reality may be committing malpractice; this is true also for trial lawyers.

Many lawyers have limited courtroom experience. A well-known attorney, Paula Young, writes on her website: "For nearly twenty years, I described myself as a litigator, but harbored an unspoken insecurity that I could not call myself a trial lawyer. 'Huh?' you say. Let me explain. For over ten years, I served as general counsel to the receiver of the then-largest property and casualty insurance insolvency in U.S. history. During that time, I successfully 'litigated' nearly $60 million in claims against re-insurers, but actually participated in one trial involving those claims."[11] Young's situation is not unique. On numerous occasions, I have worked with lawyers whose courtroom experience was nonexistent. When I was on the faculty of Wayne State University Law School, most of the law professors there had no courtroom experience. At faculty meetings I was the "authority" on what happens in the courtroom.

Truly effective trial lawyers specialize in specific areas of litigation, such as criminal law, personal injury, or bankruptcy. Such lawyers are rare. Just as a medical general practitioner would never attempt cardiac surgery, a commercial lawyer should never attempt to represent a client charged with first-degree murder.

In fifty years of forensic practice, I have testified in hundreds of insanity defense cases; only a few of the lawyers I worked with had handled more than one insanity case before they came to see me. Most did so for the first time.

Of course, there are exceptions to every rule. John Hinckley's father was a well-to-do business executive who made an effort to get the best possible legal representation for his schizophrenic son, who had attempted to kill President Reagan. He contacted his business lawyer in Colorado, who recommended Vincent J. Fuller, the lawyer's classmate from law school. Fuller had experience with white-collar crime but was not a criminal lawyer. Nevertheless, Fuller successfully presented the insanity defense on behalf of his client. He retained Dr. William Carpenter, an expert on schizophrenia who had the ability to be persuasive as an expert witness.

There are people who have unique talents.

The trial lawyer and the expert form a team. There has to be synergy between them. The team's effectiveness depends on the competence and experience of both team members. A lawyer gets the expert he deserves, and the expert deserves the lawyer he has agreed to work with.

The order of witnesses is critical to the outcome of a trial. The most persuasive witness should be presented first. By "persuasiveness" I mean not only the ability to present an opinion effectively on direct examination, but also the ability to defend it on cross-examination. Each witness is a point and counter-point, providing an opportunity to present both sides of the case. A witness for the plaintiff gives the defense an opening to present their views. A good witness for the plaintiff supports the plaintiff's position and gives little opportunity for the defense to present their version.

At the end of direct examination, lawyers often say, "Your witness." Listen to the words! Skillful lawyers can turn inexperienced witnesses for the opposing side to their advantage. I recall a case of medical malpractice tried in Ann Arbor that appeared to be an open-and-shut case for the plaintiff. I persuaded the lawyers that I should be the first witness. I arrived early, assuming that I would be the first to take the witness chair. Instead, the lawyers insisted on putting the defendant doctor first, in order to ask a "few foundation questions that would take five minutes." Two hours later, the five-minute witness finally got off the stand. The defense lawyer took the opportunity to enable the doctor to tell his side of the story. The plaintiff forfeited his advantage of going first and lost the case. I cannot emphasize strongly enough that the order of witnesses should be determined by their ability to withstand cross-examination. In many cases, I have accomplished a great deal more on cross-examination than on the direct examination. Only a foolhardy lawyer assumes that his or her opponent's case has no merit. The real issue is the balance of merit between the two sides. Because of the bias against plaintiffs in civil cases, the plaintiff must have considerably more merit than the defendant to win. Conversely, a defendant in a criminal case must have a preponderance of merit to prevail. A criminal defendant is guilty unless proven innocent.

Perfectionism is a flaw in a trial lawyer, since virtually every element of a trial is imperfect. Rarely does everything go as it should. People who claim that "failure is not an option" are incapable of imagining that they may be wrong. Failure may not be an option, but it is an ever-present possibility. Firmness in pursuit of strategy and fluidity of tactics are the hallmarks of effective lawyering. A good trial lawyer constantly changes trial tactics to advance his strategy. A witness who once seemed crucial is omitted; the order of witnesses is changed; a five-minute witness is examined for an hour, or vice versa. Each witness has a purpose that may change as the case unfolds.

Attributes that serve a nonlitigating lawyer may become liabilities in the ever-changing battlefield of a trial. The deliberateness and erudition of a lawyer adept at writing appellate briefs may be of little help in a trial, where he must have the ability to think on his feet. A trial lawyer is a strategist and a tactician.

Some lawyers are unduly concerned with contradictions in the expert's testimony; scientific opinions are often ambiguous. Scientific "truths" have limited shelf life. This fact does not stop me from having a strong belief in the validity of a scientific theory. The essence of scientific knowledge is generalization: whatever is irrelevant is omitted. The separation of relevant and irrelevant observations and inferences is necessary to any scientific formulation. Often, when I mention that something is not relevant, the opposing lawyer objects that relevance is for the judge to determine and is not the subject of expert testimony.[12] For some strange reason, some lawyers assume that the law has a proprietary claim on the concept of relevance.

The U.S. Supreme Court determined in 1993 that judges should decide what scientific testimony is relevant to a case (*Daubert v. Merrell Dow Pharmaceuticals, Inc*). The *Daubert* standard does not refer to relevancy in the legal sense but relevancy to the explanation of a scientific concept. This approach diminishes the effectiveness of scientific testimony, as a judge determines not only what the law is but what is science. The *Daubert* court established criteria for judges to screen "purportedly scientific evidence." The four *Daubert* criteria for evaluating the admissibility of expert testimony are:

1. whether the methods upon which the testimony is based are centered upon a testable hypothesis;
2. the known or potential rate of error associated with the method;
3. whether the method has been subject to peer review;
4. whether the method is generally accepted in the relevant scientific community.

The *Daubert* ruling further states "The trial judge should consider the meanings of 'scientific' and 'knowledge.' The admissibility of expert testimony is determined by the requirement that to be admissible, '[t]he subject of an expert's testimony must be "scientific . . . knowledge,"' because it is 'the requirement that an expert's testimony pertain to "scientific knowledge"' that 'establishes a standard of evidentiary reliability.' Furthermore, 'in order to qualify as "scientific knowledge," an inference or assertion must be derived by the scientific method.'"

That *Daubert* decision controls the admissibility of expert testimony in the federal courts. The decision has also been adopted by thirty-one states; thirteen states continue to rely upon the *Frye* decision, which established that in order to qualify as expert testimony a witness's opinions must be consistent with generally accepted theory in the given field.

THE IMAGE OF FORENSIC EXPERTS

The public views lawyers and forensic experts with suspicion unless they do the "right thing"—namely, prosecute criminals and defend clients against "frivolous lawsuits." Plaintiff lawyer-bashing is highly popular, as is attacking the experts who work with them.

In 1969, a group of forensic psychiatrists gathered at a Philadelphia hotel for the purpose of creating a new organization dedicated to forensic psychiatry. I suggested the name "American Academy of Forensic Psychiatry" or the "American Association of Forensic Psychiatry." My proposal was defeated. Participants objected to the term "forensic" because it implied courtroom testimony. The new organization was called the American Academy of Psychiatry and the Law (AAPL). The prevailing sentiment was that the euphemism "Psychiatry and the Law" stressed the relationship between law and psychiatry and avoided the stigma that comes with a courtroom battle of the experts.

In 1972 I published a paper entitled "Forensic Psychiatry in the Legal Defense of Murder." In this article, I wrote, "The contemporary ideal forensic psychiatrist is a man who writes extensively on the subject of law and psychiatry, but avoids tarnishing his image by entering the courtroom. The recently organized American Academy of Psychiatry and the Law took as one of its basic tenets avoidance of any involvement with courtroom testimony."[13]

Dr. Robert Sadoff, president of AAPL at that time, wrote me a letter chiding me for this comment. He said that the reluctance to be identified with courtroom testimony was not a basic tenet of the Academy. However, Dr. Jonas Rappeport, AAPL's founder, spoke of psychiatry as "the be-legaled" profession. In the early days of AAPL, Rappeport was critical of me for being too involved with the law: he called me, disparagingly, "almost a lawyer." I had begun teaching in law school in 1959.

During the 1989 AAPL convention, I entered an elevator wearing my American Academy of Psychiatry and Law convention badge. Two young women were already in the elevator, and one of them asked, "What is the American Academy for Psychiatry and the Law?" I answered, "A national association of forensic psychiatrists." The other woman asked "Why don't they call it that?" "That's a good question," I said as the two women exited the elevator.

At the 1996 annual meeting of the AAPL, I served with about ten others on the Committee on the Private Practice of Forensic Psychiatry. At the end of an animated discussion on issues relating to forensic psychiatry, the chairman asked how much time each of us devoted to the practice of forensic psychiatry. To my amazement, a colleague who was well trained in forensic psychiatry volunteered, "About five percent." I must have uttered some sound of surprise because she turned to me and asked, "What do you find so surprising about it?" My response was, "Your training and talents are obviously underutilized." I was even more surprised by her next comment: "I do not want to do forensic psychiatry more than five percent of the time." She said this with pride. No physician would call himself a cardiologist if his practice of cardiology was limited to 5 percent of his time. A psychiatrist who only occasionally sees a child in his or her practice would not consider himself or herself a child psychiatrist. The AAPL membership is what sociologists Avishai Margalit and Joseph Raz call an "encompassing group," meaning that membership is a matter of belonging rather than of achievement. One need not demonstrate competence in order to be accepted as a full member."[14] There is little space devoted in the AAPL meetings or publications to the skill of testimony.

THE EXPERT'S REPORT

Once the expert has collected all of the relevant data, he should write a report for the referring attorney. Before beginning work on the case, the expert should have secured from the referring attorney a written communication instructing him as to which issues he ought to address. I insist upon such a document, anticipating that if I testify at some point, I may be asked what my assignment was.

The expert's report has many uses. First, it summarizes the expert's work in reaching his opinion. Second, it may serve as an outline for the lawyer's direct examination if the expert testifies. Further, many jurisdictions require exchange of expert reports between the two sides. A report may induce settlement of the case, as has happened repeatedly in my experience.

If the plaintiff suffers from an illness, the relationship between the event under dispute and the patient's condition is addressed in the report. The event could be causative, aggravating, or neither. The degree of functional impairment, if any, and its relationship to the event under dispute should also be described. Prognosis and therapeutic recommendations have to be formulated because the award for damages takes into consideration future medical expenses. Pain and suffering experienced by the patient should be addressed.

Some lawyers insist that the expert should not provide a report; they are concerned that the report might contain information adverse to their claim. Other lawyers say that they do not want to provide the opposite attorney with ammunition for cross-examination. As a public document, the report will, sooner or later, become known to all concerned, so it is a double-edged sword. Only a naive expert and an inexperienced lawyer expect the report to be useful to one side only. Most reports contain some information that may be useful to the other side.

I recall a Boston attorney asking me not to issue a report in order to avoid a lengthy cross-examination. I wrote to him stating that I like lengthy cross-examinations, whereupon he asked me how I would explain my service in the German military during World War II. As a Holocaust survivor from Poland, I found this question amusing, so I asked in my letter why he thought that I served in the German military during World War II. He wrote back stating that my service in the German army was self-evident: I graduated in 1951 from medical school in Munich, Germany. A few weeks later he discovered his error and apologized for his erroneous inference.

TESTIMONY AND EMOTION

Everybody knows that emotions play a critical role in human decision-making. Yet before I take the witness stand, some lawyers plead with me to avoid showing emotion, even when the facts are heart-wrenching. They ask me to take the cross-examiner's insults with forbearance and pretend not to be offended. I tell them that I am not an actor and that my pretense would be transparent and result in my losing credibility with the jury.

The unemotional approach has one problem: it is not persuasive. Experts' testimony should be free of undignified, excessive displays of feelings, but it should be real and authentic. To be persuasive, one has to combine knowledge, reason, and passion. Testimony is a communicative art. The words used by experts and lawyers during testimony activate emotions. The words *murder* and *homicide* may be listed in the dictionary as synonyms; in real life, they may mean the difference between life and a death sentence. The word *murder* is a condemnatory judgment; *homicide* is a description of an event.

In a persuasive interaction, there are message givers and message receivers. The message itself consists of the informational content and emotional impact. If we visualize the personality as consisting of id, ego, and superego, then the question arises as to which part of the personality the message should be addressed to. Ideally, the message should be perceived at all three levels of the mental apparatus. In everyday language, that means that the message should be perceived on the gut level, be acceptable to reason, and stir up the conscience of the message receiver. All else being equal, the persuasive success of a communicator will be determined by the selection of the audience. Playing Mozart to an audience receptive only to rock-and-roll music will not lead to positive audience response. The problem is that, under average litigation circumstances, we have no way of determining the composition of the jury.

I believe that anybody, including an expert witness, can and should show feelings when it is appropriate. I base this view upon my extensive courtroom experience and the authority of Charles Darwin, who had shown in 1872 the adaptive value of emotions. Darwin described how the expressive movements of the face and body are "in themselves of much importance to our welfare. The movements of expression give vividness and energy to our spoken words. They reveal the thoughts and intentions of others more truly than do words, which may be falsified."[15]

William James, the American philosopher and psychologist who was trained as a medical doctor, believed that only through feeling is it possible "to perceive how events happen, and how work is actually done."[16] We are keenly aware that emotions may cause conflicts, but we should remember that emotions may resolve conflicts as well.

Clarence Darrow relied on emotions and reason to achieve victory in his cases. When Darrow finished his closing argument, more often than not the jury was in tears. The importance of the emotions in decision-making has been studied by many, including Dr. Paul MacLean, a senior research scientist at the National Institute of Mental Health, who in 1952 published his first paper on the "visceral brain" and coined the term "limbic system." The limbic brain is the source of emotional response and should not be ignored as a player in the decision-making process.

The neuroscientist António Damásio showed that people who are emotionally deprived have difficulty making rational decisions. He writes in the introduction to *Descartes's Error: Emotion, Reason, and the Human Brain*,

> Although I cannot tell for certain what sparked my interest in the neural underpinnings of reason, I do know when I became convinced that the traditional views on the nature of rationality could not be correct. I had been advised early in life that sound decisions came from a cool head. . . . I had grown up accustomed to thinking that the mechanisms of reason existed in a separate province of the mind, where emotion should not be allowed to intrude, and when I thought of the brain behind that mind, I envisioned separate neural systems for reason and emotion.

Damasio goes on to explain his clinical work with individuals who contradicted the traditional view of the cool-headed reasonable person. He learned that despite having perfect logic, they made awful decisions. He wrote of one such person: "But now I had before my eyes the coolest, least emotional, most intelligent human being one might imagine, and yet his practical reasoning was so impaired that it produced, in the wanderings of daily life, a succession of mistakes, a perpetual violation of what would be considered socially appropriate and personally advantageous." [17]

In his best-selling book *Blink: The Power of Thinking without Thinking*, Malcolm Gladwell extols the role of intuition in our day-to-day lives—a lesson I learned as a teenager trying to survive the Holocaust (it has served me well in the courtroom, too). In his book, Gladwell brought attention to the work of Gerd Gigerenzer, a German social psychologist who directed Munich's famed Max Planck Institute for Psychological Research and who wrote a book called *Gut Feelings: The Intelligence of the Unconscious* (the German title, *Bauchentscheidungen*, literally translates as "decisions from the belly"). [18]

Knowledge of the power of emotions plays a large part in my insistence on tape-recording or videotaping all of my interviews. I know that the patient's words and demeanor are much more persuasive to a jury than I could ever be. One of the oldest and most valuable diagnostic tools in medicine is a good history. The patient-litigant tells the story in his or her own words. In my reports I include verbatim some portions of the interview. The patient is doing the talking instead of me. "I was hit by the truck," is different than, "The truck collided with the car of Mrs. Jones." What needs to be told to the jury is the experience as endured by the patient. I cannot tell the story if I have never heard it or it has faded in my memory. Before I testify I listen to the recording, which makes an interview that took place two years ago come alive.

The biggest obstacle to a lawyer's success in the courtroom is excess aggressiveness; the biggest obstacle to an expert witness's persuasiveness is timidity. An example of poor expert witness performance is described in the book *A Civil Action* by Jonathon Harr. [19] He describes an actual trial that hinged on the effectiveness of the expert witness testimony.

In Woburn, Massachusetts, several young children developed leukemia because the drinking water was polluted with industrial waste. Two of the nation's largest corporations were accused of causing these children's deaths. Jan Schlitchmann, the plaintiff's lawyer, spared no effort in preparing his experts. Geologist John Dobrinski was the first expert witness. Schlitchmann, an outstanding trial lawyer, spent days preparing Dobrinski for his testimony. Harr says in his book that Schlitchmann called Dobrinski "a courtroom virgin." Schlitchmann established that Dobrinski was outstanding in his field and had done excellent work on the scientific aspects of the case, but Dobrinski was an ineffective witness. Schlitchmann had to instruct him what to do with his hands, which way to look, how to sit, and so on.

Schlitchmann anticipated that Dobrinski's direct examination would take three days, but Drobinski remained on the stand for three weeks. Schlitchmann was satisfied with Dobrinski's testimony because he "never once raised his voice or betrayed any irritation" when he was cross-examined by defense lawyer Jerome Facher, who accused Dobrinski of being a perjurer, being incompetent, and so on. Although none of these accusations was true, the failure of the witness to challenge the cross-examiner created a false image.

The next defense witness was Professor George Pinder, a man of outstanding reputation and the chairman of the Department of Geology at Princeton. In cross-examination, Facher abused Pinder. Consistent with conventional wisdom, Pinder was considered a good witness because he replied calmly to all insults. He was cross-examined in minute detail based upon thousands of pages of depositions that had been gathered over five days. Harr reports,

> By the fourth day of Facher's cross-examination, Pinder had lost his appetite and developed insomnia. He felt the burden of the case—the Woburn families, all the other experts, Schlitchmann and his partners and their financial investment—entirely on his shoulders. At night he would lie awake in his bed at the Ritz Carlton thinking about Facher and plotting escapes from Facher's traps. He felt lucky if he got four hours' sleep. He called home to Princeton every evening and talked to his wife. "You can't imagine the pressure," he told her. "There is no relief from it. I never had anyone try to discredit me as a human being, which is what Facher is trying to do."[20]

A skillful lawyer dealing with an honest, well-prepared witness who gives meritorious, justified testimony can still create the appearance of deception and incompetence unless the expert witness is skilled in the art of testimony from either experience or talent. In the words of Schlitchmann's associate Conway, "George Pinder is the guru, the world's greatest geology expert. He knows more about the aquifer than anyone else in the world." But Conway also said of Pinder's time on the stand, "There is nothing worse than watching your witness being raped. It is awful to sit there and not being able to do anything." Paradoxically, Schlitchmann took pride in the fact that Dobrinski was a "courtroom virgin," even as this made him the ideal target of the so-called courtroom "rape."[21]

Schlitchmann had made the common mistake of getting the world's greatest experts on the subject instead of getting a person with adequate knowledge and ability to present that knowledge in the courtroom. Schlitchmann, devastated by the debacle of the cross-examination of his star witness, spent hours preparing Pinder for redirect. This was another mistake. In Harr's words, "Schlitchmann felt he could make Pinder shine again on redirect."[22]

In reality, these efforts were quite obviously counterproductive because they made the expert more anxious and deprived him of sleep. Lawyers often try to artificially mold the witness instead of learning what the witness is really like and using the witness's existing assets to the best advantage. It borders on grandiosity for a lawyer to believe that he can transform a meek person into an assertive, self-assured witness, so why spend hours trying to do so? After all the preparations, Schlitchmann asked Pinder just before he took the witness stand, "Are you feeling okay?"

"I was feeling fine until I started talking with you," muttered Pinder. Harr comments, "Pinder did not do fine that day." Harr writes that at the end of a devastating re-cross-examination, "As the day wore on, Judge Skinner had a few more observations to make about Pinder. 'You have a hopeless witness who changes from A to B,' the judge told Schlitchmann at a bench conference. 'The spirit of his answers doesn't change from day to day, but the form certainly does.' The lawyer answered and added as an aforethought, 'Expert witnesses are born, not made.' 'But you made him an expert,' replied the judge."[23] Some people have a natural talent to be persuasive and resist intimidation. Obviously, Judge Skinner and Schlitchmann were not talking about the geological expertise of Professor Pinder, or his veracity, but about his testimonial skills. In the courtroom it did not matter how much geology Professor Pinder knew; what was essential was his ability to function in the courtroom. I believe that effective experts are rarely born; they develop their skills through experience in the courtroom.

The importance of a witness depends on the ability to give persuasive direct testimony and to withstand cross-examination, no matter how abusive. The secret of being effective on cross-examination is anticipatory scrutiny; the question on the table is a harbinger of questions not yet asked. One common cross-examiner's tactic is what I call pseudo-cross-examination. The cross-examiner "testifies" under the guise of asking questions and then demands a yes-or-no answer from the expert. The inexperienced expert falls into this trap. This creates the impression that the cross-examiner, who after all has the burden of proof, is prevailing. An experienced expert finds ways of dealing with this scheme productively. I like to respond to such tactics by saying, "This is an interesting observation. What is your question?"

COMPONENTS OF EFFECTIVE TESTIMONY

Experts, like all human beings, get tired. I am not reluctant to inform a judge that I need a break or that I can no longer continue for the day. Some judges are resistant to these requests, but I make clear to them that I cannot perform my function effectively if I am exhausted. Testimony should not be an endurance contest.

An expert should pay attention to his or her voice and to the variety of distractions that take place in the courtroom. I recall a judge in a Detroit courtroom who did paperwork during my testimony. At one point I stopped speaking and looked at him, whereupon he said, "Just because you are testifying doesn't mean that everything has to stop," to which I said to the judge, "Your Honor, I respectfully suggest that I and possibly the jury are distracted by your activities."

The American courtroom system is plagued by lengthy delays. Testimony often begins hours later than scheduled. Quite often this has to do with capricious behavior on the part of the judges. I have had a number of confrontations with judges on this issue. I recall testifying in Detroit's Recorder's Court (criminal court) for about half an hour when I overheard the bailiff whisper to the judge that the judge's dental appointment was nearing. The judge announced that court was adjourned until 2:00 P.M. In those days, I had a full-time psychotherapeutic practice, and I had been assured that I would be out of the courtroom by 1:00 P.M. I told the judge that I could not be back in the courtroom at 2:00 P.M., whereupon the judge said, "I will send the sheriff to get you."

I told him that I had heard that he adjourned because of a dental appointment that he clearly had scheduled some time ago. I told him that if I had known that I would be testifying at 2:00 P.M., I could have cancelled my patients for the afternoon. "That's your problem," the judge replied.

I left the courtroom and headed for the telephone booth and called my friend Theodore Souris, a Michigan Supreme Court Justice. I told him that I intended not to return. Ted said, "Don't do that. You'll be putting yourself in his hands. Instead, write a letter to the Supreme Court and he will be reprimanded." I had no choice but to place a notice on my office door advising my patients that I was away. Nonetheless, arbitrary delays should be anticipated by an expert, as they are often out of the expert's control.

One should also consider situations in which it is better not to testify. On March 5, 2007, while I was in Longboat Key, Florida, a Detroit radio and television personality called to interview me about a gruesome murder that had taken place in Detroit. A man had killed his wife, dismembered her body, took the torso to another location, and then brought it back. When the police came to search his home, the man left and drove to northern Michigan; he was later found wandering in the woods, barefoot in the snow and suffering from severe hypothermia.

Not many details of the case were known at that point, and they were certainly not known to me. I expressed the opinion that the homicide sounded bizarre. It didn't seem to fit the usual spousal homicide, and I said that I would need to know a great deal more before expressing an opinion. I was then asked about the influence that this tragedy would have upon the two children, who had been taken by the sister of the perpetrator and were in her care. I emphasized that sensitive handling of this situation would minimize the harmful effects that would be inevitable for the children. Depicting the father as a monster would not be beneficial to the children's development. As little as possible in terms of details should be told to the children, because they had no ability to cope with the whole tragedy.

A few hours later I received a telephone call from a lawyer who heard the broadcast. She was retained by the sister of the homicide perpetrator, who was seeking temporary custody of the children. The lawyer wanted my testimony via phone in a hearing that would take place that very afternoon in which a referee would decide who should have temporary custody of the children. I was told that my opinion would be very helpful to the case of the father's sister.

I informed the lawyer that the comments that I made in the context of a news media interview were general observations and were different from what I might give as a professional opinion in a specific case in court. There are many variables involved in any specific child-custody case. I declined to participate. The attorney said that she would play the radio recording to the magistrate (I do not know whether she did so).

The point is that an opinion should be delivered for a specific audience. When I teach medical students, I may choose to express opinions that I would not consider appropriate in a courtroom, and vice versa.

THE ART OF PERSUASION AND THE EXPERT WITNESS

Persuasiveness is the expert's greatest asset, but it hardly ever tops the lawyer's list of preferred qualities in an expert. Many professionals who are persuasive in daily interactions steer clear of persuasion in the courtroom. Most experts are willing to spend many hours arriving at scientifically valid opinions but resist devoting any time to improving their persuasive skills. To my knowledge, I was the first member in the American Academy of Forensic Sciences to offer a seminar on effective testimony. Many professionals who have limited courtroom experience downgrade persuasiveness as inconsistent with being "objective" and impartial.

Testimony, including scientific testimony, is never result-neutral. Even a material witness usually knows which side will benefit from his or her testimony. An engineering expert who testifies that a bridge collapsed because of faulty construction is implicitly telling the jury to find the defendant company guilty of negligence.

I call expert testimony "teaching under combat conditions." The adversary system disregards the meek expert, even though he may have relevant scientific knowledge. Every teacher who faces an audience is an advocate and a persuader. The teacher's goal differs from that of the expert witness, but the tools are the same. An effective expert witness must combine knowledge, persuasiveness, and a sense of strategy.

An expert witness is a person of authority. The German sociologist Max Weber identified three types of authority: rational, traditional, and charismatic.[24] An expert witness, by definition, has a claim on the first two: the expert's formulation is presumably rational and being declared an expert witness by the court takes care of the traditional source of authority. Charisma depends upon the expert's personality and passion. If you want to be persuasive, testify about something that has made you emotional or, at the very least, something that you consider a contribution to justice.

Advocating for an opinion one holds is natural and ethical. Aristotle, in his dicussion of persuasiveness, emphasized that credibility is the most powerful evidence and said it rests on the authority that comes from experience and passion.[25] Lawyers often tell experts: "Don't let them get you emotional." But if the jury perceives that the expert has no emotional commitment to his or her opinion, they are not likely to find the opinion believable or persuasive.

In conclusion, let me list eight attributes of an effective expert witness:

1. *Competence*: observers gain the impression that the witness is a responsible professional.
2. *Authority*: the witness inspires respect in the jury.
3. *Familiarity* with the details of the case and understanding of the relevant technical issues.
4. *Emotional involvement* with the outcome—the witness expresses appropriate feelings.
5. *Spontaneity*: the capacity to deal with challenges intuitively; the ability to think on one's feet.
6. *Sense of strategy*: that is, an awareness of the long-range goals of the proceedings.
7. *Courtroom presence*: the ability to command the audience's attention through demeanor and verbal communication.
8. *Structural sense of testimony*: the ever-present awareness that all elements of testimony are related. Each witness is functionally connected with all evidence that has been presented and will be presented.

EXPERTS AND MONEY

Expert witnesses, like all professionals, should be paid for their work. However, there is a strange perception that experts paid on a fee-for-service basis are less credible than experts who receive a salary (for example, a court-clinic employee or a full-time university employee). Cross-examiners often ask me: "Doctor, how much are you being paid for your testimony?" The obvious answer is, "I am not being paid for my testimony; I am being paid for the work I have done in this case."

I recall testifying in the 1980s on the opposite side of Dr. Ames Robey, the former director of the Michigan Forensic Center. The prosecutor "asked" me on cross-examination: "Unlike Dr. Robey you, Dr. Tanay, are being paid for your testimony." I answered that Robey is paid just like everybody else, including the judge and the prosecutor. The prosecutor insisted that Robey was not paid "for testimony" whereas I was in a position of being paid "for testimony." At that point, Judge Colombo broke in and said, "I take judicial notice of the fact that Dr. Robey, just like Dr. Tanay, does get paid for his time."

Some expert witnesses are not paid at all because they are not prudent in their dealings with the retaining lawyers. I learned from the following case that requiring a contractual agreement and prepayment from the lawyer is essential for a forensic expert.

A middle-aged Michigan man (let us call him "James Gardener") discovered that his daughter was sharing an apartment with two other college students. He presumed that this was a sexual affair and killed them in a fit of rage. Three lawyers were retained to defend Gardener. The defense was insanity. The lawyers produced a psychiatrist who had never testified before. During the direct examination, the lead lawyer stressed that the expert witness had never been in a courtroom. Predictably, the direct examination was not persuasive, and the cross-examination was a disaster for the defense.

The trial judge told the lawyers that they were ineffective and advised them, "You should call Doctor Tanay." I was brought into the case as a rebuttal witness to the psychiatrist for the prosecution, who testified that Gardener was sane. My final bill was three thousand dollars. The lawyers refused to pay my fee. They falsely claimed that I told them that whether I got paid or not did not matter, as I was interested in being involved in a case that dominated the headlines in Detroit. I was unable find a lawyer to sue these three lawyers. I complained to the Michigan Bar that I could not get a lawyer to represent me, and the bar appointed a well-known lawyer named Lawrence S. Charfoos. The case dragged on for a long time, since the lawyers made a great many motions to keep us out of the courtroom. When we were finally scheduled to appear before a judge, Charfoos was tied up in a trial. He suggested that a young lawyer from his firm named David Christensen would be able to represent me. I agreed.

During the trial, a well-known criminal lawyer testified that he attended a lunch at Carl's Chophouse in Detroit when the three lawyers and I were discussing my participation in the Gardner case. He described me as pleading to be given the opportunity to be an expert in this famous case. To my dismay, Christensen limited his cross-examination to one single question, "The behavior of Dr. Tanay seems to have offended you," to which the witness emphatically agreed.

Since we were the moving party, Christensen was the first one to give the closing argument. He began by saying that he does not mind lawyers putting on a witness who is lying, but he is bothered when lawyers do not instruct the witness how to lie effectively. Christensen was interrupted in his closing statement by the judge, who admonished him that he was accusing a fellow member of the bar of perjury. At this point, Christensen told the judge, "But Your Honor, this is obvious, please note." He then walked over to a blackboard and wrote down the day of the Gardener trial and the agreed upon date of the luncheon between the lawyers and me. The luncheon took place weeks after the trial. "How could Dr. Tanay plead to be an expert witness in a case that has already been concluded?" The judge had no choice but to rule in our favor, and I was paid $3,000.00. I was not surprised that David Christensen became one of the most effective trial lawyers in Michigan and partner of Lawrence Charfoos.

The point of the story is that it is essential to have a written contract with the lawyers stating that they are responsible for the fees of the expert. In many instances, lawyers do not have the necessary financial resources to live up to their obligations. No such problems are encountered when testifying for the prosecution or defense in civil cases, which usually have unlimited funds. No matter which side experts contract with, they should have retainer agreements.

If a criminal defendant is indigent (as is often the case), then an expert is limited in how much time he or she can invest, as funds are scarce. This is particularly true in Michigan and other states that do not have a public defender system. Incompetent representation of criminal defendants in such states is common. The American Bar Association reported:

Inadequate compensation for indigent defense attorneys in Michigan makes the recruitment and retention of experienced attorneys extraordinarily difficult. . . . The rule is you don't have an expert. You don't have an investigator. If you want to get one, you get $150 in Wayne County to hire an investigator to do all the investigation you need. If you want an expert, you will get $250 to have the expert meet with your client, prepare testimony, and testify. The dollar limits are wholly unreasonable. We really don't have technology support either. Many lawyers who are providing much of the work don't even have a secretary, let alone a law library.[26]

Rich defendants, on the other hand may "suffer" from experts' unnecessarily excessive time investment. The John DuPont case shows how great wealth can influence forensic evaluation in a negative way.

In January 1996, Drs. Phillip Resnick and Park Dietz participated on opposite sides in the insanity defense case of John DuPont. Resnick and Dietz described their work in the DuPont case in a joint presentation to AAPL in 1998 in Denver, Colorado, which I attended. These exerpts of their presentation are taken from the commercially available recording of this meeting. During the conference, Resnick's associate, Bosovich, described the DuPont case as follows:

The crime itself of which Mr. DuPont was accused was the murder of Dave Schultz, who was an Olympic champion wrestler, which occurred on Fox Catcher Farm on January 26, 1996. And what I would like to do prior to that is just give a very brief history of Mr. DuPont's growing up years by very briefly, like, one minute. Then I want to talk about some behavior of his in the early '90s leading up to 1996 and then give you a more detailed account of the actual day of the crime. . . .

I'm going to skip ahead now to the late 1980s. Mr. DuPont's mother died in 1988. Mr. DuPont had been known to behave erratically prior to then and to have used alcohol and cocaine. However after her death, his behavior became much more erratic. He was believed to be abusing alcohol and cocaine much more frequently. He also began to develop some unusual beliefs. For instance, he believed that there were tunnels underneath his property and, as a result, hired a company to dig throughout his property to discover these tunnels. He also became very security-conscious and hired a security company and spent thousands of dollars on security improvements for his property. He also believed that trees and buildings on his property were moving. As a result, he spent money wiring down the buildings and also spent hours videotaping trees and buildings on his property. He would then force his employees to watch the videotapes so he could try to get them to confirm his belief. He also saw faces of people on the trees. Mr. DuPont also believed that there were people in the walls of his house spying on him. As a result, he had holes cut in his wall to look for these people and, in some cases, also had razor wire put inside the walls. On at least one occasion, he fired a gun into the wall.

At some point in the early '90s, when all of this was going on, his attorney contacted a psychiatrist to investigate the issue of civil commitment. However, this never came about. By 1995, Mr. DuPont had developed the belief that he was the American Dalai Lama and also that he was the Russian Crown Prince. He also expressed some fears that the KGB and the International Olympic Committee were after him. . . .

On the date of January 26, Mr. DuPont opted not to go to the airport to say goodbye to the Bulgarian Wrestling Team, which had been visiting them. Instead, he decided to stay home. He then told Pat Goodall, who was his security chief, that he wanted to drive around the farm to inspect snow damage. Mr. DuPont drove his Lincoln Town Car with Pat Goodall as a passenger in the front seat. They pulled into the Schultzes' driveway and discovered that [Olympic wrestler] Dave Schultz was standing by his car. Dave Schultz began to approach the Lincoln Town Car and said, "Hi, Coach." At that time, Mr. DuPont pulled his gun, pointed out the window, and shot Dave Schultz twice. Pat Goodall said that when Mr. DuPont began to shoot Dave Schultz, he said, "Do you have a problem with me?" After Dave Schultz fell, Mr. DuPont fired a third shot. Before he fired the third shot, Dave Schultz's wife, Nancy, came out onto the front porch. She had testified during the trial that Mr. DuPont pointed the gun at her and she tried to retreat. She then told Mr. DuPont that she had called the police. After Mr. Goodall got out of the car—actually, he got out of the car while this was going on—Mr. DuPont sped out of the Schultzes' driveway and drove back to his manor house. When he arrived there, he told one of his employees, "If the cops come, don't let them in."

The defense called on a total of twelve "mental health professionals." A multiplicity of experts on the same issue is usually counterproductive. Multiple experts create contradictions. Resnick told us,

When I flew to Philadelphia, it turned out to be the first of 23 trips to Philadelphia that I would make from Cleveland in this case. I saw Mr. DuPont a total of eleven times and put in a total of over 700 hours into the case over the next year. I figured that out—if you divide 700 hours by 50 weeks, it occupied 14 hours a week for a year of my life and, other than my wife, there is no other case that has been that involving for me. I personally interviewed 25 witnesses, visited the *murder* site. I testified in three competency hearings and the trial itself on the issue and I helped prepare cross-examination questions for Park Dietz, which was the most difficult task of all. [emphasis mine]

After seven days of deliberation, the jury did not find DuPont insane, but rather guilty of murder without premeditation, or third-degree murder. Thus, Resnick's seven hundred hours and the twelve experts' services had failed to establish the insanity defense in a case where insanity was so obvious that a directed verdict—in which the judge instructs the jury to find a defendant insane—would have been appropriate. Needless to say, the expenses incurred by the DuPont estate were astronomically high.

The third-degree-murder verdict had actually been a compromise verdict, since DuPont was either insane or guilty of premeditated first-degree murder—not something in between. Thus, the very purpose of protecting the public from a dangerous paranoid schizophrenic—by confining DuPont to a mental institution—was compromised as well. The judge attempted to correct this failure by giving the highest possible sentence—thirteen to thirty years in prison. Neither the defense nor prosecution could claim a victory: the prosecution had failed in their effort to prove first-degree murder, and the defense had failed to prove that a grossly psychotic man who committed a bizarre homicide was insane. The cause of justice would have been better served had the prosecution accepted an insanity defense, which would have ensured DuPont's lifelong confinement. The state, the family, and the community would have been spared the ordeal—and expense—of a trial that simply made no sense.

NOTES

1. Emanuel Tanay, "Virginia Tech Mass Murder: A Forensic Psychiatrist's Perspective," *Journal of the American Academy of Psychiatry Law* 35 (2007): 152–53.

2. Federal Rule of Evidence 702 (as amended Apr. 17, 2000, eff. Dec. 1, 2000). U.S. House of Representatives. Committee on the Judiciary. *Federal Rules of Evidence*. Washington, D.C.: Government Printing Office, 2009.

3. Quoted by Rudolph Flesch in *The Art of Readable Writing* (New York: Collier Books, 1962), 36.

4. Cited by Garry Willis in *Explaining America: The Federalist* (Garden City, NY: Doubleday, 1981), 24.

5. *Ake v. Oklahoma*, 470 U.S. 68 (1985).

6. Paul MacLean, *The Triune Brain in Evolution* (New York: Plenum Press, 1990).

7. Jonathan Harr, *A Civil Action* (New York: Vintage Books, 1996).

8. Malcolm Gladwell, *Outliers: The Story of Success* (New York: Little, Brown, 2008), chapter 2.

9. Federal Rule of Evidence. 704(b).

10. J. Lave and E. Wenger, *Situated Learning: Legitimate Peripheral Participation* (Cambridge, UK: Cambridge University Press, 1991).

11. Paula Young, "As Trials 'Vanish' Alternatives Play a Dominant Role in Dispute Resolution," http://www.mediate.com/people/personprofile.cfm?auid=444.

12. See also *Kumho Tire Co. v. Carmichael*, 526 U.S. 137 (1999).

13. *Journal of Forensic Sciences* 17, no. 1 (1972): 22.

14. Avishai Margalit, *The Decent Society*, trans. Naomi Goldblum (Cambridge, MA: Harvard University Press).

15. Charles Darwin, *The Expression of the Emotions in Man and Animals* (London: John Murray, 1872).

16. http://icelebz.com/quotes.william_james, accessed January 15, 2010.

17. António Damásio, *Descartes' Error: Emotion, Reason, and the Human Brain* (New York: Putnam Publishing, 1994).

18. Gerd Gigerenzer, *Gut Feelings* (New York: Viking, 2007).

19. Harr, *A Civil Action.*

20. Harr, *A Civil Action*, 339.

21. Harr, *A Civil Action.*

22. Harr, *A Civil Action.*

23. Harr, *A Civil Action*, 338.

24. Kathy Henry, "Max Weber's Typology of Forms of Authority—Traditional, Rational-Legal, and Charismatic," http://ezinearticles.com/?Max-Webers-Typology-of-Forms-of-Authority—Traditional,-Rational-Legal,-and-Charismatic&id=507723

25. *Rhetoric* 1356a, 1377b.

26. http://www.indigentdefense.org/brokenpromise.

3

THE LITIGATION
PROCESS

THE OPENING STATEMENT AND THE EXPERT WITNESS

The moving party—the plaintiff in civil cases and the prosecutor in criminal cases—presents its case first. This is an advantage since it is easier to persuade than dissuade. An opening statement is like a first date: the lawyer must try to develop a positive relationship with the jury and establish his credibility. The jurors are in unfamiliar surroundings and likely to feel anxiety. The lawyer should explain the trial process and assist the jury in understanding their role; positive feelings will follow.

Many lawyers begin the trial with an opening statement that, if taken at face value, would eliminate the need for the trial. They tell the jury what every witness will say and portray themselves as the masterminds of the case, thus depriving the jury of a sense of discovery and undermining the credibility of the witnesses that follow. I believe that a complete narration of the drama that is about to unfold is counterproductive. It should not be a final argument in support of a case that has not yet been presented. Here is a short excerpt from defense attorney Parnham's opening statement in the case of Andrea Yates, the mother who drowned her five children in a bathtub: "You will hear testimony during the course of this case from two psychologists. Dr. Harris, Gerald Harris, who will be our first witness. Dr. Harris will tell you that he has seen Andrea Pia Yates, that he has tested Andrea Pia Yates, that he believes for a number of reasons that she does not now meet the standard of competency. Not yet. That is required of a person that's on trial for a criminal offense." Parnham's opening statement runs to a number of pages in the transcript.

The opening statement of a plaintiff's attorney in a civil case should differ from the opening statement of a defense attorney. The plaintiff's lawyer's task is to persuade the jury that the defendant is liable for the harm suffered by his client.

In contrast to the lawyer for the plaintiff, the defense lawyer's task in the opening statement is to immunize the fact finders against the testimony that they are about to hear. It is, therefore, useful for the defense lawyer to summarize the evidence that the defense will offer. The plaintiff's lawyer who gives all the details of his or her expert's testimony puts himself or herself in the role of a producer. The defense lawyer, on the other hand, by giving a preview of the plaintiff's testimony, is accomplishing a desirable result. At times it might be perfectly appropriate to indicate in the opening statement that one believes that the outcome of the lawsuit is self-evident. At other times, it might be counterproductive to do so (there are cases where it is most appropriate to limit the opening statement to an indication that there is a dispute and one merely expects the jury to listen with an open mind).

When reviewing the transcripts of some cases in which I testified, I was amazed that the lawyer in the opening statement outlined what he thought I would say on the stand. Quite often the lawyer's forecast and my testimony were quite different. In the opening statement in the trial of Robert Garwood, who was charged with treason, the defense lawyer told the jury of Marine Corps officers that I had been a prisoner of war. When on direct I did not so testify, in spite of the heroic efforts of the lawyer to get me to do so, my failure to cooperate made him angry. Being an inmate in a concentration camp for a brief period did not make me a prisoner of war.

When it comes to the order of witnesses, many lawyers put the cart in front of the horse. Who testifies when is critical to the success of a trial. In some cases, putting the plaintiff ahead of the expert ensures defeat. The same plaintiff presented to a jury after the jury has been educated by the testimony of an expert can make the plaintiff credible. The reverse is also sometimes true. There are cases where the testimony of the expert becomes credible because it was preceded by the testimony of the defendant or the plaintiff.

A trial is an education for the jury, and the deliberations and verdict are the equivalent of a final exam. Don't expect the jury to pass the test before they have completed the course. And the lawyer should pay attention to the emotional connotations of words. He should not say, "My client was injured in this accident," but rather, "Mrs. Jones suffered a closed-head injury in this crash." Likewise, he should not say "murder," but "homicide" (unless of course he is the prosecutor).

Lawyers who dominate the trial (the type I call "super lawyers") do not follow my advice on opening statement. They begin by laying out the whole case in the opening statement and rely on their charisma to prevail. The average effective lawyer should avoid this approach.

In summary, the opening statement should raise questions without providing complete answers. It should inspire the jury to do justice without telling them what they should do. The opening statement is, after all, only the beginning, and eventually the jury will be told by the judge that lawyers' statements are not evidence.

THE EXPERT'S TESTIMONY AT TRIAL

An expert's ability to give effective testimony requires collaboration with the lawyer; he or she will ask the questions on direct examination that will enable the expert to give persuasive testimony. Lawyers habitually engage in "pseudo-testimony" and expect the expert to confirm it. I urge every lawyer who will conduct my direct examination to ask open-ended questions. I tell the lawyer, "Don't ask me when did you graduate from medical school?" Instead, ask, "Doctor Tanay, please tell us about your education." This gives me an opportunity to speak for a few minutes. If I am to be persuasive, I must be given an opportunity to speak as much as possible; my direct examiner should speak as little as possible.

Traditionally, the expert's testimony begins with qualifications. Lawyers should use this phase of testimony to educate the jury about the science of the expert. When I testify that I am board certified by the American Board of Psychiatry and Neurology the direct examiner should ask me to describe psychiatry and neurology. When I testify that I am certified by the American Board of Forensic Psychiatry, the lawyer should ask what forensic psychiatry is; when I testify in my qualification phase about having written a book that deals with the psychology of homicide, the lawyer should ask me to explain what psychology of homicide involves (if we are dealing with a homicide case).

Next, my examination of the plaintiff or defendant is explored. I hope the lawyer will give me the opportunity to describe the defendant or plaintiff as a human being who functioned in an ordinary way before the injury or before the homicide.

The interactions between the expert and the lawyers are moderated by a theoretically impartial judge. The presentation is directed at an audience—the jury (unless it is a bench trial, in which case the judge is the sole fact finder). A lawyer and his chosen expert pursue the same purpose in the direct examination. During cross-examination, the opposing attorney attempts to undermine the opinions expressed by the expert on direct examination and to depict the witness as a liar and impostor, which he is not.

An expert witness takes an oath to tell "the truth and nothing but the truth." Truth, in the context of opinion testimony, means that the expert believes that his opinion is valid. An opinion is false only if the witness professed it but does not believe it. Thus, the "truthfulness" of the opinion giver does not guarantee its validity.

The courts have devised a test to determine which opinion testimony is admissible as evidence, first in the *Frye* decision[1] and later in the *Daubert* standard, described above.[2] However, the legal criteria do not prescribe the style that an individual expert adopts to make his message understandable and persuasive. When I am preparing to testify, I learn everything I can about the case. I visit the courtroom or have it described to me in detail by the attorney. I discuss with the lawyer where he will stand when conducting my direct examination. I must be able to look at the jury. Testifying is, after all, an intense interaction with the jury. If the lawyer stands in a location that makes eye contact with the jury impossible, my ability to communicate with the jury is impaired. Their faces tell me how they feel about my testimony and about me.

The testimonial process involves many players: the witness, the direct examiner, the judge, and the cross-examiner. I pay attention to the expressions of the judge and other participants in the courtroom proceedings. Verbal and nonverbal messages play a role in this process. In one case, a Detroit lawyer who was called the "Murder King" because he handled so many homicide cases was about to conduct my direct examination. I noticed a large crucifix around his neck. I asked him why he was displaying this symbol of his religion so prominently. "I wear it because I am a Christian," was his answer. "Suppose a juror is a Jew or a Muslim. Don't you think your client has enough problems?" I asked. The crucifix was put in a briefcase. Nick Simkins, a lawyer with whom I had a great many cases, was a man who liked to display his success. He drove a Rolls Royce and wore a Rolex. The first time I noticed this timepiece on his wrist, I suggested he replace it with a Timex for courtroom appearances.

Let me say again that it is useful to differentiate between the content and the process of testimony. The outcome will be determined not only by what is said but how and by whom is it communicated. "The plaintiff suffered brain damage as the result of the defendant's negligence" and "The plaintiff is exaggerating the consequences of what was merely a fender-bender accident" are the competing claims in many a civil lawsuit. Similarly, in an insanity defense case, one side argues that the defendant is severely mentally ill and that the homicide was the result of a delusion, while the other side claims that the defendant is an antisocial personality who premeditated the murder and is malingering insanity.

Neither the expert nor the lawyer has a full command of each other's field. Nevertheless, the experts have to have some familiarity with the law and the lawyers have to be on speaking terms with the subject of the expert's testimony.

The primary purpose of expert testimony is to assist the jury and/or judge in understanding the scientific issues relevant to the case. In that sense, the expert's role is comparable to that of a teacher. The opposing sides' experts may disagree on the specifics, but both should follow the general principles of a given science and testify within the same legal framework.

I have often observed competent psychiatrists functioning in the courtroom in an incompetent manner. This should surprise no one. My license says that I am a physician and surgeon. Thus, I know what is involved in the simple surgical procedure of an appendectomy. If called upon, however, to perform this operation, my lack of surgical skill would most likely lead to a tragedy and a charge of negligence. Similarly, lack of testimonial skills and absence of familiarity with the courtroom procedures, even by someone who is technically "qualified," often lead to an unjust outcome.

The expert has a dual function: to inform the jury about technical issues and persuade them to accept his opinion. He cannot accomplish either goal without both the skill of giving direct testimony and the ability to cope with the cross-examination. The validity of the expert's opinion is of little value in determining the outcome if a direct examination is unpersuasive or, if it is distorted by cross-examination. Only a skilled forensic expert can defend himself against a fierce and contemptuous cross-examiner who seeks to destroy the expert's testimony no matter how true and valid it may be.

Expert testimony involves interpreting and arriving at an opinion. The data consist of history, documents, and observations made by the expert. The accuracy of the data is open to question. The expert's inferences are based upon his or her science; thus, a new set of uncertainties—questions about the science's validity and methodology—is brought into the equation. The founder of pragmatism, C.S. Peirce, defined truth as "the opinion which is fated to be ultimately agreed to by all who investigate."[3]

Testimony does not have to be correct to be believable. However, it has to be believed by the testifier to be credible. It takes considerable acting talent and training to persuasively deliver an opinion that one does not believe. Ordinary mortals fail miserably at such an effort.

All human decisions are made under conditions of uncertainty. A jury renders a verdict in criminal cases under the standard of "beyond reasonable doubt." Preponderance of the evidence is the burden of proof in civil cases. Lawyers and judges postulate that beyond reasonable doubt is a higher level of proof than preponderance of evidence. Both terms are ambiguous, however, and it is uncertain whether jurors make such distinctions. A juror's judgment about the weight of evidence is made from that juror's point of view. Emotions and reason influence the decision-making process.

However, a witness testifying about observations or an expert witness giving opinions is expected to give testimony without expressing doubt. The expert's motto before the trial begins should be: "I am in doubt because I may be wrong." However, by the time the expert enters the courtroom, he should have prepared so extensively that his mantra changes to: "I may be wrong, but I am not in doubt." Both parts of the formulation are significant: lack of doubt allows me to give my opinion with conviction, while the knowledge that I may be wrong protects me from self-righteousness and prepares me to change my opinion if given evidence that contradicts my opinion. An effective and ethical expert has no fear of being wrong because he is able to acknowledge an error. I am not in doubt when I testify, but I respect the doubts others have about my opinions.

The courtroom is the only remaining primitive theater in our culture. In the courtroom, real people reenact real-life dramas. A witness testifying about a bank robbery attempts to convey the emotions experienced by the people present during this event. Unlike a theater or movie actor, the witness has to rely upon the communicative power of words only. Rules of evidence require that the narrative be developed in a question-and-answer manner. In the theater and in the movies, an illusory reality is created by the pictorial presentation of events. In the courtroom, reality is presented in an abstract form.

Television, watched four hours every day by most Americans, creates a world full of crime, malingering plaintiffs, and ambulance-chasing lawyers. The illusory reality of television activates brain circuits that leave a permanent imprint upon the mind. A bias against criminal defendants and civil plaintiffs is likely in the age of television.

The parties in a lawsuit and their witnesses are by definition advocating for a specific outcome. A witness who testified that the light was red when the blue car entered the intersection is advocating a verdict against the driver of the blue car. The witness who testified that the light was green is advocating for a verdict in favor of this driver. Absent other compelling evidence, the jury will make a finding of fact based upon the persuasiveness (advocacy) of the witnesses. Legal "truth" is not necessarily the same as factual truth. It is often naively assumed that one of the witnesses was lying. Those of us who study human communication by empirical means know the difference between accuracy and truth. Memory is a work in progress.

Experts are not limited to their personal observations when testifying. Forensic experts may be very helpful even where they have no personal observations at all. According to the Federal Rules of Evidence, experts may base their testimony on a variety of sources—even information that would not itself be admissible in evidence: "The facts or data in the particular case upon which an expert bases an opinion or inference may be those perceived by or made known to the expert at or before the hearing. If of a type reasonably relied-upon by experts in the particular field in forming opinions or inferences upon the subject, the facts or data need not be admissible in evidence."[4]

Traditionally, the expert focuses upon the scientific data and the opinion that he or she has derived from these data. The naive expert assumes that this opinion will receive a considered hearing after it has been fully presented. This assumption is often proven wrong. The expert may find himself unable to present his or her data in an adequate manner. A variety of side issues may be raised that will make the presentation cumbersome and confusing.

As mentioned earlier, I refer to direct examination as teaching under combat conditions. The success of this venture depends upon the level of preparation and skill of both participants. Both questions and answers are communications. The flow of direct testimony is often interrupted by objections. A lawyer can object to communicate his disapproval either of the content or form of a communication. Some objections are made just to disrupt the direct examination. Objections can be made to highlight certain messages.

Sometimes the judge may interfere with the expert's testimony. Once, in St. Joseph, Michigan, I was asked on direct examination a simple question that required a few sentences in response. The judge yelled at me, "You can answer that with yes or no." I turned to the judge and said, "Your Honor, please do not scream at me." He said, "I wasn't screaming." I said, "Your Honor, everyone in this courtroom could hear that you were yelling at me." This exchange became an issue in appeals court. I gave an affidavit that such an exchange took place. It did not, however, appear in the transcript.

"Ask no question to which you do not know the answer" is a credo of the deductive mentality fostered in law schools. Most professors of law are at home in libraries and classrooms but are strangers in the courtrooms. Effective trial lawyers have an inductive state of mind. They *do* ask questions to which they do not know the answers, because they are trying to gain information. In law school certainty is possible, but in the courtroom the lawyer must deal with unpredictable reality.

DISCOVERY DEPOSITION

The discovery deposition of an expert witness is a proceeding in which the expert is cross-examined under oath before a court reporter by the opposing attorney. The legitimate objective of a discovery deposition is to learn the expert's opinions and underlying evidence for his conclusions. The cross-examiner is also entitled to find out if the expert has some unique bias and to identify what documents he or she has relied upon. Lawyers interpret the scope of discovery deposition very broadly. Federal courts and most state courts permit questions "reasonably calculated to lead to the discovery of admissible evidence." In reality, most defense lawyers use the discovery deposition not to discover what the expert's opinions will be at trial but to create material that can be used during the trial. Many lawyers use the discovery deposition as a fishing expedition.

For an experienced expert, the discovery deposition is a two-way street: the lawyer discovers what the expert's opinions are and how he handles himself on cross-examination, while the expert discovers what the lawyer's approach is and how he behaves as a cross-examiner. I am pleased when the opposing lawyer schedules a discovery deposition, because it subjects my reasoning to a critical examination that will improve my presentation during the trial. I particularly enjoy giving discovery depositions for lawyers who don't know me and expect an inexperienced expert whom they can use to advance their cause. They usually leave disappointed.

An effective expert witness uses the discovery deposition to his or her advantage. This requires careful preparation and extensive discussions with the retaining lawyer. Sometimes the case is settled based upon the quality of the expert's performance in the discovery deposition. Occasionally, the deposition may be used to eliminate the expert as a witness or even dismiss the whole case.

One common gambit of defense lawyers in civil cases is "bleeding the plaintiff" by taking experts' depositions all over the country. The average plaintiff's lawyer can hardly afford the expenditures associated with multiple discovery depositions and sooner or later may capitulate by settling the case. Lawyers sometimes inflict harm to their own cases by taking discovery depositions. This is what happened in the Lomnicki case.

In 1995 I was consulted by the Roseville Community School District attorney on how to cope with a pedophilic teacher, who had been in the school system for thirty years. I was given extensive information about his past behavior. There were a number of prior complaints against him. The school board had reprimanded the teacher on a few occasions for sexual behavior with students such as touching, hugging, and a variety of other suggestive moves. When I was contacted, the teacher was facing criminal charges for overt sexual abuse; however, he was still teaching. My report was brief, but I made it clear in office conferences that the teacher was a pedophile and should be fired.

Eight years later I received a call from attorney William Goodman, son of legendary Michigan lawyer Ernie Goodman, with whom I had worked many times. Goodman was representing Lomnicki's victims in a lawsuit against the school board and wanted to take my deposition. Lomnicki was at this point serving a long prison term. I told Goodman that I could not speak to him because my obligation was to the party that had retained me. Goodman nevertheless noticed a *de bene esse* deposition, a deposition that can be presented to the jury as a substitute for live appearance of the expert. I notified the school board lawyers and we had a two-hour discussion. I recommended to them that they should oppose my deposition because my testimony would be harmful to them. They tried to convince me to testify in a manner that would protect them, which I would not do.

Two days before the scheduled deposition by the plaintiff, at which I was going to simply say that I could not testify, I received a surprising subpoena from one of the defense lawyers representing the school board. I refused to honor his request because of the shortness of time and a conflict in schedule, as I had a patient and a lecture that I was going to deliver that day.

The lawyer threatened me with the judge and I told him that I would welcome his contacting the judge because I thought his behavior was unprofessional. "You don't expect an expert witness to be ready on two day's notice," I said. Furthermore, he sent me a fifteen-dollar fee as if I were a material witness. I refused to give a deposition.

As a consequence, there was a hearing before the federal judge and an order was entered that the defense's discovery deposition of me should precede the plaintiff's deposition on the day originally scheduled by the plaintiff. Thus I was being converted by the school board lawyers who had originally retained me into an adverse witness, which I think was a tactical mistake. During the deposition the lawyers argued about the validity of the order of the court. The defense tried to persuade me that the judge's order did not entitle the plaintiff to ask me questions about my opinions. My reading of the order was that I was to answer every question.

The attorney for the school board began his discovery deposition with a tactical blunder. He asked, "You are unable to diagnose Mr. Lomnicki as a pedophile because as you said, you were in an advisory role and not in a clinical role?" I asked him if he wanted to know if I had an opinion of whether Mr. Lomnicki is a pedophile, and he said "yes." My answer was that there could be no doubt that Lomnicki was a pedophile (documents I had available described him as performing cunnilingus upon his students).

The lawyer tried to invoke the Goldwater Rule of the American Psychiatric Association (APA), that prohibits expressing opinions about individuals one did not examine. However, what the lawyer did not know is that the Goldwater Rule is not applicable to forensic evaluations. I knew that was the case because I had filed an APA ethics complaint against myself to test that rule and received an opinion from the APA that it was indeed ethical for me (and presumably for any other forensic psychiatrist) to give forensic opinions without personal examination.

This was all a futile approach for the defense, since the material I had was irrefutable proof that Lomnicki was a pedophile. The lawyer was needlessly converting me into an adverse witness. There was little doubt that the discovery deposition was counterproductive for the defense.

During the subsequent deposition by the plaintiff, the defense decided to treat me in a hostile manner. When I refused to answer certain questions, they called the federal judge on a speakerphone and misrepresented the reasons for my refusal. When I tried to interpose my version of why I refused to answer an inappropriate question, the lead defense lawyer claimed that as a witness I had no right to address the judge, whereupon the federal judge said, "It will be my privilege to hear what Dr. Tanay has to say." Then the judge instructed the defense lawyers to go on with the deposition and drop the topic they were pursuing. The moral of the story is that a bad situation can be made worse.

Discovery depositions of inexperienced experts are an opportunity for the cross-examiners to practice the not-so-gentle art of shaping experts' opinions through paraphrase. The lawyer, under the guise of asking a question, tries to get on the record a distorted version of the expert's report or testimony. At the end of the redacted version, the lawyer tacks on, "Yes or no?" The naive expert or lay witness often falls into this trap. The following is an example of a lawyer's efforts to shape my testimony.

I was the expert for a plaintiff suing a major corporation for a woman who suffered major burns in an accident. I was asked to address the issue of pain and suffering. The discovery deposition was conducted by Mr. Hightower, the lawyer representing the corporation. Here is an example of inventive paraphrase:

Q: It indicates that you had received all of [the plaintiff's] medical records from UT Galveston and you had reviewed them; correct?

A. Where did you read that?

Q. In your report.

A. Where?

Q. Right there, first page.

A. That's not—you're not reading it right.

Q. Let me see it. I don't have a copy of it because I have never been provided a copy of it so?

A. So why are you making it up if you don't have it? You just said to me that you were reading from it.

Q. Sir, I've read it at a break, okay? I've looked at it and it does say you got the records?

A. But you are now pretending that you're read it and this is not accurate. You can't do that kind of thing to me. [This was on video and would be shown to the jury.]

The next gambit was the lawyer's attempt to limit my testimony when I testified in the courtroom.

Q. Can you tell the jury what you've been asked to do in this matter?

A. I have been asked to express an opinion regarding the pain and suffering that has been endured by [the plaintiff] as a result of this event.

Q. And is that your—is that your only role as you understand it?

A. My role depends on what questions are posed. . . . Whoever asks a question that I consider within my competence, I will express an opinion on that question.

Q. What I'm asking you, sir, is—and let me just object nonresponsive. What I'm trying to figure out is in reviewing all the documents that you brought here today, did you understand early on that you were reviewing those documents for the purpose of expressing an opinion about whether or not [the plaintiff] suffered pain and mental anguish and if so to what extent as a result of the accident that we're here about today?

A. That is true, I have reviewed the case, but other questions might arise that I may or may not be able to answer.

Q. My question, though, is that's—you look at all the documents that you review with the intention of expressing an opinion about whether or not [the plaintiff] experienced physical pain and mental anguish as a result of the accident and if so to what extent; is that fair?

A. I already gave you an answer. You asked me the same question. One more time. You want me to repeat the previous answer or do you hope that I will change my answer?

Once again, this attorney tried to put words into my mouth.

Q. Okay. And can you tell the jury what training or experience that you have that you believe makes you or puts you in a position superior to the jury in terms of deciding one's credibility? . . .

A. I never said that I have superior[position]. That is something that I believe is your opinion. You're not attributing that to me, I hope. I have not ever said nor intend to say that I am in some way superior to the jury. I wonder where you get that idea from.

Q. So basically what you're saying is that the jury, they have the same ability as you have to determine a witness' credibility, is that fair? . . .

A. That is a statement that you make. That is your opinion.

Q. Well, do you agree with that?

A. No, I don't agree. I don't agree with your attributing to me in the form of a question something that you have dreamed up.

An expert witness should expose the efforts of the cross-examiner to distort or shape the expert's opinions. Some applied scientists have a social aversion to challenge cross-examiners because they consider it advocacy, which they erroneously believe is not consistent with the role of a scientist.

DIRECT EXAMINATION

The direct examination of an expert should communicate to the jury the expert's qualifications and the data that the expert relied upon. Most lawyers are better at cross-examining an adverse witness than enabling their expert to give a good direct testimony. Yet the direct testimony is the most important contribution an expert can make to the case. Direct examination should answer in a narrative form five questions:

1. Who is the expert and what is his or her science?
2. What was the extent of the expert's work in this case?
3. What kind of information did he or she gather and consider?
4. What is the expert's opinion in this case?
5. What is the basis for the expert's opinion?

The success of direct examination depends upon both the lawyer's and expert's levels of preparation and skill. Direct testimony is a collaborative effort. Some lawyers prepare a list of questions, but this method is usually counterproductive because the lawyer may ask all the questions on his list and hardly listens to the answers.

Some lawyers view the expert as their mouthpiece. On November 30, 1989, I wrote a letter to Mr. Ivan M. F., an attorney who was about to conduct my direct examination. "Dear Mr. F: I have received via fax your direct examination questions. Since I have not been asked, I will not comment upon the questions that you propose to ask. I do, however, object to answers being provided in the material submitted. I realize that you may have fashioned the answers based upon my report. Nevertheless, I find this method of preparing an expert witness not acceptable." In reality I found the fact that the lawyer provided answers insulting and had serious doubts that I could work effectively with this attorney. Obviously he had little faith in my competence and integrity.

In the direct examination of an experienced forensic expert, the lawyer plays a supportive role, asking questions and scrupulously avoiding leading questions. Leading questions diminish the persuasive value of the expert's testimony. I am amazed when lawyers try to circumvent the prohibition of leading questions during direct examination. The expert should do the talking; the fewer words the lawyer speaks, the better. The expert as an educator has to testify in narrative form. The lawyer is accustomed to giving quasi testimony disguised as questions when examining a material witness. The change from an interrogation-based format to a narrative-based style of testimony is not an easy task for most lawyers. Yet the expert's persuasiveness depends upon this metamorphosis.

The credibility of direct testimony given by an expert will vary depending upon the manner displayed by the lawyer toward his witness. If the lawyer dominates the expert, he is contradicting his or her credentials. If the attorney shows a lack of respect for his own expert, the jury is not likely to find the expert credible. For example, an attorney should not begin the inquiry of the expert by asking, "What is your name, witness?" as many a lawyer has addressed me, but say instead: "Dr. Tanay, would you give us your full name." This is not only more respectful, but also more natural, because obviously the lawyer knows the name of his expert.

The lawyer should show confidence in the expert by asking general questions. He should not lead the expert witness; this is not only contrary to the rules of evidence but also counterproductive. One cannot claim that the expert is an eminent scientist if one treats him like a schoolboy who has to be kept in a highly structured framework of questions. The lawyer should give the expert as much freedom as the rules of evidence, the judge, and the opponent will permit.

According to the Federal Rules of Evidence, experts may base their testimony on a variety of sources—even information that would not itself be admissible as evidence. Unfortunately, some lawyers and judges treat experts as if they were material witnesses, limited in the scope of their testimony to observations.

In the final analysis, the competence of the lawyer and the expert determines the quality of the direct examination. An ineffective lawyer and an effective expert witness are likely to produce a mediocre direct examination. An effective lawyer and an ineffective expert will produce ineffective testimony. It takes an effective lawyer and an effective expert to create persuasive direct examination.

The Federal Rules of Evidence state that leading questions are not permitted on the direct examination of a witness unless they are necessary to develop the person's testimony. In real life these rules are frequently interpreted in a manner that discourage a witness from telling a story. Some transcripts consist of the lawyer "testifying" in the form of questions and the expert playing a confirmatory role. An expert witness who is not passive in the courtroom is labeled an advocate. The term "advocate" applied to a lawyer is a tribute, as in "he is a strong advocate for his cause." The same term applied to a witness is disparaging, as in "he's not a witness, he is an advocate."

I was an expert witness on damages testifying about the severe brain damage suffered by William Schwartz, not his real name. The defendant was the City of Inkster, Michigan, whose police were accused of causing a collision by running a stop sign while on an emergency surveillance mission without any lights. An additional complication was that Schwartz and the driver of the car he was riding in were beaten by the police. During my direct testimony I was prevented from testifying about the emotional impact of the police abuse upon Schwartz. No opportunity to testify on this issue occurred during cross-examination by Milton Lucow, a prominent defense lawyer. The same was true on redirect examination. It seemed that my testimony was over, and I never did convey to the jury the abuse inflicted upon the innocent victims of a mishap caused by the police. Lucow rose from the defense table one more time, and while walking to the podium asked me, "Doctor then in your opinion the whole damage was the result of the car accident . . ." "No sir, car accident and the police beating" was my answer, to which Lucow objected, claiming it was hearsay. I replied that everything I had related so far was hearsay because, after all, I was not present at the collision. Lucow turned to the judge for help, but the judge said, "You opened it up and the doctor certainly can tell you what he has been told and what his opinion is." I expressed the view that being beaten by the police subsequent to the accident was psychiatrically significant. Lucow did not appear to be pleased when he announced, "No more questions of this witness."

The *Detroit Free Press* reported on November 2, 1993, "A jury Monday awarded $3.8 million to William Schwartz, disabled in a 1990 accident caused by a speeding Inkster police cruiser that ignored a stop sign. Schwartz, then 24, was a passenger in a truck hit by the squad car. He has permanent spinal and brain injuries. The jury held the City of Inkster liable."

CROSS-EXAMINATION

A lawyer warned me forty years ago, "Doctor do you realize that whenever you take a witness stand you take your whole career in your hands?" The friendly lawyer's concern did not materialize, but his apprehension was well-founded. Many experts have been trapped into career-destroying statements by cross-examiners.

John Henry Wigmore, a legal authority on cross-examination, wrote, "Cross-examination is the greatest legal engine ever invented for the discovery of truth." The presumption of this statement is that witnesses lie on direct examination. However, few lawyers have the good fortune to confront fraudulent, exaggerating, and unreasonable expert testimony. Therefore, lawyers try to use a variety of stratagems to create the appearance of deceptive testimony.

John Wigmore also said, "The witness stand is a slaughterhouse of reputations."[5] Yes, cross-examiners can "slaughter" the reputation of meek experts, regardless of the merit of the testimony. A cross-examiner can question anything I have said and expect an honest, courteous answer. However, my attitude will change if the cross-examiner becomes unfair or nasty. Lawyers routinely advise their witnesses to maintain composure at all times. This approach is self-defeating: people who fail to defend themselves suffer a loss of credibility. An expert witness who is subjected to abuse by a cross-examiner cannot help but feel angry.

The 2004 presidential campaign enriched our vocabulary with a new verb: "swiftboating." The tactic of character assassination has been studied by neuroscientists and is relevant to the cross-examination of experts. Sam Wang and Sandra Aamodt, two distinguished neuroscientists, write that, "A false statement from a non-credible source that is at first not believed can gain credibility. All it takes is time to reprocess memories from short-term hippocampal storage to longer-term cortical storage."[6] People forget the source and remember the information. On cross-examination, any accusation that has not been refuted discredits the witness.

When I testify in civil cases for the defense, the plaintiff is likely to imply that I am a hired gun of the defense. When I testify for the plaintiff, the opposing lawyer tries to paint me with the same brush; this time I am a hired gun for the plaintiff.

James Becker, a defense attorney, once began his cross-examination of me by saying, "Good morning, doctor, it's nice to see you *again*." The implication was that I testify often and am therefore a hired gun and not a credible witness. I said, "Nice to see you again." Becker continued, "You're not a stranger to the courtroom, are you?" I responded, "That is true, I am not." "You testify often?" "I certainly do," I replied. Becker then said: "You always testify for plaintiff's lawyers, don't you?" "No, that is not true," I said emphatically. "I examine and testify for both sides." "Whenever you and I have encountered each other in the courtroom, you were on the plaintiff's side," Becker said. "Mr. Becker," I replied, "the reason for this is that you always work on behalf of the defense, whereas I examine for either side."

Cross-examining an experienced forensic expert witness is a risky undertaking. More often than not, it is preferable to forgo cross-examination. An effective expert witness rebuts an accusation in a way that reminds the decision makers of his credibility and self-assurance. Credibility is lost when timidity is the response to an ad hominem attack.

I welcome cross-examination because it raises doubts about the reasons I gave for my opinion on direct examination. Some jurors will have the same doubts in the privacy of the jury room without my ability to explain my reasoning. An effective expert witness adroitly elaborates on his opinions during the cross-examination. Cross-examiners often present a claim in the form of a question and expect the witness to respond with a yes or no answer. Yes or no responses are a poison pill to an expert's testimony. I often respond to a claim disguised as a question by saying, "This is a claim and not a question." Or "Maybe yes and maybe no."

I classify cross-examiners into one of three categories:

The Dragon Slayer: This lawyer is on a mission to destroy the witness, to expose him as a biased individual who sells his opinions to the highest bidder. Since these accusations do not describe me, an encounter with such a cross-examiner will be a confrontation in which I am likely to emerge victorious. I have evidence that I am a respected member of my profession, while the cross-examiner has no proof for his demeaning claims. The dragon slayer is most successful when dealing with meek expert witnesses. The various excerpts of cross-examinations that I provide later in this book prove this point.

The "Friendly" Cross-Examiner attempts to co-opt me as his witness. If he is successful at the end of cross-examination, the jury will be not be sure if I was opposing his version of the case or supporting it. My task is to make clear that I am not his witness.

The Effective Cross-Examiner: This individual picks out items that he knows that an ethical and competent expert witness will agree with even though they diminish his opinion. I have testified on a few occasions in cases of closed head injuries against Nick Simkins, with whom I have worked on many cases. He cross-examined me effectively by focusing upon areas that were not in dispute. The issue in the closed head injury case was the extent of the damage suffered by the plaintiff. Simkins carefully avoided areas where I could reinforce my direct testimony.

The real challenge for the cross-examiner is an expert witness who has hurt the lawyer's case without lies and exaggerations and is capable of defending himself in the courtroom. Cross-examination that aims to show that such a witness lied, exaggerated, or was unreasonable is likely to be counterproductive with a forensic expert.

A forensic expert who testifies frequently is unlikely to get away with unethical conduct for any length of time. I believe that the experts who have testified in opposition to my testimony were mistaken, but I cannot recall any instance where I believed that these opposing experts were committing perjury.

The so-called battle of the experts is about opinions and rarely about facts. An opinion of an expert is no more objective than the verdict of a jury or the ruling of a judge. An opinion is probable or improbable, but never certain. It might be a fact that defendant Jones perpetrated a homicide, but it is an opinion that Jones committed manslaughter or first-degree murder or is legally insane. Facts exist in the real world; opinions and ideas dwell in the minds of the people who hold them.

Some experts inexperienced in the courtroom can be made to appear biased or dishonest even though they are competent and ethical; however, a seasoned forensic expert is much less vulnerable to ad hominem attacks. Robert Lyons, a Sarasota lawyer representing the plaintiff, retained me in an obvious medical malpractice case. The cross-examiner asked me:

Q: Do you base your opinions or conclusions on the truthfulness of the history that Mrs. Brase gave to you?

A. Well, you know—

Q. Just yes or no, please, Doctor.

A. There is no yes or no to this kind of question, sir.

Q. Doctor, let me stop you.

A. No, no, don't stop me.

Q. If you answer my question, then you can explain it, okay?

A. No, sir. Sir, you asked me a question. Don't tell me I have to answer yes or no because there is no such thing as yes or no when it comes to opinions, that is what you are asking me. Accuracy or truthfulness? So I have to understand your question before I can say yes or no.

Q. Can you tell me what you mean by truthfulness. Accuracy, I am assuming that all of her assumptions are accurate?

A. No, I don't. Is she truthful in the sense that she's not telling me lies? I believe she is not telling me lies.

In this exchange, if I answered "yes," any inaccuracy of Mrs. Brase's statement would undermine my opinions. A "no" answer would weaken her credibility and the basis for my conclusions.

Adverse witnesses can be separated into two categories: those vulnerable and those who are invulnerable to cross-examination. A truthful and effective witness is likely to provide testimony that may be useful to the cross-examiner because such a witness may share areas of agreement with the opposing side. That information, when revealed in the cross-examination, will not undo the harm of the direct examination, but it will prove of some benefit; above all, it will not make a bad situation worse.

I recall a criminal case in Macomb County, just outside of Detroit. The defense had a very strong insanity claim. The defense lawyer with whom I was working was concerned about the comments of the young assistant prosecutor, who predicted that he would "destroy Tanay on cross-examination." When I entered the courtroom, there were two large file boxes marked "Tanay Materials" on the prosecutor's table. The direct examination was rather short because the lawyer wanted first to hear the cross-examination and then "rehabilitate the witness" on redirect (a strategy that I had advised against). After I finished my direct, the young prosecutor stood up, looked at me, and said, "No questions of this witness." It was the most devastating cross-examination I had experienced in a long time. The judge declared a recess. As I was walking out of the courtroom, I complimented the prosecutor, who looked familiar. He responded, "I took your class." He understood that an effective expert can use cross-examination to reinforce the message of direct examination.

Some cross-examiners are very effective in shifting the debate from the case to some other issue. The issue may be irrelevant to the case, but some judges accept the lawyer's claim in the courtroom that they "will tie it up later."

If my direct examination harmed the cross-examiner's cause he may be on a mission of revenge or damage control. Whenever I am cross-examined, I try to determine the cross-examiner's intentions. Does he wish to undermine the opinions I expressed on direct, or is his goal to undermine my credibility? Usually one or the other is the primary objective. The cross-examination must be witness-sensitive. A personal attack may offend the jury if the witness has established a positive relationship with jurors on direct examination.

Some cross-examiners conceal their aggressive intentions with pseudo-friendliness. The implied message of this friendly demeanor is that the cross-examiner is motivated by an impartial pursuit of the truth. For example, a cross-examiner may ask a friendly sounding question that contains a negative imputation. Many experts answer the question and leave the innuendo unchallenged.

"Dr. Tanay, isn't it true that you testify mostly for plaintiffs in civil cases?" This is a statement that many cross-examiners have "asked" me. In reality, it is an accusation that I am biased in favor of plaintiffs. I have said in one case "I have never declined to examine for the defense and have done so on many occasions. I have testified so often for the defense firm representing General Motors that I was given a supplier discount on the purchase of my Cadillac." Some cross-examination questions are the equivalent of: "When did you stop beating your wife?" For example, these are pseudo-questions:

- "Doctor, if you assume that the defendant knew that it was wrong to kill, then he was not insane? Yes or no?"
- "Doctor, if you assume that the plaintiff is malingering, then he is not suffering from closed-head injury? Yes or no?"

Occasionally I will say, "If I assume what you ask me to assume, then I agree with your statement." Sometimes I say, "The answer to your question has to be yes, but this is not my opinion." Whatever the response, the jury should get the message that this was a trick question.

Another common cross-examination tactic is the presentation of a false dilemma. "Doctor, have you ever made a wrong diagnosis?" If you say "yes," then you imply that you might be wrong in this case. If you say "no," then you sound arrogant. The expert witness's response should expose this question as a ploy.

The friendly cross-examiner is a much more formidable opponent than the overtly hostile one. When the cross-examination begins with "Doctor, how much are you getting paid for your testimony?" the hostile intentions are obvious and more easily countered. Showing annoyance in response to an insult is appropriate for all humans, including expert witnesses.

My responses to an aggressive cross-examiner depends in part on the quality of the direct testimony we gave. (I say "we" because the persuasiveness of direct testimony is the result of collaborative efforts of the lawyer and the expert.) If the direct examination was persuasive, I will limit myself on cross-examination to the protection of those gains. Some cross-examiners are subtle in their efforts to undermine the expert; they might ask, "You do admit that most of your practice, Doctor, is limited to forensic work?" This question implies that forensic work is a shady activity. I answer, "No, sir I am not admitting this. I am proudly saying that I am a forensic psychiatrist."

Lawyers like to quote an expert's published work out of context or use it to make innuendoes. Lawyers who cross-examine me often bring up a comment I made in a paper entitled "The Forensic Psychiatrist as a Teacher." I wrote, "Many a courtroom disaster could have been averted had I spoken up." The lawyers who bring up this paper in court ask me disapprovingly, "You think it is your job to tell lawyers that they are making a mistake?" These lawyers erroneously believe that just because lawyers would hold that against me, a jury would, too.[7] When the cross-examiner confronts me with quotes from my publications or prior testimony transcript, I use that as an opportunity to expand upon the issues. The more I elaborate, the bigger the overall impact of my testimony.

In cross-examination, the question and the response are a unit; quite often the question is a persuasive argument and it calls for a counter-argument. Many expert witnesses are unable or unwilling to cope with this challenge.

The expert has a burden of rejoinder. This does not mean that the cross-examiner's every contention must be refuted. When cross-examiners make allegations under the guise of questions, it is only fair that the experts be permitted to respond. However, judges often preclude the expert from dealing with the cross-examiner's argument by saying, "Your lawyer will give you an opportunity to respond." In those situations, I protest that "Mr. So-and-So is not my lawyer," or I point out that the question was not really a question. At times I have responded to a cross-examiner's lengthy pseudo-question by saying, "That was an interesting argument, but I do not agree with it."

An expert who submits meekly to the cross-examiner inevitably loses credibility with the decision makers. Some cross-examiners make defamatory statements. I am under oath, but the cross-examiner is not. I have often responded to an obvious slander by saying, "You would not say that if you were under oath like I am." One frequent comment from cross-examiners is, "Doctor, you agree with me that if you did not have this opinion, you would not be called upon to testify, yes or no?" I unmask the implication by saying something like, "I resent your implying that I am committing perjury."

The American Academy of Psychiatry and the Law (AAPL) conducts a peer-review presentation as part of its annual meeting. At this session, a forensic psychiatrist presents his testimony in the form of a transcript or video. A panel that has previously reviewed the testimony then presents a critical review of it.

At the 1998 Annual Meeting of the AAPL in New Orleans, Louisiana, I presented a case in which I testified for the plaintiff. The case involved a lawsuit against the city of Lansing, Michigan. A schizophrenic patient came to the police station in the early hours when the temperature was well below zero wearing only a shirt. "I am a veteran, take me to the Battle Creek VA Hospital where I am a patient," he said. This obviously psychotic man was given a jacket and told to get lost. A few hours later, the police received a call that a strange man was looking through the windows of a school. A squad car was dispatched and brought the same man back to the station. He was arrested. During the booking procedure he refused to face the agent behind the counter, because he was afraid of being shot in the back by the two policeman who stood behind him. He was wrestled to the ground and hog tied, and died in the process. The victim was black and the six police officers were white. The whole interaction was videotaped by the camera operating in the station. The case was tried in a federal court before Judge Richard Alan Enslen with an all-white jury in the city of Kalamazoo.

The AAPL audience watched my video-recorded testimony. The official discussants were rather critical of my performance; they found me unduly argumentative, emotional, and too forceful when attacked on cross-examination. One senior colleague found my blue-striped tie inappropriate for the court. Many more critical observations were made.

I asked the panel to guess the trial's outcome. The panel unanimously agreed that the jury delivered a no-cause verdict. I then turned to the large audience and asked them to anticipate a favorable or unfavorable verdict for the plaintiff, by a show of hands. The overwhelming vote was for an unfavorable outcome. There was general astonishment when I told them that the jury returned a $13 million verdict, which was believed to be one of the largest verdicts up to that time in the Kalamazoo Federal Court. Most professionals who testify occasionally are devoid of testimonial skills which are acquired, like surgical skills, with practice.

Prosecutors are often hostile to experts testifying on behalf of criminal defendants. I once testified on behalf of a bizarre psychotic indigent defendant named Nowitzke in Sarasota, Florida. The prosecutor, a man named Frank Schaub who had previously been the elected judge in the same jurisdiction, was quite aggressive and accused me of lying under oath when I testified that I charged $150 an hour in public defender cases. The prosecutor waved what he claimed was a bill showing that I had charged $600. I insisted that he show me the document. The judge directed me to answer but I again insisted on seeing the document. It turned out that the $600 was for four hours. I berated the prosecutor for misleading the jury.

Some time after this acrimonious cross-examination I received a handwritten note from Roger Craig, an attorney in Naples, Florida stating, "Even in Florida the word on the street is don't f. with Dr. Tanay!" Craig had enclosed a Florida Supreme Court decision dated May 13, 1993, titled, "The Florida Bar, Complainant v. Frank Schaub, Respondent. Number 79759." The Supreme Court of Florida was acting in response to the complaint I had filed against Schaub for his behavior in the above trial. The court made the following finding:

> In a disciplinary proceeding, the Supreme Court held that prosecutor's improperly eliciting irrelevant testimony, inserting personal opinions on psychiatry and insanity offense (sic) into questioning, and improperly eliciting testimony concerning average time of confinement for someone committed to hospital as criminally insane, warrants suspension from practice of law for period of 30 days. . . . Based upon matters occurring at the trial, the referee made the following findings:
>
> 1. During cross-examination, Schaub improperly elicited irrelevant testimony from the defense's expert psychiatrist, Dr. Tanay, that a

non-testifying expert had classified him as a "hired gun." Later, in summation to the jury, Schaub again referred to Tanay as a "hired gun."

2. Schaub accused Dr. Tanay of charging $600 per hour for his deposition testimony. Yet, Schaub had a copy of the itemized bill showing Tanay charged $150 per hour.

3. Throughout his cross-examination, Schaub insulted Dr. Tanay, ignored the trial court's rulings on defense objections, and inserted his personal opinions on psychiatry and the insanity defense in to his questioning.

The prosecutor's reckless efforts assisted by the judge succeeded with the jury, but the appellate court reversed the judgment of guilt. The court held that Nowitzke was denied a fair trial due to Schaub's prosecutorial misconduct, which led to the admission of irrelevant and deliberately misleading evidence.[8]

NOTES

1. *Frye v. United States* (293 F. 1013 (D.C. Cir. 1923).

2. See chapter 2, "Science and the Law."

3. *Writings of Charles S. Peirce: A Chronological Edition*, Vol. 4: 1879–1884. (Bloomington: Indiana University Press, 1989).

4. Federal Rule of Evidence 703 (as amended Mar. 2, 1987, eff. Oct. 1, 1987; Apr. 17, 2000, eff. Dec. 1, 2000). U.S. House of Representatives. Committee on the Judiciary. *Federal Rules of Evidence*. (Washington, D.C.: Government Printing Office, 2009).

5. Franklin D. Strier, *Reconstructing Justice: An Agenda for Trial Reform* (Westport, CT: Quorum Books, 1994).

6. *New York Times*, June 28, 2008.

7. For a crafty example of distortion of prior publication see section on discovery deposition earlier in this chapter.

8. State v. Nowitzke, 572 So. 2d 1349 (Fla. 1990).

II

GUILTY UNLESS PROVEN INNOCENT

THE CAUSE AND MODE OF DEATH

A Mistaken Determination of Suicide

A death certificate gives cause and mode of death. The mode of death can be natural (disease), homicide, suicide, or undetermined. A scientifically valid and uniform determination of mode (or manner) and cause of death is essential for public health and criminal investigations, and mortality statistics are essential to medical research. Finally, yet importantly, the mode of death is emotionally significant for the family, friends, and community. It makes a difference to survivors whether a loved one died as a result of an accident or was the victim of suicide or homicide. This will become obvious when I describe the case of fourteen-year-old boy who died due to an accident but was determined to be the victim of suicide by a man holding the title of medical examiner who was a fireman.

The statement "the mode of death was natural" is another way of saying that the death was due to nonviolent causes. In contrast, homicide and suicide are associated with a variety of detrimental consequences. For example, many life insurance policies do not pay death benefits in a case of suicide, and homicide results in a criminal investigation and possible criminal charges. There are also religious repercussions associated with suicide and homicide.

When the cause of death is uncertain, it is established by an autopsy performed by a pathologist. However, in the past, mode of death was determined in many jurisdictions by coroners who had no formal training and were elected. The determination of mode of death requires the gathering of data that cannot be ascertained by examining the body of the deceased alone. Relevant data to the determination of mode of death, be they biological or psychological, requires scientific training and academic degrees.[1]

Errors in determination of the mode of death can have far-reaching consequences. As the result of misdiagnosis, innocent individuals may be criminally prosecuted, the peace of a community could be seriously disturbed, and lengthy litigation may follow. Conversely, when a natural cause of death is erroneously certified, guilty individuals might escape criminal and financial responsibilities.

Ascertaining the mode of death frequently benefits from collaboration between the forensic pathologist and the forensic psychiatrist. This is particularly true in homicide, suicide, and accidental death cases. The frequency of errors can be decreased through such collaborative efforts.

In the 1970s, I was the psychiatric consultant to the Wayne County Medical Examiner in Michigan's most populous county, which includes Detroit. The medical examiner was Werner Spitz, M.D., an internationally recognized forensic pathologist. I participated in weekly conferences with the department staff that determined the manner and cause of death. The most intense discussions involved distinguishing between accidental and suicidal modes of death.

SUICIDE

Suicide is a major public health problem; it ranks as the eighth leading cause of death in the United States. There are more than thirty thousand suicides each year.[2] The accuracy of suicide statistics has significant public health implications and is of great emotional significance to the family of the suicide victim and the community. This is particularly true if the victim is a child.

The scientific study of suicide has been influenced by the cultural and religious attitudes that prevail in a given society. The term suicide did not appear in Robert Burton's 1652 edition of *Anatomy of Melancholy*. Samuel Johnson's 1755 *Dictionary of the English Language* did not list the word either. In those days, English speakers used such ambiguous terms as "the act" or "self-destruction."[3] It is noteworthy that etymologically, the English word *suicide* is a combination of two Latin terms. By contrast, other languages are more explicit. In Polish, for example, the word for killing oneself in an intentional manner is *samo-bojstwo*, which means "self-killing." In German, the word *Selbstmord* is combination of "self" and "murder." These words connote hostility and violence; they evoke more of an emotional response than the foreign-sounding "suicide."

According to Émile Durkheim, suicide is a social fact and a subject for sociological study.[4] Sociological data might suggest in which cohort suicide is more likely to prevail, but it is not as useful as a diagnostic tool in individual cases, which are the domain of the psychiatrist. A clinician who makes decisions involving a suicidal patient based upon sociological data alone is committing malpractice.

Psychiatric disorders are the most significant factor leading to suicide. More than 90 percent of people who commit suicide have a recognizable psychiatric illness. Medical illness and substance abuse are some of the other conditions; substance abuse is particularly a factor among young suicide victims. Some of the precipitating causes of suicide are separation, unemployment, legal problems, and other major stresses. The most important risk factor is depressive illness. The majority of the suicide victims have not only been diagnosed as depressed but also have a history of psychiatric treatment within a year of committing suicide.

Retrospective diagnosis of the deceased's suicidal state of mind depends primarily upon information from those who knew the victim. Physical evidence and autopsy results may be consistent with suicide but are not necessarily diagnostic. Psychosocial information is essential for diagnosing depressive illness, which is the underlying cause of most suicides. The interpretation of relevant psychosocial data requires a skilled professional.

Suicide is usually a manifestation of an illness. Therefore, before the mode of death is entered on the death certificate, one has to reach a conclusion about the underlying illness that gave rise to the suicide.[5] Previous suicide attempts are often part of the history of someone who successfully completed suicide. Suicide is an attempt to get relief from severe mental suffering. The illness that most often gives rise to suicide is called major depression. It is not a rare condition; therefore, one would expect that someone who has a professional responsibility for making a determination that a given death was suicide would be familiar with mental diseases. The "professional" in the case I now describe had no such familiarity.

SUICIDE OR ACCIDENT:
THE CASE OF RAYMOND SHERMAN, JR.

When a parent dies, you lose your past; when a child dies, you lose your future.

— Anonymous

The grief of bereaved parents is the most intense grief known. Bereaved parents feel that the death of their child is "the ultimate deprivation."[6] "A wife who loses a husband is called a widow. A husband who loses a wife is called a widower. A child who loses his parents is called an orphan. But there is no word for a parent who loses a child, that's how awful the loss is!"[7] I will now describe a case in which the pain of the loss of a child was compounded by professional ineptitude.

At the Annual Meeting of the American Academy of Forensic Science in February 2005, Yvette Sherman, the wife of the Green Bay Packers coach, her lawyer, Avi Berg, and I presented a panel discussion on mode of death determination and the tragic death of Sherman's son, Raymond Sherman, Jr. I gave the history of the heartbreaking story and played excerpts of my tape-recorded interview with the mother of the fourteen-year-old youngster. Yvette Sherman gave a moving presentation that was described in the *Proceedings of the American Academy of Forensic Sciences* as designed "to increase the empathy of the forensic community for the parents of a child who suffered untimely death."[8]

On May 18, 2003, at about 5:30 P.M., Raymond Sherman found his fourteen-year-old son, Raymond Jr., in the garage with a gunshot wound to the head. The forensic pathologist who performed an autopsy confirmed that the gunshot wound was the cause of death.

Before the police completed their investigation, and without interviewing the family, Al Klimek, the medical examiner for Brown County, pronounced the mode of death to be suicide. Klimek was a full-time firefighter appointed to the position of "medical examiner" by the county executive. The police investigation concluded that the youngster's death was an accident, but nonmedical medical examiner Al Klimek issued a press release declaring that the youngster's death was a suicide.

To my knowledge, Klimek made the determination of Ray's mode of death as suicide based only on the autopsy, which made suicide and homicide equally possible. In the absence of evidence of suicide and homicide, accident was most likely.

A joint conference with the family, the police, and Klimek took place on June 10, 2003. During the meeting Klimek said, "Even though I don't believe your son intended to take his own life, I had to rule suicide based on a statute." Yvette Sherman, the boy's mother asked, "Even though you don't believe our son intended to take his own life, you had to rule suicide based on a statute?" Klimek answered "Yes." Yvette Sherman asked, "What statute?" Klimek told her, "Statute number 97." Thus, according to Klimek the youngster committed an unintentional suicide as matter of law. The family's efforts to persuade Klimek to change the mode of death from suicide to accident were unsuccessful.

The difference between suicide and accident for parents is enormous. Suicide is a symptom of mental illness of some duration that should have been treated. When parents are told that their child died due to suicide they feel they are being accused of neglect. In our society there is still a stigma associated with suicide. Suicide has been condemned by Judaism, Christianity, and Islam. In many countries, suicide attempts are punishable by law.

Parents often feel guilty when a child commits suicide, always wondering "what could I have done to prevent my child from killing him or herself?" They believe that a youngster depressed enough to take his life would show signs of impending disaster that parents should recognize. Suicidal depression has a number of emotional, cognitive, and somatic symptoms, which would be readily recognized in a close-knit family.

Avi Berg, the attorney retained by the family, read my chapter "Psychological Autopsy" in the *Handbook of Forensic Sciences* edited by Cyril H.Wecht, and called me.[9] Berg retained me as an expert witness and supplied me with extensive documents for review. I also requested an interview with the parents of the youngster.

Interview with Mrs. Yvette Sherman

On April 9, 2004, I interviewed Mrs. Sherman who is an intelligent, articulate woman. At the outset of the interview, she was very poised and casual. I was aware of her reaction to the traumatic subject from our telephone call, and I avoided touching upon the death of her son at the beginning of our meeting. She described to me the background of her husband and her own family. I found out that there was no history of any genetic predisposition to mental illness and no history of suicide in either parental family.

Raymond's history was covered in detail. It was obvious that he was an adored child with a great many talents. He was highly popular and was an above-average student. There was no history of any traumatic events or significant family conflicts in his life. He was an outgoing, expressive, and loving youngster, and he was well accepted and loved by neighbors and peers. We discussed in considerable detail the last few days before Raymond's death. Instead of paraphrasing the account given to me by Mrs. Sherman, I will let her speak for herself. I started by asking her to go back a few days before Raymond's death.

A. Raymond, that week, had a track meet, he broke the track record. He had sports acceleration practice. During his track meet, which was at Edison . . . in Green Bay . . . he and his teammates broke two track records that week. He also had his talent show performances. . . . I remember that week with all of his buddies; they were doing a Stomp routine, which he started when he came in at sixth grade. He created that along with one of the other teachers, because he had seen it in Minneapolis . . . he wanted to bring that whole Stomp concept to Green Bay,[10] so he started in sixth grade. So, they had performances in sixth grade, seventh grade. Eighth grade was a big performance and a lot of his friends—who were athletes and some performers—he wanted to make sure that they all dressed in certain costume and he had me there saying, "Mom, help me out with this." . . . He did his Stomp routine, which he was very proud of, because he played the drums and the theme for his performance was—they were in a locker room. . . . They started using a basketball. They bounced the basketball and one of them had a hockey stick. He and his other buddy had drum sticks and they started playing.

Q. In terms of the community or the neighborhood, how did he fit in?

A. Raymond fit in any place and every place he has ever been. He was, and I would have to say that I don't know of any parents who would disagree with me on this . . . he was probably the most loved child in that community in terms of people that knew him and this is from boys and girls. Raymond, because he was loved and was so kind to everybody . . . some of his friends said to me "Mrs. Sherman, you know, there were kids around Raymond that we would never think of even associating with," but Raymond never turned, he was popular. . . . He could do everything. He was smart. He was intelligent. He was a comedian. He knew how to make somebody feel good, who was feeling bad. He was never cruel. He was always kind to people . . . and he could do whatever it is he needed to do.

Q. Go back to that Friday.

A. At the dance he said he had a soccer match that weekend, so I said you can go to the dance Friday night. Anyway, so he went to the dance. He and his other buddy went—they were dropped off and I went to pick him up. I said I'm going to pick you up at ten o'clock, because you have to get up early in the morning to go to your soccer match. [He said] "Okay, mom." So, I went to pick him up . . . this was Friday night. Of course, I'm out there waiting, waiting, waiting—he wasn't standing at the door . . . so I walked into the dance and I know a lot of those kids . . . they were all in their dancing and there were parents there standing around while I just walked right in and out on the dance floor and I said, "Raymond, we have to go." [He said] "Oh, mom," you know, "can't we stay here longer?" I said, oh no, honey, we have to go and [he said] "Okay." So, he starts leaving and we're walking out and he's talking—they're both talking, joking . . . about how much fun they had . . . he and his friend, Olin. . . . We left and we were walking out and he was talking about the dance and the party and how it didn't get started until he got there . . . what a good time they had and, I remember, after dropping his friend off, when I got to the house that night—earlier that evening we were at the neighbor's house—we were having a bonfire. My girls were down there and . . . all the neighborhood kids. We were down there and we [were] all singing around the campfire. . . . I had picked up Ray . . . this is still Friday night. This is still after I dropped the other kids off and we were going home . . . this was earlier. I had been sitting at the campfire—we were singing songs. The girls were all playing with the neighbors and Ray, of course, was at the party.

Q. Did anything else happen Saturday?

A. No. Saturday he spent the night at his friend's [Olin's] house . . . because they had another game on Sunday—no they won that [soccer game], so Sunday morning, the day he died, they had lost that game and we were all outside again and Olin's dad was out and we were all sitting around talking again about the party and Raymond we were talking about the dancing—I remember that—and how some of the kids were dancing and I told him that I don't want you dancing like that [laughs] . . . the new style that the kids are doing. . . . they dance pretty close . . . I said I don't want you dancing and that happening with you and he said, "I know mom . . . I'm going to have a respectable girl . . . I wouldn't do that." I said you never know whose mother of those daughters would come in and I don't want you in that situation where they see you dancing like that with their daughter. So, we just kind of talked about that. This was Sunday morning. We talked again about losing his soccer game that morning.

Q. Was he going to a movie on Sunday?

A. He was going to go, my gosh; he was going to go to the movies to see *The Matrix* . . . He had been waiting over two months to see this movie. . . . My husband had been out of town all of this time—he had been in Puerto Rico, so he was back. He was going to take Raymond to the movies and Raymond called him, oh, there is so much that happened during this time, but he called him on his cell phone. Ray had rushed back—before they went to the movies my daughters were in a dance recital. They had a noon performance and they had another one that evening, so Ray had gotten back just in time to come in the house. He asked Ray where the tickets were and so he took the tickets and left and went to the performance. Actually, he went—when they came back, Ray was having a conversation with his dad about the movies and Ray had called them. He said, "I'll take—you get the movie times," so during that time Ray had called his dad on his cell phone. Raymond had looked all the movies times up and he left all the movie times on there. "Dad, there's a five o'clock, a six o'clock, a seven o'clock" . . . all the way to probably the last performance, because everything was *The Matrix*. He was so excited about this movie. He was into it. Not just *The Matrix*. Any movies that Ray was into, he would always act out whatever characters he was going to see. The movie before that was *Spiderman*, so Raymond would be Spiderman in the house. . . . He was like that from the time he was a little boy. But that day he was going to the movies with his dad and when we came home after the recital we were talking and I had gotten on the phone . . . this had to be around 4:30/5:00. Around 4:30 or so, because the first thing I did was get on the telephone . . . also calling parents at that time, because we were going to have a meeting about the eighth grade dance and delegating responsibility, seeing who would bring what and do what . . . just that typical preparation. So, Raymond looked at me, because he knew I was on the phone calling these parents, then he went out into the garage and that was the last time—

Q. What time did he go into the garage?

A. It had to be around . . . between 4:30 and 5:00 he went in there . . . it was daylight.

Q. He talks to you and goes into the garage. Was there anything unusual you noticed about him before he goes into the garage? Did you hear the gunshot?

A. No. I was on the phone and my mom was on the porch and the girls were in there watching television. I'm on the phone calling parents and God dog-it, no, I didn't hear it.

Q. How did you discover him? Did you discover him?

A. No. My husband—I remember him walking to the garage door saying "Raymond, you almost done?" and Raymond said, "Yeah, dad. I'm almost finished."

Q. Your husband comes home and he goes into the garage?

A. Yeah. He had walked in there and Raymond, I guess, was just finishing up whatever he was doing and he said "Okay, dad. I'm almost ready."

Q. Almost ready for what?

A. To go to the movies. Ray had opened the door, he saw him and he said "I'm almost done dad putting the last of these things together." Whatever their conversation was and he said "Okay" and they were getting ready to go to the movies.

Q. So your husband comes back inside the house?

A. He comes back inside the house. You know it's really something, Dr. Tanay, because I regret this to this day. My husband wanted to go in and help Ray . . . pick up the stuff in the garage, because there were a bunch of tables . . . he was going to help him clean up the garage. . . . My mother and I said no, don't help him. Let him do it himself. The reason that I did that was because about a week or two before that, when we were talking about . . . going through Ray's curriculum for high school down here . . . and I'm thinking that you're going to be fifteen years old in August and he plays sports, music and he wanted to get into drama classes. He had just talked to me just a week before saying, "Mom, you have to call this Nickelodeon, they have auditions."

Q. So your husband leaves him in the garage to finish cleaning up. What's next?

A. I just want to tell you why I had him go in there, because we knew he couldn't have a job after school, because of sports and activities, so we came up with—how about cleaning up garages. Call your friend Mika when you get down here and start a business on Saturdays cleaning out garages. I told Ray, my husband, to let him finish and then we were going to go in and critique him to get him ready for his "job." . . . What happens next is Ray comes in and a few minutes later Raymond didn't come out, so Ray opens the door and he says, "Oh my God, call 911," so I have the phone (I hang up) and I walk out there and I look down [lengthy pauses and begins to cry loudly] and I see my son laying there in a pool of blood and I said, "Raymond what did you do?" [regains composure] I'm talking to myself—I'm talking to him like you hit your head, the tables were in there.

Q. It didn't occur to you that it could be a gunshot?

A. Oh, God, no. No, no. So, I thought maybe he hit his head from playing, because he was always jumping off stuff. I said did you hit your head? I didn't know. So anyway, I'm looking at my phone trying to get 911. I look up and I see my neighbor across the street. She was sitting out there. The garage door was open at that time. I think Ray was opening . . . it had to be open, because I saw my neighbor. My husband evidently opened the garage door; probably after he saw Raymond or I did—I don't remember. Ray was moving stuff out of the way. I said can you call 911, because I was trying to call it and if I make a mistake [starts to cry] that means it would take more time and I didn't want to make a mistake. I was trying to focus on those three numbers and I said will you call 911 and tell them to get over here as fast as they can [crying harder] and then I got 911 and I didn't know at that time what had happened.

Q. But you still don't know that it is . . .

A. No, no, and then someone was there. I think it might have been one of the paramedics. . . . I don't know what they said, it's a gunshot wound (uncontrollable crying). It was a gun and the first thing I said to myself was, because the guns were in there and I said oh my God, he was in here pretending to be the Matrix and he shot himself and I told my husband, because when Ray had walked out there I guess a week or so when they were cleaning out the garage getting ready for the garage sale, Ray had checked those guns and I told him to put them away and he said, "I should have put them away" and it dawned on me that he was playing with those guns, because the one thing he would always do whenever he would become a character he tried to be as real as he could without becoming that and he would study things and study movements over and over again, but he always . . . with toys, it wasn't just guns—it was anything. So, I said, oh, my God and the guys in there said he was dead. [Crying loudly] I knew he was getting ready to go see that movie. I'm so mad at myself.

Q. You're mad at yourself for what?

A. Because, why didn't I move them. Why didn't I move them? I asked my husband and I know he was going to do it, but he thought, he said, "I told Raymond—don't play with them, these are dangerous." He told him he would teach him how to use them. He would take them, because that was the first time he'd ever had a real gun and Raymond was very visual.

Q. Let me now ask you what I said before I was going to ask you and that has to do with the fact that you suffered a terrible loss [Mrs. Sherman crying loudly] and you know, that kind of a loss is a horrible burden for a parent to carry. Nothing worse can happen to a parent than something of that nature. Have you had any help?

A. I've had some counseling, but I haven't been able to . . . I've been so focused on this case. Everything. . . .

Q. This case is in a way insignificant. I have professionally no doubt that this was an accident. What is significant is to help you to deal with what happened to you.

A. [uncontrollable crying continues] I lost my son. I lost my best friend and I lost my only son and he was so good. He was so good, he was so kind, he was so loving, and I loved him and I should have protected him and I didn't. Dr.

Tanay, we talked about everything. We talked about drugs, we talked about alcohol, we talked about relationships, we talked about sex, we talked about everything a lot of parents don't talk about with their sons. I didn't talk to him about guns—I didn't know anything about them and I missed that [Mrs. Sherman crying intensely while talking].

Q. Let us stop now. I think that since I cannot be of much help to you, let me just say to you one thing. I think you, like any parent in this situation, you need help. Let me tell you, aside from patients, I had friends who lost children, not in such a tragic way, but due to illness and that was a profound trauma to them and they needed help and you need help. We will stop on that—you need help and calling it an accident, which it certainly was, is not going to change the reality of your loss.

Following this interview, I was convinced that Raymond Jr. had not taken his own life. He showed no signs of major depression; his enthusiastic involvement in sports and social events in the days immediately leading up to his death, and eagerness to see a popular movie, all point away from suicide. His death was clearly an accident.

Based on my unopposed expert testimony, a trial judge changed the mode of death on the death certificate of Raymond Sherman Jr. to "accident." One might assume that a medical examiner would have the qualifications to appear in court as an expert witness when mode of death is at issue. However, Klimek did not meet the qualifications to be an expert witness on mode of death because he had no relevant credentials in that area.

A person entrusted with making a determination that a child committed suicide should make such judgment with a high degree of certainty. The Sherman family and the Green Bay community suffered emotional and social harm by the pronouncement that Raymond's death was suicide. The nightmare of losing a child to a gun accident in their own home was magnified by Klimek's designation of suicide. The Sherman family suffered this additional trauma because they lived in the city of Green Bay; had they lived in Milwaukee or Madison, where medical examiners are required to be physicians, most likely the case would have been adjudicated as an accident.

In light of all that has transpired, one might think the state of Wisconsin would have taken steps to prevent such problems in the future. But this is not the case. Klimek continues to be the medical examiner for Brown County. He provides the same services for Oconto County, which, according to the *Green Bay Press-Gazette* of August 7, 2006, will abolish its coroner's office. Mr. Klimek also handles death investigations for Door County.

NOTES

1. "Determination of Cause and Mode of Death before and after Medicolegal Autopsy: A Comparative Study," M. Segerberg-Konttinen, March 1, 1988, *Journal of Forensics Sciences*, online.

2. All statistical data taken from the standard psychiatric textbook, *Kaplan & Sadock's Comprehensive Textbook of Psychiatry* by Benjamin J. Sadock, Virginia A. Sadock, and Harold L. Kaplan. 8th ed. (Philadelphia: Lippincott Williams & Wilkins, 2004).

3. Antoon Leenaars, *Suicide Notes* (New York: Human Sciences Press, 1988).

4. Steven Lukes, *Emile Durkheim: His Life and Work, a Historical and Critical Study* (Stanford: Stanford University Press, 1985).

5. The unique cases of so-called rational suicide are an exception. See Glenn C. Graber, "Mastering the Concept of Suicide," in *Suicide, Right or Wrong*, ed. John Donnelly (Amherst, NY: Prometheus Books, 1998).

6. Joan Hagan Arnold and Penelope Buschman Gemma, *A Child Dies* (Philadelphia: Charles Press Publishers, 1994).

7. Susan Neugeboren, *An Orphan's Tale* (New York: HRW, 1976).

8. *Proceedings of the American Academy of Forensic Sciences*, vol. 11 (2005): 12.

9. Cyril H. Wecht, *Handbook of Forensic Sciences* (New York: Mathew Bender, 1990).

10. Percussion group performance using various objects, originated in England.

5

A KILLING IS A KILLING IS A KILLING— UNLESS IT ISN'T

Varieties of Homicide

Gertrude Stein famously said, "A rose is a rose is a rose," but what is true of roses is not true of homicides. Yet there was a time when every killing, including accidental killing, was the same in the eyes of the law and was punishable by death. Fortunately, cultures and societies have evolved to become more nuanced in their treatment of homicide. Indeed, the ability to perceive differences in human behavior is a developmental landmark for individuals and societies.

Contemporary justice involves proportionality—the severity of the punishment should correspond to the nature of the crime; thus, modern law distinguishes between varieties of homicides, depending on the motivation of the perpetrator.[1] There are good psychosocial reasons to separate premeditated killing from an impulsive act that results in death. The former is first-degree murder, punishable by life in prison or the death penalty. The latter is third-degree murder or manslaughter, and is punishable by relatively short imprisonment. Distinguishing between types of homicide is one of the most important functions of a forensic psychiatrist..

Law enforcement and forensic psychiatry deal with an administration of justice that is based upon suspicions, evidence, and opinions. The term *suspect* describes a member of large class of people who could have possibly committed the homicide under investigation. A defendant is a person who, based upon evidence, is believed to have committed a specific crime.

In our justice system, the police and the prosecution determine who becomes a defendant in a criminal homicide. The power to determine who is a suspect and who is a defendant has great consequences for the individuals affected.

Our law enforcement agencies are fragmented and devoid of even the minimal uniformity essential to competence and effectiveness. We have somewhere between 40,000 and 50,000 different police jurisdictions, and the training level varies widely among them. In some jurisdictions, police have virtually no training.

Most professions have members of varying competence, but no other profession has such widespread differences in the level of training as the police in the United States. I have encountered many police officers whose only preparation has been on-the-job training. In my forensic practice, I have come across cases where police officers were inadequately trained even in handling weapons and had injured and killed other police officers.

After the police arrest a suspect, a prosecutor determines the nature of the charge. Unfortunately, many prosecutors are more interested in publicity than justice. Prosecutors sometimes file first-degree murder charges with little regard for the evidence or the public interest. The first-degree murder indictment is often based more on creative interpretation of the law than on evidence. The following is an illustration of how police and prosecution work together to produce a miscarriage of justice.

Susan Smith (not her real name) was at a country club with her girlfriends when her friends recognized that she had had too much to drink and should not drive home. They asked a male friend to drive Smith home. The man took her to the entrance door of the club and went to get the car. In the meantime, a valet drove up in a car, which Mrs. Smith, who was intoxicated, believed to be hers. She got into it and drove away. Believing that she was pulling into her own driveway, Smith ran the car into the garage door of Kathryn Griffith, a seventy-one-year-old woman who lived alone. Mrs. Griffith was reading the newspaper in her bedroom at the time. She got out of bed and called the police, believing herself to be the victim of a break-in. She suffered a cardiac death, presumably because of the excitement. The Oakland County prosecutor at the time, Brooks Patterson, declared Griffith's death to be a fright death. Oakland County, Michigan's most affluent region, has a population in excess of million people.

Smith was a mild-mannered person, and this was her first significant encounter with the law. Smith had caused property damage and was guilty of driving a vehicle while intoxicated. Prosecutor Brooks Patterson had the discretionary power to charge Smith with a misdemeanor. Regrettably, Patterson was not content with pursuing the misdemeanor charge. Through sheer legal sophistry, he transformed the misdemeanor into murder. Death caused in the process of committing a felony is regarded as "felony murder," which in the state of Michigan is the equivalent of first-degree murder and is punishable by life in prison without parole. The felony in this case was "stealing" a car.

I was contacted by Attorney Fessler, who was also a Republican state senator from West Bloomfield Township, with a request to evaluate Susan Smith. He told me he requested a copy of Griffith's autopsy report from the medical examiner's office and was told it was being retyped. He then inspected Griffith's death certificate on file with the city of Troy and found that the word "natural" had been erased and replaced with the words "see me about this." It was later revealed that the medical examiner changed the cause of death on the death certificate from "natural" to "undetermined," clearing the way for a court to determine whether Griffith was murdered.

Prosecutor Brooks Patterson issued a warrant charging Smith "with murder, auto-theft, breaking and entering and destruction of property." This is a classic example of a prosecutor seeking publicity by "manufacturing" charges including murder.

I testified on behalf of Susan Smith. Joyce Todd, an assistant prosecutor, devoted a great deal of time and effort to convict Smith of felony murder. Todd was a competent and effective lawyer wasting her time and taxpayer money to advance a legalistic murder charge. Smith's lawyer was just as effective, and I gave persuasive testimony. Smith was convicted of a second-degree murder, which was a partial victory for the defense.

In a system interested more in justice, this accident would have been adjudicated as just that—an accident. Justice was not served by this outcome, but the injustice of life imprisonment without parole was avoided. Smith did not commit homicide, even though she caused Griffith's sudden cardiac death.

THE PSYCHOLOGY OF HOMICIDE

The human mind, according to Sigmund Freud, can be divided into three components: id, ego, and superego. His "anatomy of personality" has been generally accepted in psychology. In nontechnical terms, we can speak of these three elements as unconscious (id), reason (ego), and conscience (superego).

Attention, perception, memory, and conscious control of behavior exemplify the normal consciousness. An altered state of consciousness, called a dissociative state, occurs under certain stressful circumstances. In a dissociative state, behavior is not under the control of the ego (self) or of the superego (conscience). Instead, the id (unconscious) controls behavior, and impulsive decision-making dominates action. This condition accounts for many homicides.

Dissociation can be induced by chemical, neurological, and experiential factors. It is widely accepted that chemicals (alcohol, illegal drugs, and some prescription drugs) can lead to dissociation. Emotional stress and overwhelming life experiences can also produce dissociation.

The standard psychiatric textbook by Kaplan and Sadock states that dissociation is often misconstrued as split personality.[2] The term "split personality" is used by laypeople as a synonym for schizophrenia. A dissociative episode is a transient psychotic experience.

All behavior is psychiatrically categorized as egosyntonic, egodystonic, or psychotic. These terms can be translated as self-harmonious, self-disharmonious, and psychotic behavior. For example, a parent instructing a child is acting in an egosyntonic manner, the self-image of a parent involves assisting and teaching the child. However, when the parent loses self-control and beats the child and inflicts injury, this is egodystonic behavior, since it is inconsistent with parents' self-image as caregivers and protectors from harm.

In 1969 I proposed a classification of homicides as egosyntonic, egodystonic, or psychotic.[3] John Hinckley's attempt to kill President Reagan is an example of a psychotic homicide attempt. In his delusional state, the schizophrenic John Hinckley believed that killing President Reagan would secure for him the love of Jodie Foster. Hinckley's behavior was neither impulsive nor rational, yet it was consistent with his delusional thinking.[4]

Egosyntonic homicide is a killing committed without disruption of personality. The egosyntonic homicide is a rational, goal-directed act, committed in order to fulfill a consciously acceptable wish.[5] Killings by police, soldiers in combat, and those acting in self-defense are egosyntonic. Killings committed by criminals are also in the same category, even though they are the result of the antisocial motivation.

Egodystonic homicide is often the result of a sadomasochistic relationship between two individuals whose personalities and life situations determine the deadly outcome. The passive participant in the sadomasochistic relationship has failed the developmental task of transforming infantile rage into the adaptive anger of adulthood. He or she fluctuates between passivity and breakthrough rage, during which egodystonic violence takes place.

Modern neuroscience makes it is possible to show that there is a difference between different types of homocide. Some impulses bypass the neocortex and the behavior of the actor is the result of activation of subcortical parts of the brain. Thus, first-degree murder and manslaughter differ not only legally but neuroscientifically.

In the egosyntonic homicide, different areas of the brain are activated in order to bring about the physical actions designed to cause the victim's death; these are areas that deal with intentionality.

There is a common failure to distinguish between anger and rage; in common usage, the two terms are often used as synonyms. But anger, unlike rage, is not likely to lead to egodystonic violence. However, people who habitually suppress anger are likely to suffer from explosive outbursts of rage and occasional violence. Rage is often viewed simply as an exaggerated, more intense, form of anger; however from a psychological point of view, there is a vast difference between these two emotions. Anger is within the control of the individual, while rage overwhelms a person's mental apparatus.

A homicide in a sadomasochistic relationship represents an explosive resolution of a long-term conflict. The killing takes place during a disruption of the ego and is often precipitated by a seemingly insignificant provocation. I use the term "homicidal process" to describe the progressive intensification of the sadomasochistic relationship between the future perpetrator of homicide and the victim.

The type of weapon used in a homicide and the duration of the homicidal rage are directly proportional. Time is a critical factor because the homicidal impulse between intimates has a very short duration. An enraged homicidal husband or wife using a firearm can carry out a homicide in a few seconds. Using a knife would take a longer time, a blunt instrument would take even longer. The very act of lifting a knife or a blunt instrument provides discharge of aggression and often leads to termination of the homicidal rage. Obviously, there are exceptions. I recall a homicide perpetrated by a young woman with a flimsy fruit knife. She became enraged at her husband and attacked him with this relatively harmless-looking weapon. Unfortunately, one quick stab left of the breastbone landed directly in the husband's heart, causing death. On the other hand, I also recall a husband who raised a large butcher knife against his wife and collapsed in tearful apology.

Often, the proximity of an emergency room or a surgeon's skill determines whether a given homicidal assault leads to the victim's death or survival. The perpetrator's mental state and motivation may be identical in both cases, but the legal consequences will be significantly different. Attempted murder is legally quite different than actual murder.

SPOUSAL HOMICIDE

Husbands do kill wives and wives do kill husbands, but rarely in the premeditated way we see depicted in the media. Spousal homicide is usually impulsive and happens after years of aggressive tension within the marriage. A sudden increase in hostility may result in an altered state of consciousness, popularly known as "rage," that leads to a physical assault. If a knife or gun is readily available, a homicide may result.

Paul Davis and his wife, Kate (not their real names), are a classic case of spousal homicide. On Friday, August 20, 1971, Davis arrived at home to find his three children on the living-room couch. A packed suitcase of his clothes was nearby. His wife of twelve years was standing with a man and her mother in front of the children. The man, a bailiff, handed Davis an envelope of divorce papers.

As Davis described it, "The man handed me the divorce papers, and from there on I was irrational. I went into a shock, you might say. We'd been married twelve years—what else can I say? All I could see was the big word—divorce—divorce—divorce."

Kate sent the three children outside to play in the yard, and Davis begged his wife not to go through with the divorce. He followed his mother-in-law to her car and asked what she thought of the situation. When the mother-in-law told him that Kate was serious about the divorce, Davis feared what he might do next and told his mother-in-law that he would be upstairs packing his suitcase. The mother-in-law left.

Upstairs, Davis opened the suitcase that Kate had packed. On the top, she had placed his deer-hunting license. Upon seeing his license,

Davis went to a nearby drawer for his lip ice (used in the woods when cold wind chaps one's lips). Next to the lip ice was Davis's six-bullet revolver. He put the gun in his suitcase and closed it.

He then went down to the kitchen and asked Kate if she planned to feed the dog. The divorce papers were on top of the refrigerator, and he pulled them down and opened his suitcase to take them with him. When he opened the suitcase, he saw his gun, impulsively picked it up, walked toward his wife, and asked her, "Kate, won't you change your mind?"

Kate called for her mother (who was already gone) and pushed the gun out of the way, but, as Davis described it, the gun went off almost automatically. He does not remember pressing the trigger. He only remembers shooting her once in the middle of the forehead. Davis mentioned that after he shot his wife he thought there was a bullet left in the gun and tried to use it to commit suicide. But when he put the gun to his head, there was no bullet. "That's how I knew I had shot her six times," David said. "I always kept the gun fully loaded."

The children heard the shots and came into the kitchen. They screamed and ran across the busy road to their neighbor's mobile home. Davis leaned over to kiss his wife on the cheek and said, "Kate, it doesn't matter. I still love you." He then followed the children and told his neighbor, "She's dead. You can't help her." When the neighbor called the police, he took the phone from the neighbor and said to the state trooper, "My name is Paul Davis. I live at . . ." and he gave the address. He then said, "I'm sane now. I've shot my wife six times. Don't come with a bunch of sirens. I know I killed her." The police troopers who testified at Davis's trial said he was calm and submissive at his arrest.

Davis's lawyer asked me to interview his client and give a psychiatric opinion as to his client's sanity at the time of the homicide. When I met Davis for our interview, he was thirty-two. He told me repeatedly that he was very much in love with his wife, and I believed him. On a number of occasions during the interview he became quite emotional and cried. He expressed profound remorse, depression, and suicidal ideas.

Davis described a childhood of strict work and parents of whom he spoke highly; he said they had instilled a strong conscience in him. He had had an uneventful childhood and had been in only one schoolyard fight. Davis married Kate, his high school sweetheart, in 1959, shortly after she graduated from high school. He said their marriage was difficult from the start. Kate had left home several times to stay with her mother. Davis described their sexual relations as "like a job," and a frequency of intercourse that went from once a week early in the marriage to every month or two in later years. He described a period after the birth of their first child where his wife had asked for a divorce, but they reconciled and Davis perceived that things were "pretty good" after that, except for the limited sexual relations.

Before the homicide, Davis said, he did not doubt his wife's fidelity. However, he described finding evidence afterward that she had been unfaithful. A photo album turned up of Kate with other men and the places they had visited, and Paul remembered a trip Kate had taken up north where she claimed to be visiting "a girlfriend" but was likely meeting another man. The Davis's neighbor also testified in court that she had seen a man visiting Kate at the Davis home, but she had not mentioned this to Davis. His denial notwithstanding, it was apparent that on a subconscious level he was aware of Kate's infidelity.

Like many killers of spouses, Davis used a gun that was already in the house. Because guns kill quickly, they are essential in impulsive homicides because they shorten the duration of the homicidal episode. Davis was a gun collector and said in our interview that he had fourteen guns. At one point in the interview I said to him, "You should be afraid of guns. If the gun had not been there, most likely you would not be here now."

"Probably not," he replied. "Probably if the gun hadn't been there, I think I'd have walked out. Because I was on the way out. I was coming downstairs with the suitcase."

The gun is a weapon and a stimulant of aggressive impulses. Davis's history was typical for an individual with an overdeveloped superego (conscience) and masochistic tendencies. His marriage was a sadomas-ochistic relationship that satisfied his own needs and those of his wife. In my opinion, Davis was not psychotic, but at the time of the homicide he was in a dissociative state. At that time Michigan had the "irresistible impulse" defense, which Davis's lawyer pursued. This case stands out in my mind because the insanity defense prevailed. Since Davis was not psychotic, he was back home within a rather short period of time. My wife and I visited him with our young son David on our way to our northern Michigan vacation home. Davis showed us around and took us upstairs to see his three children's empty bedrooms. The children's maternal grandparents had custody of them, yet the bedrooms were exactly as they had been when the children left. My four-year-old son, David, began to play with the model train that was on the floor in one room. When Davis saw that he began to cry. This case is emblematic of the many spousal homicides that I have encountered in the last fifty years.

In 1983, when I was an associate editor of the *Journal of Forensic Sciences*, I was assigned to review a best-selling book entitled *Fatal Vision*, on the Jeffery McDonald case. Dr. McDonald was an army doctor who in 1970 was convicted of murdering, in a brutally sadistic manner, his wife and two children. The author of the book, Joe McGinniss, portrayed Dr. McDonald as a psychopath. McGinniss had befriended Dr. McDonald during the long time between McDonald falling under suspicion and the actual trial. McGinniss was less than honest with his "friend." He professed to believe that McDonald was innocent, but quietly he was writing a book that was exposing McDonald as a sadistic killer. After I read the book I was convinced that the description of a planned killing by McDonald of his pregnant wife, Colette, and the stabbing of the daughters, Kimberly, age five, and Kristen, age two, to eliminate eye-witnesses, made no sense to someone familiar with the psychology of homicide. Last but not least, McDonald himself was assaulted, but the prosecution claimed that the wounds were self-inflicted. The prosecutors told the jurors that McDonald committed the murders in a state of paranoid rage. However, they had no evidence to prove it; nor did they have psychiatric testimony. The efforts to rebut the accusations were barred by the court. I wrote in my review, "The prosecution's case against Dr. McDonald was in large measure built upon character assassination. . . . Every possible indiscretion that Dr. McDonald committed over a lifetime had been paraded before the jury time and time again. Paradoxically, the psychiatric testimony offered by the defense was kept out because it was ruled to be 'character testimony.' This was clearly unfair."[6]

McDonald was a gregarious, Princeton-educated doctor and a loving, doting father. There was nothing in his history to indicate sociopathic tendencies. Dr. McDonald is still in prison. All efforts on his behalf failed. But I am convinced that he is innocent. My reasons for believing that Dr. McDonald was innocent are quite simple. There was no evidence that he committed these brutal murders, merely suspicions. Furthermore, it takes a certain personality or a psychotic illness to become a sadistic killer of one's children and wife. Dr. McDonald was neither a psychopath nor a psychotic. A dedicated husband and father, a man without history of criminality, does not suddenly become a sadistic multiple murderer.

KYLLEEN HARGRAVE-THOMAS

In May 2005, at the Liberty Athletic Club in Ann Arbor, Michigan, I noted a discarded front page of the *Detroit Free Press* with the headline "With Judge in Her Corner, She Hopes for Clemency." When I read that Michael Reynolds was the assistant prosecutor who tried the case, I immediately suspected that an injustice had occurred. I picked up the newspaper and read the article's first paragraph. "Kylleen Hargrave-Thomas, a dental receptionist, was accused of stabbing her boyfriend, forty-two-year-old Joseph Bernal, a Ford Rouge rail yard worker, in his home. According to the prosecutor, Ms. Hargrave-Thomas was enraged that Bernal had called off their wedding, entered his home at night in a rage and stabbed him in the heart, then returned at 5 A.M. to set his mattress on fire to cover up the evidence."[7]

This was an unlikely scenario for a impulsive (rage) homicide. As soon as I got home, I printed the fifty-some page opinion of Federal District Court Judge Paul Gadola written in 2002. I was amazed by Judge Gadola's strong language in overturning Hargrave-Thomas's 1993 state-court conviction. Clearly, his sense of justice had been offended. I had personally testified in Judge Gadola's courtroom when he was a Michigan trial judge in Flint, and I found him to be a strong conservative and tough on crime. It had not surprised me when President Reagan appointed him to the federal bench.

Judge Gadola wrote in his August 2002 opinion that Hargrave-Thomas's lawyers "were manifestly and flagrantly ineffective"—failing to investigate, interview, call witnesses, or even to present evidence. He called the case a travesty and said Hargrave-Thomas was likely innocent of the murder. After a few hours of reading about the case, I, too, was convinced that Hargrave-Thomas was innocent. The 1993 defense had been grossly inadequate. A bench trial in this type of a case is unheard of—yet on November 5, 1993, Judge Wendy Baxter had found Ms. Hargrave-Thomas guilty of first-degree murder and arson.

Before she became a judge, I knew Wendy Baxter as a zealous prosecutor. In the Hargrave-Thomas case, Judge Baxter's novel contribution to jurisprudence was a unique piecemeal conduct of the trial. She took testimony on seven different days spread out over five months. In fifty years of forensic experience, I have never heard of taking testimony in a first-degree murder trial in such a fragmented manner. I doubt that any judge could keep track of testimony presented in this fashion.

Prosecutor Reynolds had argued to the judge—without any supporting evidence—that Hargrave-Thomas killed Bernal in a rage. However, Reynolds's own version of events contradicted a rage-type homicide. He claimed that Hargrave-Thomas was the last person to have seen Bernal alive: they had parted around midnight and she went home. This inference could not be proved or disproved, but it was the bedrock of the prosecution's case. Reynolds further argued that she returned to Bernal's residence between 5:00 and 7:00 A.M., entered the house through the garage, found a kitchen knife, crept up to his bedroom, and stabbed him to death. If Hargrave-Thomas had killed him in this manner then it would not have been a rage reaction but a carefully planned first-degree murder. If she killed him in a rage, it was not first-degree murder but manslaughter. The prosecutor was pursuing two contradictory claims.

After killing Bernal, according to the prosecution, she went home and got her two children ready for school. Around 7:30 A.M., Hargrave-Thomas arrived at her son's school for a meeting with a school counselor, who later testified that Hargrave-Thomas appeared perfectly normal and composed. While Reynolds's scenario of a person returning to his or her usual composure just after committing a bloody murder and arson might be plausible for a mafia hit man, it has little resemblance to a murder committed by a "woman scorned," which was the theme of the prosecution. The claim that a right-handed woman in her late thirties could, with her left hand, expertly stab a forty-two-year-old able-bodied male factory worker was far-fetched. Presumably, Bernal would have struggled, and Hargrave-Thomas would have had blood not only on her hands but also on her body.

Potential witnesses never called to the stand included a co-worker who signed an affidavit saying that Bernal had proposed to Hargrave-Thomas (undercutting the prosecution's theory that Hargrave-Thomas killed Bernal after he refused to marry her), her sons (who saw nothing unusual in her behavior that morning), and a newspaper deliveryman who saw someone standing outside Bernal's home around 4:30 A.M. (the deliveryman noted Bernal's open garage door and asked the man, who was wearing what appeared to be a police uniform, what was going on; the man mentioned a small fire—almost three hours before neighbors reported a fire in Bernal's home).

From a psychiatric perspective, it is inconceivable that Hargrave-Thomas killed Bernal. Law-abiding people do at times kill each other, but this typically occurs impulsively. Here, the prosecution posited a rage-based killing carried out in a premeditated, sadistic manner, followed by a masterly cover-up by a perpetrator with a cool demeanor. Hargrave-Thomas was not a seasoned criminal capable of such exploits.

According to the federal judge, Hargrave-Thomas's defense lawyer, Rene Cooper, did no investigation, did not interview potential witnesses, filed no motions challenging the evidence, and did not call any witnesses at the trial. The failure to respond to accusations, as a practical matter, is the functional equivalent of a guilty plea. The defense lawyer has the burden of rejoinder; this did not take place in the trial of Hargrave-Thomas.

Cooper relied upon the presumption of innocence and offered no defense on behalf of her client. She had decided on a bench trial, although lawyers are typically reluctant to place the fate of a client charged with first-degree murder in the hands of a judge. Judges have to consider political ramifications when they are the sole fact finders deciding guilt or innocence of a defendant charged with murder. The judge who rejects the prosecutor's claim runs the risk of being labeled soft on crime.

Judge Gadola ordered a new trial and released Thomas from prison pending a new trial. However, the prosecution appealed Judge Gadola's ruling and a federal appeals court reversed his decision. The U.S. Supreme Court refused to review the case. On September 17, 2006, after four years of freedom, in which Hargrave-Thomas had obtained a college degree and worked for a local Christian service agency, she was going back to prison to serve a life term without parole. Although Judge Gadola stated that Hargrave-Thomas was most likely innocent, he did not overturn her verdict, in compliance with the 2004 decision of the U.S. 6th Circuit Court of Appeals.[8]

The only way to undo the injustice in this case was by commutation; that is a reduction of a sentence by the governor. If Hargrave-Thomas had committed manslaughter, it is unlikely that she would have been sentenced to any prison term longer than the ten years that she had already served. Therefore, whichever approach one takes in relation to this case, there can be no doubt that an injustice occurred. I found out that law professor Andrea Lyon, associated with the Chicago Center for Justice in Capital Cases, was handling commutation efforts on behalf of Hargrave-Thomas. Professor Lyon was teaching at that time at the University of Michigan in Ann Arbor. We met for lunch and decided that I would try to persuade Governor Granholm to commute Hargrave-Thomas's sentence. My friend, former Attorney General Frank Kelley, who had been re-elected ten times and had served in this capacity for thirty-seven years, personally delivered my letter to the governor, but our efforts were unsuccessful. Political considerations outweighed Governor Granholm's concern for justice.

The next move of Professor Lyon was the Michigan Parole Board; she organized testimony and written recommendations from many people. I wrote a lengthy letter. The board recommended parole unanimously and Governor Granholm had little choice but to take action. In August 2008, a banner headline in the *Detroit Free Press* informed its readers "Convicted Killer Gets a Break." The article described the belated commutation of Hargrave-Thomas's sentence. The first paragraph announced: "An Oakland County woman who has spent nearly 11 years in prison for killing her ex-boyfriend will be released next month, after Gov. Jennifer Granholm commuted her sentence."

I could hardly believe that the author of this brazenly sensational piece was David Ashenfelter, the same reporter who wrote the May 2005 article that got me interested in the plight of Hargrave-Thomas in the first place. I had no doubt that Kylleen Hargrave-Thomas is innocent, but the average reader would likely have believed that Hargrave-Thomas was a dangerous killer and that a politician soft on crime had let her loose. Now I could better understand Governor Granholm's reluctance to intervene.

INNOCENT AND GUILTY OF FIRST-DEGREE MURDER

Upon retirement, my best friend, Dr. James Graves, moved with his wife, Sue, to the Upper Peninsula of Michigan. In April 2008 Jim and Sue came to Ann Arbor to attend my eightieth birthday party. During this visit they asked my opinion about a murder trial that was in progress before Judge William Carmody, who is their neighbor. After I heard the details, I told them: "The man is innocent but he will be found guilty by the jury." Jim was a distinguished psychiatrist and neuroscientist, and he was puzzled by my prediction of a guilty verdict because there was virtually no evidence to support the charge of murder. He wanted to know what I relied upon in making my prediction. "Imagination and politics are more important than evidence," was my answer.

Here are the facts of the case. On June 22, 2006, Juanita Richardson fell to her death from a 140-foot cliff at Pictured Rocks National Lakeshore. Juanita's husband, Thomas David Richardson, forty-six, was charged with killing his wife. The Richardson couple had traveled from their home in McBain, a community of under a thousand residents in Northern Michigan, to the popular tourist attraction when the accident, according to the husband, or criminal homicide, according to the prosecutor, took place. In my experience, a criminal defendant is guilty unless he can prove his innocence, and there was no way that Richardson could prove that he did not lure his wife to Pictured Rocks National Lakeshore with the intention of pushing her off the cliff.

A week later, I received a call from Jim, who said, "I am amazed about your ability to anticipate the verdict." After this conversation, I decided to explore the case in more detail. The *Mining Journal* was my source of information for Jim about this case.

On April 16, 2008, the *Mining Journal* reported that the jury convicted Richardson of first-degree murder. "The jury of seven women and five men deliberated for about 11 hours over two days. They found Richardson guilty of the most serious of the possible charges, first-degree murder. He could have been convicted of second-degree murder, voluntary or involuntary manslaughter." All of these crimes were included in the charge to the jury.

This is a strange combination of contradictory claims, an extravagant inclusion of charges of "everything but the kitchen sink" variety. In my fifty years of forensic psychiatric experience, I have never encountered such smorgasbord of charges in a spousal homicide.

Prosecutor Karen Bahrman delivered her closing argument with a color portrait of Juanita Richardson facing the jury. Bahrman spoke for nearly four-hours. Here is a short excerpt:

> I will be asking yourselves at various times, to put yourselves in the shoes of a logical innocent person, in many of the situations that the defendant was in. For example, we'll ask you to pretend that you just saw your spouse of 23 years, the mother or father of your children, fall from a cliff.

You're running for help and in that five minutes, does it occur to you to lie about what you saw? Do you even think about what you're going to tell people?

And the defense on the other hand, will be asking you to put your-selves in the shoes of a logical murderer. And this you cannot do because there is no such thing. A person who would decide to take the life of an-other human being, in such a cruel manner and for such selfish reasons, has already crossed that line between normal and abnormal. We can't expect him to act normally or logically or rationally. He doesn't think like us and we have nothing in common with him. So it's not supposed to make sense, from that perspective.[9]

Thus it makes sense that Richardson committed premeditated mur-der because it makes no sense. The prosecutor displayed an elementary absence of knowledge of the psychology of homicide. The prosecutor, in her closing argument, summed up the case by saying: "We have no idea what happened out there."

Thus to this prosecutor, *the absence of evidence* did not prove in-nocence but guilt. The *Mining Journal* describes defense attorney Karl Numinen as displaying a drawing on a screen in which people see two decidedly different things, depending how the image is viewed. He said:

We see what we want to see. The same picture, if you look at it close enough and long enough, you can see either way. You can see a young beautiful woman or you can see an old, ugly woman. The picture is de-signed that way. We see what we want to see. And this case is one great example of that. The police see what they want to see. When Deputy Webber stands there, or sits there, and testifies he's only looking for items of interest, he's looking only for what he wants to see. When they ask only questions that they're interested in, and don't write down the answers to things they're not interested in, they're only seeing what they want to see. I think witnesses do that too, sometimes—sometimes consciously, sometimes unconsciously. The prosecutor's engaged in that. She sees things only the way she wants to see. But she also has tried to get other people to change the way they want to see things, so that they can see it her way.[10]

This was an accurate depiction of the prosecutor's approach, but the de-fense lawyer functioned as his own expert. Lawyer's statements are not evidence. This case called for an expert on the psychology of homicide.

Prosecutor Bahrman spoke about the power of circumstantial evidence in this case. The so-called circumstantial evidence is an inference from the facts that possibly or likely justify a certain conclusion. It has to be distinguished from *direct evidence;* circumstantial evidence relies upon reasoning not observation. In this case there were no facts that would justify making inferences. In reality there was no evidence, direct or circumstantial, only speculations. Circumstantial evidence is a claim based upon an inference. For example, from the evidence that a person was seen running away from the scene of a crime, a jury may infer that the person committed the crime. As far as I could find out, the only circumstantial evidence was the speculations about the behavior of the husband after his wife fell to her death. For example, he ran for help instead of running to the body, he cried but there were no tears, and so on. From this fact several unsupportable inferences were made: "Prosecutor Bahrman said the prosecution believes Richardson distracts his wife, perhaps with the idea of taking her picture after she took his, then he gets her to move close to the ledge and he pushes her, or uses some other means, like a walking stick or choke hold, to subdue her."

Bahrman continued:

The cumulative nature of circumstantial evidence isn't just about coincidence, it's about the convergence of separate coincidences in the same place, and that's what makes it so compelling. It's also a process of elimination. So you're going to conclude that the defendant caused Mrs. Richardson's death, that he did something to set her fall into motion, via exactly the same process that you used to conclude that the planes that hit the World Trade Center on 9/11 did not do so by accident.[11]

The reference to 9/11 was irrelevant and prejudicial.

The prosecutor went to extraordinary lengths to convict Richardson. The police wired a cellmate of Richardson with a recording device. On March 5, 2008, it was reported that:

A former cell mate of Thomas David Richardson testified Monday the accused murderer allegedly offered his Corvette and boat as payment to jail inmate for killing Alger County Prosecutor Karen Bahrman. Dylan Bonevelle, 23, who is serving a county jail sentence for larceny, said he was part of conversations in March in which Richardson claimed he wanted Bahrman dead. "He had a Corvette and a boat he was willing to trade to have you killed," Bonevelle told Bahrman Monday. At one point, he said you'd be the next bitch to go off the cliff.[12]

I presume this "evidence" was not deemed credible since no charges were filed for Richardson's alleged effort to kill the prosecutor.

Numinen, the defense lawyer, said that he wondered what kind of a man it would take to kill his wife in the manner Juanita Richardson died and he concluded, "It would take an evil man to throw his wife off a cliff. Tom's not an evil man." In my opinion it would take a sadistic psychopath to kill a person in this manner. This case does not fit the spousal homicide category.

On Sunday, June 28, 2008, Jim Graves called me and told me that the television news program *Dateline* would cover the Richardson murder. I viewed the *Dateline* story and was positively shocked by it. The prosecutor's argument to the jury was shown in part, as well as the testimony of the police and other witnesses. The reasoning of the police and the prosecutor seemed to me ludicrous. Whatever the defendant said or did was "proof" that he is guilty. The rangers and the police officer interrogating him found his reactions suspicious. The fact that he cried and then would be perfectly normal was obvious proof to them that he is guilty. The fact that his stories were contradictory was proof that he was guilty. The picture that his wife took of him just a few minutes before the tragedy happened showed him to be grim like someone who is about to commit murder. I have examined hundreds of people who have committed a homicide but I do not know how someone looks who is about to commit murder. Mr. Richards was not a sadistic murderer. In the next chapter we will look at someone who was.

NOTES

1. *Solem v. Helm*, 463 U.S. 277 (1983).

2. *Kaplan & Sadock's Comprehensive Textbook of Psychiatry* by Benjamin J. Sadock, Virginia A. Sadock, and Harold L. Kaplan. 8th ed. (Philadelphia: Lippincott Williams & Wilkins, 2004).

3. Emanuel Tanay, M.D., with Lucy Freeman, *The Murderers* (New York: The Bobbs-Merrill Company, 1976).

4. "Psychiatric Study of Homicide," *American Journal of Psychiatry* 125, no. 9 (March 1969).

5. Emanuel Tanay, M.D., "Psychiatric Aspects of Homicide Prevention," *American Journal of Psychiatry*, 128, no. 7 (January 1972): 815.

6. "A Review of *Fatal Vision*," *Journal of Forensic Sciences*, 31, no. 3 (1986): 1163.

7. David Ashenfelter, "With Judge in Her Corner, Michigan Woman Seeks Clemency," *Detroit Free Press*, May 12, 2005.

8. Gina Darmon, "Convicted Killer Back in Prison: Verdict in '93 Trial Is Questioned," *Detroit Free Press*, September 17, 2006.

9. John Pepin, "Richardson Case Winding Down," *Mining Journal*, April 15, 2008.

10. Pepin, "Richardson Case."

11. Pepin, "Richardson Case."

12. Kim Hogum, "Richardson Trial in Second Day," *Mining Journal*, March 5, 2008.

6

TED BUNDY
The Pleasure of Cruelty

In the 1970s, a series of murders of attractive young women stretched from California through Colorado to Florida. Bite marks on their breasts left no doubt that a sexual sadistic serial killer was at work. When an Ann Arbor nurse was murdered in Aspen in this manner, the Detroit news media repeatedly asked for my comments. Little did I know that I would be involved as an expert in this case for the next ten years.

This chapter is a warning about the risk of being manipulated by a psychopath. The malevolence of a psychopath and his duplicity is not readily recognized by the untrained observer. In this chapter, we will see how Ted Bundy successfully manipulated policemen, lawyers and, naturally, his victims. The transcript of portions of my interview with Bundy shows the need for an examiner to attune himself or herself to the psychopath's style.

Serial killers are exceedingly rare but they stir disproportionate interest in the general public. I have examined countless homicide perpetrators over the past fifty years; among them were only four serial killers, two of whom attracted public attention, namely, Ted Bundy and the so-called Angel of Death of Cincinnati who allegedly killed 54 patients in a VA hospital. When I use the term serial killer I am referring to the sadistic variety of psychopaths who kill for pleasure. Ted Bundy is the classic example of this type of a killer.

In 1941 in *The Mask of Sanity* Dr. Hervey Cleckley identified 16 distinct clinical criteria for diagnosis of psychopath, among them: hot-headed,

manipulative, exploitative, irresponsible, self-centered, shallow, unable
to bond, lacking in empathy or anxiety, likely to commit a wide variety
of crimes, more violent, more likely to recidivate, and less likely to respond to treatment than other offenders. As the concept of psychopathy
evolved, the emphasis shifted from traits to behavior, and in 1952, the
word "psychopath" was officially replaced with "sociopathic personality."
By 1968, "sociopathic personality" yielded to "personality disorder, antisocial type."[1] What ever diagnostic label one chooses, Theodore Bundy
fits them all.

When I was first asked to examine this notorious serial killer there
was the expectation that I would find him psychotic and eligible for
insanity defense. It didn't require much of my time to determine that
Bundy was a classic psychopath. I recommended to the public defender
to bring into the case Dr. Cleckley who confirmed my diagnosis. Dr.
Hervey Cleckley knew a great deal more about psychopaths than I
did; however, it soon became apparent that I was more at home in
the courtroom than this venerable pioneer. To his credit he quickly
acknowledged it and did seek suggestions from me. He appeared only
once in the long Bundy legal story.

A sadistic serial killer's success depends upon his appearing normal.
Psychopaths are typically charming and persuasive, which enables
them to manipulate the people around them. Their sadistic behavior is
bizarre; however, their day-to-day behavior is normal and arouses no
suspicion. Bundy raped and tortured his victims before killing them.
He is connected to thirty murders, but the total number of his victims
is believed to be much higher.

Ted Bundy's court-appointed public defender, Michael Minerva,
contacted me regarding the 1978 Chi Omega murders. Two sorority
sisters had been killed and two others injured in Tallahassee, Florida.
Bundy was identified as the perpetrator. Minerva asked whether "there
are grounds to seek a court-ordered psychiatric evaluation of Mr.
Bundy."[2]

Attorney J. Victor Africano of Live Oak, Florida, contacted me also;
he represented Bundy in the July 20, 1978, indictment charging him
with the first-degree murder and kidnapping of Kimberly Diane Leach,
a twelve-year-old girl. The autopsy findings were consistent with torture and sexual abuse. To my knowledge, Leach was Bundy's only child
victim—he generally preferred to prey on young women.

On April 27, 1979, I told Minerva that a psychiatric evaluation of his client was essential even though Bundy objected to it. I wrote:

In view of the seriousness of the charges facing your client, it would appear that proceeding to trial without psychiatric evaluation would constitute a significant omission.

At the same time, it does not appear likely that forensic psychiatric evaluation would offer the promise of beneficial legal results for your client. Let us assume that a psychiatrist reached the opinion that there was a basis for insanity defense. Such a defense is not likely to prevail without some degree of cooperation of the client, who as far as I can gather from your letter, rejects the insanity defense as a possibility. It is, therefore, not likely that you can persuade Mr. Bundy to cooperate by logical arguments, which evidently you have tried.

Mr. Bundy's insistence to represent himself attests to his self-destructive tendencies. The adage that "a lawyer who represents himself has a fool for a client" is even more valid when applied to a defendant. Defendants who represent themselves usually end with disastrous results.

Obviously any citizen is entitled to poor judgment and even stupidity. In this case, however, the question is whether the decisions made by Mr. Bundy in regard to his defense are dictated by psychopathology or by ordinary poor judgment. It would seem to me that in view of these considerations, both the prosecution and defense would want a judicial determination of competency to stand trial prior to any other criminal proceedings. . . . My recommendation is that Mr. Bundy should undergo a psychiatric evaluation independent of his wishes. I believe there is ample legal precedent, even requirement, (*Dusky v. United States*) to establish ability to stand trial when there is doubt on this issue.

Based upon my letter, Minerva petitioned the court to appoint me as an examiner to assist the defense at public expense.

On May 18, 1979, I examined Ted Bundy in Tallahassee and prepared a report based on our tape-recorded interview and my review of documents. The text of the report follows.

May 21, 1979
Re: Theodore Robert BUNDY Case no. 78-670
Dear Mr. Minerva:
Pursuant to the order of the Honorable Edward D. Cowart, Circuit Judge, I have examined the above-named individual at the Court House

of Leon County in Tallahassee, Florida, on May 18, 1979. The issue to
which this report addresses itself is Mr. Bundy's capacity to stand trial.

The data upon which my conclusions and opinions are based are the
documents that you have submitted to me consisting of [a long list of
documents and transcripts of interviews with police are omitted for the
sake of brevity]:

Psychiatric forensic opinion has to be given in the context of prevailing
legal criteria. I have therefore reviewed significant, relevant legal decisions dealing with this particular subject.

At the outset, I wish to stress that in this case, we are dealing with a
very complex situation made even more complicated by Mr. Bundy's
psychopathology.

The interview was conducted in a conference room of the court house
that was pleasant and well-lighted. I believe there were five deputy sheriffs guarding the only exit.

Mr. Bundy is a 32-year-old, handsome-looking man, dressed with
the casual elegance of a young college professor. He was meticulously
groomed, from well-cared-for fingernails to freshly washed hair. He was
in total command of the situation. The deputy sheriffs appeared more
like part of his entourage than policemen guarding a prisoner.

The conference room had many comfortable chairs. Two chairs, however, were particularly comfortable looking; these were taken by the
deputies into the hallway for their own use. Mr. Bundy, in a very firm
and definite manner, instructed the deputies that this arrangement did
not meet with his approval. They not only complied with his request to
return the chairs, but seemed to be apologetic.

I was accompanied to the conference room by Mr. Minerva, Public
Defender for the Second Judicial Circuit, who has a large staff of lawyers
working for him. Observing the interaction, however brief, between Mr.
Bundy and Mr. Minerva would lead one to believe that Mr. Minerva was
Mr. Bundy's assistant.

Mr. Bundy made a few pointed inquiries to Mr. Minerva about certain work to be done and made a few polite but firm suggestions as to
future work. In my brief visit prior to the examination to the offices of
the Public Defender, I heard a lawyer whose name I don't know telling
Mr. Minerva that he went to visit Mr. Bundy in jail but never did have
a chance to speak to him because Mr. Bundy was busy on the phone.
Based upon various observations, I have reached the impression that the
Public Defender's office is dominated, to a large degree, by the issues and
controversies involving Mr. Bundy's case.

At the outset of the interview, Mr. Bundy commented upon the security precautions, saying that they were the result of "the Bundy mys-

tique" that has developed as a result of news media activities. This was presented in the manner of a complaint; it was, however, my impression that Mr. Bundy was taking narcisstic pleasure in what he called "Bundy mystique" and what in reality was criminal notoriety that might cost him his life.

In the nearly three hours that I spent with Mr. Bundy, I found him to be in a cheerful, even jovial mood. He spoke freely, but meaningful communication was never established. [Bundy treated me as if I were a news media personality and not a psychiatrist who might assist his lawyers in defending him.] I asked about his apparent lack of concern that was out of keeping with the charges facing him. He acknowledged that he is facing a possible death sentence. However, he stated, "I will cross that bridge when I get to it."

In contrast to the eloquence that Mr. Bundy displays when talking about abstract matters, he has little interest in discussing his past life history or his interpersonal relationships.

His early childhood was fatherless; he is an illegitimate child. At the age of five he acquired a step-father who appears to have made a minimal impact upon him. He professes no difficulties in childhood or adolescence and specifically denies any type of antisocial activities. When confronted with the information contained in the file that as an adolescent he was involved in forging skiing tickets, he gives a detailed account of that particular venture. He described this enterprise with laughter and obvious delight. He does admit the irrefutable, like his stealing of cars, credit card misuse, etc.; however, this occurred only after his "unjust" conviction in Utah for kidnapping, and according to Mr. Bundy, is to be attributed to the influence of his fellow inmates. Stealing and forgery were completely alien to him prior to his incarceration. In a manner typical for a psychopath, he presents information that, with his intelligence, he must know I would find not credible. When I confront him with evidence to the contrary, he readily admits his misrepresentation and fabricates another explanation.

His presentation of the evidence in the Utah kidnapping case against him is psychiatrically significant for diagnostic purposes. At first he presents it in a manner which places him in the role of being the victim of a gross miscarriage of justice perpetrated by a prejudiced judge. He was convicted because he drove a Volkswagen, and the perpetrator of the kidnapping drove a Volkswagen also. He omitted that additional identifying items irrefutably connected to the crime were also found in his Volkswagen. However, when Mr. Bundy becomes aware of the fact that I am familiar with evidence used during that trial, he rationalizes away every piece of evidence that linked him to the crime. The victim described a crowbar, pantyhose, handcuffs, and other items which were found in his Volkswagen. It just so happened that Mr. Bundy, at the time of his arrest, had all of the above items and was also identified by the victim. Mr. Bundy is unable to recognize the significance of evidence held against him (see below).

It would be simplistic to characterize this as merely lying, inasmuch as he acts as if his perception of the insignificance of the evidence was real. He makes decisions based upon these distorted views of reality, he is neither concerned nor distressed in what would be an appropriate manner, given the charges facing him.

The interactions of Mr. Bundy with the police and the whole criminal justice system have been discussed at length with him and his attorneys. It is my opinion, based upon a variety of data, that his dealings with the criminal justice system are dominated by psychopathology.

Transcripts of the many hours of his conversations with police officers constitute a variety of "confession." When I pointed that out to him he does not dispute my inference; he merely provides a different explanation. Whatever the explanation, the consequences of the verbal games that Mr. Bundy played with investigators were counterproductive to his defense and occurred against the advice of his counsel. Bundy was primarily interested in keeping the interaction with the police going; therefore, from time to time, he offered them some juicy tidbit.

Mr. Bundy "confessed" to the crimes while maintaining his innocence. The denials and admissions are quite apparent from the tapes and transcripts of his conversations with the investigators. The same attitude was maintained during the interview with me. . . Thus it could be argued that Mr. Bundy does have a factual understanding of the proceedings, but lacks a rational understanding of what is facing him. The needs of the moment dominate what he does. The consequences play a secondary role.

The interview, the conference with defense counsel, and the documentary material reviewed reveal that Mr. Bundy functions in the role of "chief counsel," and the public defender has been consistently manipulated to the role of "associate counsel." Mr. Bundy makes motions in open court, passes judgment in open court on adequacy of legal research of points raised by the defense, and schedules depositions that sometimes conflict with plans made by his defense attorneys.

In his decision-making process, Mr. Bundy is guided by his emotional needs, sometimes to the detriment of his legal interests. Mr. Bundy's pathological need to defy authority and to manipulate his associates and adversaries supplies him with "thrills" to the detriment of his ability to cooperate with his counsel.

Mr. Bundy's activities are damaging and disruptive to a great many people who come in contact with him, in whatever capacity. This fact in itself would be of little relevance to the issue of ability to stand trial. However, the same activities are also, in some instances, self-destructive and represent an interference with his defense.

Mr. Bundy placed himself in a rather disadvantageous position by his non-confession confession. He talks to the crime investigators about "my problem," but refrains from doing so with his attorneys and the expert they have chosen.

If one assumes that Mr. Bundy has committed the crimes with which he is charged, then psychiatrically, the possibility of mental derangement at the time of the acts would be a definite consideration. I have reference to the brutality of the assaults and the infliction of severe bites including biting off the nipples. The bizarreness and brutality are often associated with mental states that may qualify for the insanity defense. [I stressed with the lawyers that insanity defense as a practical matter was not a consideration; the goal was to prevent execution, and a death sentence was inevitable if the case went to trial.]

On the face of it, the denial of having committed a terrible crime is adaptive and self-serving; however, in the present context it appears to be self-defeating. I realize that it could be argued that Mr. Bundy has some chance to prevail on the claim of his innocence. I consider that exceedingly unlikely, not only because of the evidence that the prosecution has against him but also due to Mr. Bundy's behavior in the past and in the future. I would anticipate that in the unlikely event that the prosecution's case against him would weaken, he would, through his behavior, bolster the prosecution's case. I have much less doubt about Mr. Bundy's capacity to assist the prosecution than his ability to assist his own counsel.

If one assumes that his sadistic acts, including homicides attributed to Mr. Bundy in Tallahassee, were carried out by him, then psychiatrically it would be likely that various other similar acts have been perpetrated by him. It could then be argued that he is effective in concealing his criminal activities. Such an argument would be only partly true. It would be more accurate to say that he is of two minds on this issue—he attempts to conceal and reveal his involvement. He masterminds escapes with a great deal of ingenuity, and arranges for his apprehension.

I have discussed with Mr. Bundy his appraisal of the evidence held against him. It is his view that the case against him is weak or even frivolous. This judgment of Mr. Bundy's is inaccurate according to his defense counsel and, most likely, represents a manifestation of his personality disorder. (Psychopaths have no fear.)

In view of the fact that on conviction he faces the death sentence, the acceptance of an offer of a life sentence in exchange for a guilty plea was something to be considered seriously. This option was precluded by Mr. Bundy's view that the prosecution's case against him was weak. This is at least his explanation of why he was unwilling to consider this particular approach. However it is my opinion that he is driven by his deep-seated need to have a trial, which he views as an opportunity to confront and confound various authority figures. In this last category I include, for his purposes, not only judges and prosecutors, but also his defense attorneys.

In a certain sense, Mr. Bundy is a producer of a play that attempts to show that various authority figures can be manipulated, set against each other, and placed in positions of conflict. Mr. Bundy does not have the capacity to recognize that the price for producing this "thriller" might be his own life. Mr. Bundy the Lawyer does not recognize that his client, Bundy the Defendant, is not being adequately represented. We have here an individual who has had a history of antisocial behavior during his adolescence. There is history of poor occupational performance and antisocial behavior during adult life—one felony conviction in Utah and the unfinished trial for homicide in Colorado. Furthermore, there is an undisputed history of forgery, stealing of cars, etc.

In the interview situation there is no symptomatology consistent with psychotic illness. The overall demeanor is typical for an individual suffering from a personality disorder.

Whether or not this condition is considered mental illness for criminal law purposes is a subject of controversy within law and psychiatry. In the past this particular condition was called psychopathy; at the present time the term "antisocial personality" is more commonly used. There are those who believe that this condition is merely a variant of normality, whereas others insist that this is a genuine illness. It is my view that sociopathy, if sufficiently severe, is an illness inasmuch as there is impairment of a variety of psychic functions. Among others, sociopaths have a peculiar sensitivity to intoxicating substances, particularly alcohol. Many of the more bizarre crimes committed by sociopaths are in response to alcohol consumption. The psychopathology of a sociopath is not easily recognized because they do not provide symptoms easily recognized by a lay person or even a psychiatrist. Sociopaths understandably arouse a great deal of hostility and there is therefore a tendency to view them more as "bad" than as sick. Furthermore, they themselves deny that they suffer from an illness. Be that as it may, severe personality disorder does not justify an insanity defense. The insanity defense requires "severe mental illness" which usually is interpreted to mean psychosis.

I have carefully reviewed the Florida provisions dealing with incompetence to stand trial. I have serious doubts that Mr. Bundy has "sufficient present ability to consult with his lawyers with a reasonable degree of rational understanding." In view of this fact, it is my recommendation that a judicial determination of Mr. Bundy's ability to stand trial be made.

The following are excerpts from my nearly three-hour examination of Bundy, which served as the basis for the above report. The preliminaries have been omitted.

Tanay (Q.): What school did you go to?

Bundy (A.): I went to, it was Stanley Elementary School and we had, we were playing marbles once as I recall, I, ah, there was some infraction of the rules there and I, ah, walloped the kid, the first and only time, yeah the first time I ever hit anyone, and we had a scrap you know, he and I, the teacher found out about and she rapped our knuckles with a [inaudible], and, ah, we had kind of a, a rough crowd, I say rough in those days—today, of course, it would be mild, but I think as kids, we ran around and caught frogs and whatnot, and it was the, the non-Catholic kids ran around in one group and the Catholic kids ran in another group. It was fairly—

Q. Any difficulties like getting in trouble—with the police, for example—as an adolescent?

A. I can remember the biggest adventure was a fellow who I guess was, in my mind, one of the more adventuresome older kids—said that if I got him some comic books from the drug store, he would give me his pocketknife, so I, you know—

At this point, Bundy does not know how much of his history I am familiar with; thus, he avoids telling me that the many hours he spent chatting with the police were essentially a indirect confession of being a perpetrator of sadistic sexual murders. He gave some evasive answers but I tried to get him to talk about his current charges.

Q. And that had to do with a homicide investigation?

A. That had to do with at first attempting to evade a police officer, and then the investigation expanded, and then I was, I was charged in October '75 with kidnapping. So I don't know—that's jumping ahead quite a bit, but that was the first time I had any encounter with the police—that is, where I was the, you know, I was the arrestee—

Q. The first time, it was in '75.

A. Yes.

Q. Anything unusual up to '75 that you can think of?

A. Talking about the policeman?

Q. Generally about your life. Anything that you would consider a problem or other people would consider a problem?

A. Well, I suppose in retrospect it's easy to say, well, here is an area where I, you know, if I'd only gone this way or been a bit more disciplined, and not, you know, lost a straight-and-narrow path—ah, you know, I wouldn't have taken so long to get done what I wanted to get done. For instance, ah, if I think the problem in a general sense was that I was never willing to commit to a specific discipline, as it were, in in [sic] college—I couldn't, I felt no driving force, no commitment, no desire for anything particular. One time I started out college at University of [inaudible], just a general liberal arts major, nothing real exciting, and I was going to college because that was sort of an expectation of my family's as much as it was my own, and just to, you know, in general—

Q. Yeah, you were telling me about your vocational pursuits—they shifted from one area to another.

A. Right.

Q. Law School, foreign studies.

A. Law school came later down the road a piece. But ah, first, it was Chinese and then I just, I think that in my own mind was the low point, what you might call the crisis point in my own intellectual and emotional development when I reached 20–21, because I went to Stanford and I just had no desire to learn; I'd rather play tennis all day. I didn't go to language labs and I [inaudible], I did very well in Chinese, but I just lost it, and when I came back to Seattle after that summer, I—

Q. What do you attribute that change to, since you must have been pretty ambitious to begin with, to achieve what you have achieved?

A. I don't know. There were several things working on me. . . . The more I learned Chinese, the more I knew it was a [inaudible] mastery . . . and I felt I was slowly losing my ability to converse in English, for goodness sakes—it was kind of, it bothered me in a way, because I was becoming less articulate in my native language at the same time I was bumbling around in an alien language, and I was beginning to question how I was going to apply that language. . . . It would be difficult for me to identify every factor that sort of led to a total breakdown in my, not total, but a breakdown in my discipline, in my goal-oriented kind of behavior, where I just sort of drifted that summer—and I'd also gotten, earlier that year, my spring quarter at Washington, which would have been 1967, I got involved with a girl.

Q. What was her first name?

A. Diane . . . and you know, she was a very beautiful girl and a very—

Q. That was in—

A. It was in Seattle, University of Washington. I spent a lot of time with her, and I started neglecting my studies and we had a great time. We slept together and did all those things, and it was really a marvelous experience.

Q. And what happened to the relationship?

A. Well, she was a year ahead of me in business, a very strong-willed person. More than that, she was her father's daughter; she was the only child; her father was a vice-president of a corporation, a very dynamic, achieving individual, and she sort of felt the burden herself of fulfilling her father's expectations in that regard, and she always, we were always discussing the agony over it—fears and failures when it came to father. So, but, ah, she stayed at the University of Washington that summer; she lived in San Francisco out at Stanford; and then we sort of drifted apart, and . . . my own academic world became more muddled. I began to hold more tightly to, ah, the image or fantasy of Diane and my relationship, and I saw how futile that was, and that our relationship sort of, I would say, evaporated.

Q. Who terminated it, you or Diane?

A. I'm not so sure who did, but I would say, under the circumstances, it was sort of by default, as it were. She was a very mobile person, an exciting individual, and, ah, lots and lots of people were attracted to her, and she is a very involved person and always on the go, and here I was, losing my own, my own momentum, ah, and I just when I came back to the University of Washington, I—

Bundy was able to maintain number of relationships with women that did not involve sadistic behavior. The inability to discuss with him his homicidal sadistic activities precluded gaining an understanding of the critical factors in this selectivity.

Q. But what accounted for this transformation that you keep referring to, some kind of a change occurred at that particular point in your life—

A. Sure, uh-hmm.

Q. Ah, we're talking about 19-what?

A. 1967

Q. 1967. Anything unusual that happened then?

A. Well, I probed more deeply into it and I thought back on it several times, because, as I say, this is the low end of my life, or at least the low point where I sort of—

Q. Was Diane a factor in that metamorphosis?

A. I think it was, what it was, Diane—Diane had high expectations for a man she was with because of her father's position and of [her] own expectations, because her parents wanted her to be involved with a successful business-oriented-type person.

Q. Which you did not—

A. Which I was certainly was not, I was not.

Q. Why not, didn't you have the potential for success in whatever you went into?

A. Oh I did, but I just didn't have an idea of what that would be. [Laughs.] So I felt at that time, I just, I was dropping back from everything.

Bundy was in a situation that one would expect to generate distress. Neuropsychological testing of individuals diagnosed as antisocial personalities demonstrates cognitive impairment and autonomic nervous system hypoactivity.

Q. You know, I'm struck by something as we talk, you seem to be very much at ease, very casual, and you even dress like a college professor, a young college professor or something like that, and you [are] very comfortable, and yet you [are] facing a terrible, terrible situation. How come you're so unconcerned?

A. I'm not unconcerned.

Q. I can only go by what I see.

A. Sure.

Q. You are very casual, pleasant, even charming and animated, witty, all of this, you laugh, and yet you're in such a horrible predicament. Isn't it?

A. It is. Ah, well, believe me, I've gone through hell in getting here. When I was first arrested in August of '75, and arrested for kidnapping, believe me, I cried like a baby and, ah, laid awake at night shivering. I've gone through a metamorphosis in the past three-and-a-half years, almost four, and it's not that, maybe I've become harder, but also I've become accustomed to all the pressure, become accustomed to the accusations. I know who I am, I know what I am and—

Q. You say "accusations." You know, not to go into the specifics of it, but some of them are not mere accusations, but facts accepted by you.

A. For instance? I mean—

Q. You know, the credit cards, the car—if one looks at your life and your past aspirations, and even if you set aside the homicides—

A. Uh-hmm.

Q. You really made a mess of your life. Forget the homicides. If they find to-morrow that Joe Blow did it and you are entirely innocent of it, but there is still—I know a little bit about it just from the material that was made available to me in the last, what, four or five years—you have been in a lot of difficulty.

A. Yes, yes I have. Uh, I'm—

Q. How do you explain that?

A. Well, I explain—the start, I can explain and I don't mean to say "rationalize" . . . but explain it as really and as objectively as possible, my conduct since I was found guilty of kidnapping in Utah, simply on the grounds of surviving and conditioning.

Q. Okay, let's look at this, your being found guilty in Utah. How is it that you were found guilty in Utah?

A. Well, I was convicted in a bench trial following a trial.

Q. Bench trial.

A. Instead of having a jury, we had a judge.

Q. Yes, I understand that would have been your option.

A. Right.

Q. Why did you decide to have a bench trial?

A. Well, because I thought the case was such that, ah, the facts clearly pointed to my innocence, and I was assured by my counsel that we had the best judge in a trial bench in Salt Lake City—because I was very concerned that the pub-licity had tainted the community, that even if we found a jury of persons who would be willing to say they were free of any prejudice, that, in fact, that—

Q. But what makes you think that a judge is free of prejudice?

A. Well, that's, ah, the chance I took.

Q. Why?

A. Because, I guess, because I believed, I believed that a man [as] conditioned as Judge Hansen—I was always led to believe that Judge Hansen was condi-tioned to follow the law and apply those to the facts no matter—

I believe that Bundy was being guided by his need to have an encoun-ter with an authority figure. I doubt that a lawyer would have recom-mended a bench trial in view of the overwhelming evidence that the prosecution had.

Q. Didn't he follow the law? I presume he did.

A. I don't think he did. I think that he found the pressure too great.

Q. The evidence against you was not persuasive?

A. Well, it was to him, but absolutely not.

Q. What, what was the evidence?

A. The evidence was that, ah, that the young woman who had been abducted identified me as the person who had abducted her.

Q. Uh-hmm.

A. That was the long and short of it. But the case is a bit more obvious, is a bit more complex, than that, and that, ah, she was abducted in November of '74 and did not make an identification of me until October of '75. Ah, it was a very sketchy identification, one which we had attempted to prove as the result of influence, both direct and indirect . . . by law-enforcement officers.

Q. Wasn't there some other evidence also, or was this the identification was the only—

A. Well, ah, she was abducted in a car, in a Volkswagen she described as light blue. I owned a beige Volkswagen, and the Volkswagen she was in had a tear in the backseat, and my Volkswagen had a tear in the backseat. Ah, all Volkswagens have tears in the backseat. [Laughs.]. . . . Ah, let's see what else, a crowbar was found in my car. The person she struggled with had what she believed to be a crowbar, although she couldn't, she said she'd never seen it. The person who abducted her placed handcuffs on her wrists, and she escaped. A search of my car in August 1975, they detected, they seized a pair of handcuffs, and those are the collateral, circumstantial kind of things they used to corroborate the identification.

Q. So there was strong circumstantial evidence tying you to the case, is that right?

A. Yeah, ah, in all fairness, you didn't have to say that. I mean, I will admit that circumstantial evidence, such as it was, did exist, although it was subject to a good deal of clarification, as it were.

Notice that Bundy perceives a gentle confrontation with reality as unfair.

Q. But that was the first one.

A. Uh-hmm.

Q. But then what were some of the subsequent events?

A. Subsequent, my conviction?

Q. Yes.

A. Well, then I was incarcerated in prison, where I learned to how to respond to an entirely different culture of people that I have never had any contact with before. I learned how to live among people who were potentially violent, who had [an] entirely different code of ethics and morals . . . than I had myself. I learned how to hotwire cars, how to use credit cards, how to hang paper [issue fraudulent checks], all kind of things I never knew before, and, ah, just, and I accepted it everyday—people who were rapists, murderers, bank robbers, petty thieves. Prior to my arrest in August of '75, I had never known any of it or even gone to jail. I mean, I was a young Republican going to law school—that was essentially my background. . . . I had to survive amongst an entirely different group of people, a new environment—a new, you know, I had to learn the ropes, so I learned them; I learned how to get along, how to survive. I was then, I was, ah—

Q. You know, let me ask you another thing that comes to my mind. You describe [that] you were a young Republican going to law school who didn't know anybody who had any problems with police. But in your discussions with the police—I read some of them—you seem to admit to them all kind of wrongdoings, including the homicides.

A. I don't know

Q. I mean, you don't make a confession, but you sort of play with them, isn't it?

A. Well I don't know exactly what you're referring to, but I have a general idea. Mike, Mike [Minerva, his defense lawyer] has alluded to that, and I've read some of the transcripts myself and, ah, I can appreciate the interpretation because that's quite frankly [the] interpretation that I was giving to the police. . . . My goal was to get back to my home state of Washington. I was, ah, I was back in custody again and, ah, I had one goal and it was unrealistic in the big picture, but I was hoping to convince them to use as—I'll say, but that's not the word, but kind of like tantalizing them—[Euphemism for manipulation]

Q. Are you that suggestive? I mean, you are telling me before, you said you were in jail, and there were these criminals, and suddenly you acquire a habit of hanging paper and stealing cars and, ah, operating stolen credit cards, I mean you were really a quick learner.

A. Yeah. I don't see that I'm any more of a . . . quick learner. However, I am a survivor, and when in Rome, you have to do as—

Q. Yeah but you were an outsider; Rome—

A. I was, I was, I think it would be fair to admit if I'd been able to stick to the straight-and-narrow and, ah, stay inconspicuous and live at a poverty kind of level for a while, I would have avoided these bad, these habits that I've seemed to acquire—that I wouldn't be here now. . . . I should have, I should have gone to law school in 1973 instead of starting in 1974, you know. [Laughs.] I don't know, I guess I could say we're talking about innumerable paths one could travel down life just by making one decision or not making a decision. Ah, I can't say, ah, I mean, it's nothing. I'm not sitting here because of a lifelong pattern, so to speak, of behavior. I am not sitting here because of something I have done, maybe because of things I haven't done. As I say, maybe it's because I didn't get married when I should have gotten married. Maybe it's because, ah, I should have, ah, worked for the Republican Party instead of going back to law school. I—

Q. How did the first year in law school go for you?

A. Oh it was it was a bitch. [Laughs.]

Throughout the interview Bundy related to me as if it was a social visit and not an examination initiated by his lawyer. He showed typical focus on the here and now and disregarded whatever contributions I could make to save his life. On some level he must have been aware that he was facing the likelihood of being executed.

Q. Which law school did you go to?

A. I started out at the University of Puget Sound. It was a night school, a part-time program that just wasn't my cup of tea. Too much commuting and all, so I went to the University of Utah for my first full year of law school in Salt Lake City, and it was, it was more than I bargained for. I mean, the subject matter—on the one hand, [it] strikes me it shouldn't be that difficult, but it is. It was very difficult. But once, after the end of the year, when I started to get a handle on it and started to pull it together, it made—

Q. But then didn't you shift into psychology at one point? That preceded the law school?

A. Well, see, after I went to Stanford, a real quick summer, and I went to Stanford and came back to the University of Washington and, ah, left the Chinese department, tried to get into architecture, got into urban planning, registered for a whole bunch of courses, never went to any of the courses, worked as a busboy at this lake yacht club, dropped out, didn't go to any courses, didn't take any exams, dropped out of school in January of 1968, traveled, went skiing in Heavenly Valley and Aspen, and then went back east to Philadelphia and then came back. Worked in politics in '68, urban campaigns, and went to Temple University [in] the early part of '69, and then I bounced around a little bit more. But at least I was pulling myself together.

Q. How were you supporting yourself?

A. Well, ah, busboy, waiter, worked in a logging mill, ah, worked in political campaigns where I got paid. Worked as a [inaudible], served legal process, ah, worked with [inaudible]. I started back to school in June of '70, University of Washington. My major was psychology and I graduated with, three years later, with a bachelor's of science in psychology.

Q. That would have been what year?

A. That was June of '72.

Q. And I understand that you worked for a while in a psychiatric clinic?

A. Well, for a stance I did. First I worked at Seattle Crisis Clinic, which is sort of when people call in distress and they need help, and it was a fantastic experience for me, reaching out to people and communicating with people. It matured me a great deal . . . working with violence, since I never had. Then I went to work after graduating. During the summer I worked I worked at a psychiatric outpatient clinic at Harborview Hospital; it is a teaching hospital for the University of Washington Medical School. And after—it was a summer grant—when that grant expired in early September of '72, I, ah, immediately jumped into a gubernatorial campaign, ah, and worked in politics from that time until November. Then I worked at the crime commission and then I got a personal contract to research, to do some research for a large commission.

Q. You certainly were an active young man.

A. Well, I did a lot of different things, but I never seemed to focus in on anything. Ah, and there was really nothing I wanted to focus in on. Ah, but I had my contacts, did a lot of things. I think I enjoyed politics more than anything, 'cause I had a lot of friends.

Bundy was a sexually sadistic psychopath who charmed, abducted, raped and killed beautiful women. There is the natural presumption that such a person would be intuitively recognized as a malevolent creature. Unfortunately that is not the case. There is a striking disparity between the sadistic behavior of psychopaths and their charming demeanor in everyday interactions. The relationship between Ted Bundy and Ann Rule is emblematic for the capacity of a sexual sadistic psychopaths to present normal demeanor.

In her book *The Stranger Beside Me,* Ann Rule describes how Bundy and she worked together at the Seattle Crisis Clinic. "Rapport, an almost instant rapport, made us friends." She writes, "Ted has been described as the perfect son, the perfect student, the Boy Scout grown to adulthood, a genius, as the bright light in the future of the Republican Party, a sensitive psychiatric social worker, a budding lawyer, a trusted friend, a young man for whom the future could surely hold only success." Ms. Rule was not a naïve person but an experienced crime reporter and former police officer. The friendship she speaks of was one-sided: Bundy was incabable of friendship, compassion, altruism, and empathy.

I discussed with Bundy his relationships with women, particularly Diane (mentioned above) and Liz, with whom he had had normal sexual and romantic relationships that did not lead to sadism or homicide. I found it significant that he had a number of such relationships without any danger to the women's lives. His victims were women with whom he had no prior relationship. It seems as if being a stranger was a prerequisite, just like a certain appearance, for becoming a victim.

Bundy's ability to be charming and manipulative was not limited to women. I have never encountered a prisoner in custody who exercised such influence as Bundy did upon the policemen who were interrogating him and prison guards in whose custody he was. Bundy was treated with deference by jail personnel. The usual contempt was absent. We touched on that in our interview.

Q. Let me just comment about this. I notice that you have such a casual relationship with the police officers, the guards—

A. Yeah.

Q. Whatever they are referred to as here.

A. Yeah, deputies.

Q. Deputies. They are from the Sheriff's Department, is that right?

A. Yes.

Q. You seem to have a very collegial relationship with them, almost, don't you?

A. Oh yes, I understand what you're saying, and it's the only way to relate to them. You can't be, ah, they have all the muscle power, and the best way, most pleasant way for everybody, is just to be nice. And they've been around this for so long.

Q. But it's more than being nice. You're actually being, I notice—I'm not sure what would be the term—it's very, a kind of camaraderie, as if you were a fellow deputy, you know, just joking and—

A. Well, I don't, it's—I relate to them as if they're, as if they are fellow human beings. And because I have very little opportunity for that kind of contact in jail, and the times and people that [I] often have to deal with in jail, well—they, too, are people and can be friendly, just at different, oftentimes, different people—

A segment of the interview dealing with Bundy's interactions with fellow prisoners has been omitted. At that point we turned to his intentions to represent himself in the trial.

Q. You know, in terms of the defense—are you going to let this be conducted by your attorney, or are you going to represent yourself, or what's the situation?

A. Well, I think I'm looking at a hybrid situation where, recognizing my own limitations and my own skill and experience, I will accept Mike Minerva's counsel to a degree, but I'll also insist upon putting in my two cents' worth when I think its necessary. And so to that extent, I will stand up in court if I want, when I want, and—

Q. Has that been productive or not? Your own participation?

A. I don't think it's been counterproductive to—not [to] debate your question, but I don't know what has been productive, honestly. I don't think that I've been any less productive than my attorneys have been, so in that respect, I'm not shy and don't feel that my performance has been sub-par. I think I can do very, very well. . . .

Next I tried to explore the presence of symptoms consistent with psychiatric illness. He made some reference to being depressed during his time at Stanford. Although he speaks of having friends or being depressed, I doubt that he has the capacity to experience the emotions associated with these concepts; these are just words that he uses.

Q. I have no doubt that you can win some battles, but can you win the war? . . . I mean, it [the depression] did not render you incapable of functioning.

A. It rendered me incapable of doing work at school, I must say, but beyond that—

Q. Effective work, but you continued school?

A. I more or less continued, but I didn't attend classes. But outside the area of school, I functioned fairly well. I just decided to leave school alone for awhile and try to put my head together and see if some time away would help things out. It did. It took a couple years.

Q. You know I have written a report to your lawyer. Was that made available to you?

A. No.

Q. So how does the situation work out where you sort of co-counsel on your own case?

A. Well, Mike [Minerva] is uncomfortable with that because he is a very good attorney, but he is a traditional attorney and a cautious attorney, and he doesn't know how to share responsibility with a defendant. Basically, he's very skeptical of that kind of a relationship because, like most attorneys, he would like to have total control of the case and I would—I would, too. I mean, I wouldn't want some joker in a jail cell telling me what to do, but I try to make it as easy on Mike as I can [laughs], and without being overbearing or being obnoxious and demanding, I just let him know that I expect to be informed, and when I feel things are not going right, I let him know. And ultimately I feel that if something is going to happen in this case that I want to happen, it will happen. It has to. I mean, there is no way Mike can do anything in this case that I really object to. Ah, and so I feel more or less in command of the defense—or I think I have the ultimate veto. And it's comforting because I don't feel like so many defendants feel—that they're just at the mercy of the system that's alien, and it's attacking them, and they don't understand what their attorneys are doing and they don't understand what the system is doing to them, and it really is a source of a good deal—

Q. Well, there is some difference in relation to you, I would agree, because . . . one has to acknowledge the fact that you are a man of considerable intelligence and sophistication—and familiarity with the law, too. So that is a factor to be considered.

A. Yes, it is. It is. It helps me. I mean, I sleep well. [Laughs] I don't, I really don't lay awake worrying about it.

Q. What do you think of the fact that, after all, there is a chance that you might get convicted and the penalty is what?

A. Death, execution, whatever they call it.

We then discussed Bundy's escape from the courthouse in Aspen, Colorado, where he was being tried for killing a nurse from Dearborn, Michigan. He was apprehended when he ended up back in Aspen after getting lost on Aspen Mountain. He was then incarcerated in nearby Glenwood Springs, Colorado, from where he also escaped. Bundy had starved himself until he became thin enough to fit through the vent opening. He had been the only prisoner and arranged the bedclothes to make it appear as if he was still in his cell, sleeping. His escape was not noticed until a few hours later. In his first escape, in Aspen, he jumped from the second floor of the courthouse onto the bushes below. He suffered no injuries. During our interview, he described his escape and apprehension.

A. A pedestrian down the street saw me jump, and then they calmly walked down to the Sheriff's office, which is on the ground floor of the building, and said that someone jumped out of the second story of the courthouse. The woman said, "What?"—and she ran upstairs to the court clerk . . . and said, "Where's Bundy?" And she [the clerk] said, "My guess is in the courtroom," and she went up and talked to the officers and said, "Where's Bundy?"—and he says, "Well, he's in the courtroom." [inaudible] And so that's, they gave me about fifteen minutes.

Q. Well, you know, you relate that with obvious pleasure.

A. Well, I mean [laughs], I do, I do, uh.

Q. You know, aside from everything else here, you do have fun with all of that, don't you?

A. Well, I had fun with it, yes. I mean, I'd much rather not [have] had to go through it at all, to be honest with you.

Q. And yet, and yet, you say you sort of get yourself into these entanglements with the authorities.

A. Yeah. I don't do it intentionally, believe me.

Q. You could have done it as a lawyer.

A. Oh, surely. [I'd] much rather, I mean, I would have been practicing two years by now.

Q. Yeah. You can challenge authority, too, but then it's legitimate.

A. Oh, definitely. Oh, I'd much rather [be] doing that. This is not my idea of a weird kick. I don't enjoy it. I'd much rather be free. I didn't want to be apprehended, and when I was apprehended, I wasn't trying to be apprehended.

Q. Let's focus upon this for a minute. Aside from the homicides—which we can't really discuss, because either you didn't do it or you won't talk about it—so lets set that aside.

A. Uh-hmm.

Q. But there are a number of events which were antisocial; we'll use that worn-out phrase. How that comes about, that a man with your background and your intelligence, that you get engaged in this kind of activity—and in a manner in which you have done it, it was quite provocative, like even with the credit cards—

A. Well, let's think about the credit cards and the stolen car. Ah, you know, prior to my arrest, I would have no more thought of stealing a car or using a stolen credit card then I would of cutting off my hand, and that is the honest-to-God truth. Ah, the thought never even occurred to me—I mean, that's how straight I was, it never even occurred to me; it was impossible as something to do. But once I got out or escaped, I felt that to a certain degree, society's laws respecting those kinds of things no longer applied to me.

Bundy makes it sound as if his antisocial activities and sadistic violence did not begin until his incarceration. The reality was that antisocial behavior was part of his personality structure.[3]

I asked Bundy about his early antisocial exploits.

Q. Yes. I got it. Ah, you put together a forgery ring.

A. Ah.

Q. Where they were making their own [ski] tickets.

A. [Laughing.] Again that's kind of a glorified, extreme term for it. When I was in high school, I was a skiing fanatic. I loved to ski. I had a whole group of kids, guys who skied and, ah, went up every weekend, and ski tickets then were only $5 a day, and that was a fortune then. Now they're of course $10 or $11.

Q. $12 now.

A. $12, terrible. We used to go up every weekend and we all went Christmas vacation, spring vacation—this cost money. I mean, you know, we're talking about $5 a shot. Well, we were an enterprising group, and all of them—shoot, one guy was president of the student body, and the rest of them were honor-roll kind of guys, and I'm not saying that that justifies it, but we weren't a group of hit—I guess you could call us white-collar criminals. [Laughs.] They took these, and I enjoy it, I enjoy telling you this story, too. [Laughs.] At Crystal Mountain in Washington, we took these passes and when they issued them, they had these little different color codes at the bottom: blue, yellow, red. And each day they'd stamp them a different color, like R3 would be purple; they'd staple it on. Well, we found out what stamp company made the rubber stamps and we went up to Seattle—we lived in Tacoma; we went up to Seattle—and bought a set of the stamps and all different kinds of ink pens. And at the end of the day, we'd ask people for their old lift tickets, so we had the selection of all the different color-coded tickets: red, blue, green, yellow, etc. And then we'd bleach out the stamp on there. There was a special procedure we had for bleaching out the stamp on the part of the ticket, and we'd come that morning, and we'd walk up to the skiing—whatever it was, vendor—and see [what] it was—they were issuing red tickets with, ah, T12 on it, and, ah, and blue, and we'd go back to the car and pull out our red tickets and get out the stamp T12 and put it in a blue blotter, and we were gone for the day. And they never stopped us in two years. We saved a heck of a lot of money. Now [laughs]—I don't know—

Q. Any questions you have that you would like to ask me? You know, I'm a psychiatrist who has some experience, or maybe even considerable experience, in these legal matters. Any kind of question that you have that you would like to ask me?

A. Well, first of all, I've gone through, I've spoken to different psychologists, psychiatrists at different times, particularly in Utah. I've worked, I say, I worked under psychiatrists before, I've worked with psychologists, so I've seen all different facets of people in their line of work. Ah, I'm constantly around people who are, lady psychiatrists are trying to figure me out. Well, I came in here with kind of a strong objection that I was going to register with you, and I still will register with you. Ah, I'm concerned that even for the limited purpose that you're here to talk to me today that, ah, [a] two-hour visit, for example, to me is not sufficient for determining anything one way or the other, or even developing a number of hypotheses, and I—I mean, I just—

Q. You think if we talked six hours, we might get somewhere else? 'Cause that can be arranged, you know. We can meet tomorrow morning.

A. Well, where, I mean, I'm not here to try to impress you one way or another. I mean, I honestly welcome the opportunity to tell someone how I'm feeling, what I'm thinking, what I've done. I really am—it's inconceivable to me that we could touch on things—

Q. Suddenly, you seem to have gotten sad.

A. In two hours—oh, well, it's because I'm really thinking now. Ah, I don't know if emotional is the word. I'm reflecting back on other interviews with other psychiatrists, psychologist-types, and I guess the sadness or the emotion is due to what I feel is a wham-bam-thank-you-ma'am treatment that I was given. And granted, however, that the persons . . . spent hours with me over the course of months. But still, I felt even after all that time they took with me, I'm afraid they succumbed to their own prejudices, and/or, in a caution, you know—I guess the institutional psychiatrist says, "When in doubt, ah, err on the side of safety," which is for incarceration, you know. They say, "Well, we didn't get to know this person. You may have the report."

Q. Yes, I have.

A. I don't feel like I know it, and therefore he's hiding something.

Q. Well you, don't you think that you have kept me fairly much at bay anyway?

A. Well, I don't know how—I mean, we haven't had a chance. What have I refused to talk to you about?

Q. You haven't, you haven't.

A. And I'm not trying to woo you with words or gloss things over, but there's a lot—

Q. But you see, only in the last few minutes, you have sort of changed a bit. You are more engaged.

It was my impression that Bundy was experiencing separation anxiety in the manner of a child, as if to say, "Let's play a little more." Bundy's impressive intelligence coexisted with the immaturity of a child whose ability to postpone gratification is very limited.

From the beginning of the case, the insanity defense was on the lawyers' minds. I had to point out to them that, theoretically, the insanity defense was not applicable to someone who suffered from a severe personality disorder. For legal purposes, as previously stated, a personality disorder does not qualify as "severe mental illness," which usually means psychosis. A personality disorder is comparable to a physical deformity, whereas psychosis constitutes a true disease. Furthermore, even if the insanity defense had applied to Bundy, no jury would have found him insane. Last but not least, Bundy maintained his innocence—a prerequisite for claiming the insanity defense is the acceptance of having committed the crime.

I contended that Bundy's competency to stand trial (especially his ability to represent himself, as he insisted on doing) required psychiatric and judicial scrutiny. Bundy's psychopathology required me to clearly distinguish between three different competency issues: competency to stand trial, competency to represent himself, and competency to plead guilty. I did not have a definite opinion about him being not competent, but I did feel that there was enough doubt that a judicial determination of his competency was in order. I had no difficulty saying that he was competent to plead guilty. I was of the opinion that he was not competent to represent himself if he pled not guilty.

Since neither the defense nor prosecution wanted me as a witness, the judge declared me a witness adverse to both parties and I became an expert of the court. During the hearing, the judge took my direct testimony, but neither the prosecution nor the defense cross-examined me. Bundy, who represented himself with the assistance of Minerva, stood up and said, "Tempting as it would be to cross-examine Dr. Tanay, I will not do so because I do not recognize him as a witness." I was the expert chosen by his lawyer who, like me, wanted to save

Bundy's life. But Bundy's goal was to play games and therefore in his mind I became his adversary. Since there was no cross-examination, my testimony on Bundy's competency was much shorter than anticipated. Neither side accepted my opinion that Bundy's love of celebrity status and the enjoyment he gained from manipulating and playing games with everyone involved in the trial precluded his acting in his own best interest or accepting the advice of competent legal counsel.

When I learned that a guilty plea agreement was being negotiated, I told Minerva and Edward Harvey (Minerva's assistant) that they were engaged in a futile exercise, that Bundy would never willingly give up a trial, which would gratify his need for a big show. Bundy promised his lawyer that he would enter a guilty plea that would save his life but preclude a trial. Minerva dictated a confidential memorandum on the guilty plea on May 29, 1979: "I had doubts about Ted's competence to stand trial because of Ted's unwillingness to accept a plea agreement for a life sentence. If Ted agrees to the plea, I should call Dr. Tanay to find out if this would alter his opinion, and if it would, ask him to write a supplemental opinion for the record."

I told Minerva that no matter what the agreement, at the last minute, Bundy would renege on his guilty plea. Minerva wrote me a lengthy letter describing the arrival of Bundy's mother, girlfriend, and some friends in the courtroom for the taking of the guilty plea by a judge. Millard Farmer, the prominent defense lawyer whom Bundy had recruited to assist in the case, also made a special trip for the occasion. The news media were in full force to witness the guilty plea that would save Bundy's life. Bundy approached the witness stand—apparently to accept the guilty plea—and instead distributed a document castigating his lawyers. He expressed his outrage that they had no faith in his innocence and had tried to induce him to plead guilty even though he was not guilty. It was another spectacular show—one that would cost him his life.

Subsequent to the trial, which could result only in conviction and a death sentence, one of the most prominent law firms in Washington, D.C., Wilmer, Cutler, and Pickering, contacted me about the case. In the tradition of Clarence Darrow, major U.S. legal firms often devote some resources on a pro publico bono basis, sometimes taking on nearly hopeless death-penalty cases such as Bundy's. These contributions are a well-kept secret in the sense that they are rarely talked about or publicized, since the idea of pro bono work does not fit the stereotype of money-hungry lawyers.

After the fiasco of taking the lifesaving guilty plea, the public defender no longer represented him. Two lawyers from Wilmer, Cutler, and Pickering, James E. Coleman, Jr., and Polly J. Nelson, took on the task of preventing Bundy's execution by securing a life sentence.[4] I worked with them until the last moments to save Bundy's life.

Since I was convinced that Bundy was a sadistic serial killer, one might wonder why I worked with lawyers who were dedicated to saving his life. I am absolutely opposed to the death penalty. I have good reasons to be fearful of a state that has the right to kill people. For five long years I was on death row, I was one of the bad people that a nation sentenced to death—I am a Holocaust survivor from Poland. Despite this fact, I opposed the execution of Adolph Eichman in Israel and I am alarmed by the power of American government to impose the death penalty.

As a forensic psychiatrist who has examined hundreds of homicide perpetrators, I am no stranger to murder. But I believe that the death penalty does not deter homicide. And trying a death-penalty case can be very, very expensive. In the case of the Cincinnati Angel of Death, who killed more than 50 helpless patients, I testified for the prosecution because a wise prosecutor decided not to seek the death penalty and accepted a guilty plea to a life sentence without parole. This was accomplished at a cost of a few thousand dollars. The federal government spent millions to execute Timothy McVeigh, and what did we gain? Some people talk about closure for the families. The execution of the Nazi leadership did not bring closure to the Holocaust survivors. My father, Bronislaw Tenenwurzel, was tortured and killed in front of the entire camp Plaszow by Amon Goeth, the anti-hero of *Schindler's List*. Goeth was sentenced by a Polish court to death and hanged. The execution of Amon Goeth did not bring closure to me. Killing the killers validates the belief that killing solves real or imaginary problems.

The right to kill people a nation deems bad is a dangerous concession to the totalitarian conception of a government. It is bizarre that a country that does not trust the government to regulate health care is willing to entrust it with the right to kill.[5]

Polly Nelson, the lead lawyer, attempted to save Bundy from execution by a wide range of approaches. She first tried the Florida Supreme Court; when this failed, she filed a habeas corpus petition to the U.S. District Court, which was denied. But she was permitted to appeal to the 11th Circuit Court of Appeals in Atlanta. Nelson argued that, acting as his own counsel, Bundy was not competent to control the proceedings. Critical to Nelson's argument was my testimony that Bundy's pathological need to direct the proceedings in a self-destructive manner prevented adequate representation. This was a persuasive argument for the 11th Circuit Court of Appeals in Atlanta.

On December 12, 1987, Nelson deposed me in preparation for filing the habeas corpus petition. The beginning of the deposition largely confirmed the opinions that I expressed in my report to Minerva. In this excerpt from the deposition, Nelson makes reference to that report.

Nelson: . . . You state, "It is my opinion, based on a variety of data, that [Bundy's] dealings with the criminal justice system are dominated by psychopathology." Are you referring there merely to the alleged crimes or to Mr. Bundy's other behaviors?

Tanay: Both. He was doing the same thing, he was being the same psychopath when he dealt with his victims that he tortured and killed as when he was dealing with lawyers who were helping him, or investigators who were trying to solve the crime. . . . He was destructive to himself. My observations were that he was manipulating people around him, including his lawyers, even though it was destructive to him. Ultimately he was the victim of it all, but he was victimizing other people even while he was in jail.

Q. In your opinion, was this behavior of Mr. Bundy's under his conscious control?

A. No, it was not. This was part and parcel of his maladaptive personality structure. He was doing what was dictated by his personality disorder.

Q. This psychopathology that you note, with which he deals with the criminal justice system, was that a temporary phenomena or was it a chronic condition?

A. It was a lifelong pattern. It was not a temporary phenomenon. It was an expression of his basic personality structure.

I testified that Bundy would not cooperate with the defense team who were trying to save his life, and Nelson asked me to elaborate.

Q. Cooperate in what manner?

A. With the advice of his lawyers—including, even, Mr. Farmer, who supposedly Mr. Bundy greatly respected and admired—and that he would take the guilty plea, because it was my view that he would not, because that would terminate the show, his ability to be the celebrity would come to an end, he would be just someone who was spared from the death sentence, and the show would be over. Whereas, his need was to have the proceedings go on and on in order to gratify his pathological needs.

Q. If Mr. Bundy made the decision to reject the plea bargain, in your opinion, would that have been a rational decision?

A. No. It was, in my opinion, clearly an irrational decision, even though I anticipated it—not because it was rational, but because it was consistent with the psychopathology, the mental disorder from which he suffered. In fact, had he done what his lawyers advised him to do, that would have been rational, since it was foreseeable that he would be convicted and face the death penalty.

Q. Was Mr. Bundy's behavior with his attorney and his actions in terms of self-representation and other defense matters, was that an integral part of his psychopathology?

A. Very definitely so. He behaved like a typical psychopath with his lawyers, and, for that matter, with me.

Q. You testified at the competency hearing of June 11, 1979. At that hearing, did Mr. Bundy's competency counsel, Mr. Hayes, explore your opinion to develop facts on which to make a decision as to Mr. Bundy's competency?

A. No one did that. To be very simplistic about it, my feeling of that hearing was like someone who dressed up for the party and arrived and they canceled the party. I was asked very few questions, and very little information about my knowledge of Mr. Bundy or the case was placed on the record.

Q. In your experience as an expert witness, was this proceeding unique?

A. I have testified—I believe the first time was thirty years ago, and I have testified on many occasions since—but this is the only case like that, where I have been declared an adverse witness to both parties, and where information that I had was really not developed by an adversary proceeding. Normally, one side pulls in one direction, the other side pulls in the other direction, and considerable information is elicited. I always consider cross-examination to be essential to develop a point of view that I am presenting.

Q. Did you feel that your opinion was adequately presented in this hearing?

A. Not at all. Not at all. There was no exploration—that was my impression, I made some notes of it—that was my impression of what happened, and when I read it now that just confirms that my considerable work invested in the case was not utilized in that hearing. I mean, I did not develop my opinion and explain my opinion in this case. An expert witness, unlike a lecturer in a classroom, cannot function on his or her own. He or she is completely at the mercy of whoever takes the testimony.

Q. Did you have an opinion at the time of the hearing on June 11 whether or not Mr. Bundy was able to assist his counsel?

A. Considering the nature of the functions that he was to perform as a defendant claiming innocence, it was my opinion that he was not able to stand trial. When you say assist his counsel, he was his own counsel.

Q. Was he capable of changing that behavior and not becoming his own counsel?

A. In my opinion, he was not. He was predictably unpredictable. What I mean by that is that one could anticipate that he would be guided more by showmanship than prudence.

Q. Was Mr. Bundy able meaningfully to assist his counsel at that time?

A. He was not.

Q. Referring to the first factor in the Florida rules of criminal procedure governing competency to stand trial, do you have an opinion as to whether Mr. Bundy was able to appreciate the charges?

A. Yes, I do have an opinion that he was able to appreciate the charges intellectually.

Q. When you say "intellectually," do you mean that there was some way in which he was not able to appreciate the charges?

A. That's true. I'm of the opinion that he did not appreciate the seriousness of the charges. He could intellectually tell you what the charges were, but he just dismissed them as . . . insignificant—based on his rich imagination of law enforcement—which was not the case. Clearly the charges were based upon solid evidence, but that was not his view.

Q. Dr. Tanay, when you say that Mr. Bundy dismissed the weight of the evidence against him, was that merely carelessness on his part, or was that due to an emotional or mental factor?

A. It was part of the illness, his attitude was the product, the outcome, of the nature of the illness.

Q. Looking to the second factor of the Florida standards, was Mr. Bundy able to appreciate the range and the nature of the possible penalty?

A. Again, intellectually he was. As I pointed out in my report, he said that he would cross that bridge when he came to it, when I was asked him, "Do you know that you are facing the death sentence?" He could intellectually acknowledge it, but he sure didn't act like a man who was facing a death sentence. He was acting like a man who did not have a care in the world. . . . He was cheerful and acted more like a man who was not in jail, but was onstage.

Q. Was that fact psychiatrically significant?

A. Yes. It's consistent with the diagnosis that I have previously described, of someone who is a typical psychopath or suffers from a personality disorder.

Q. Dr. Tanay, did you ever observe Mr. Bundy with Mr. Minerva?

A. Yes. As I indicated in my report, Mr. Bundy was acting as if Mr. Minerva was his third assistant and not a lawyer representing him.

Q. Did you in June of 1979 have an opinion as to Mr. Bundy's ability to assist his attorneys in planning his defense?

A. I did have an opinion.

Q. And what was that opinion?

A. That he was unable to assist in planning his defense. To the contrary, he was interfering with whatever meaningful plans the defense made. He sabotaged pretty consistently what the defense lawyers had worked out. His conduct was symptomatic of his illness, and it was outside his control.

Q. What was your opinion as to Mr. Bundy's motivation to help himself in the legal process?

A. He was not motivated by a need to help himself. He was motivated by the need to be the star of the show, as I pointed out in my report. He was the producer of a play in which he was playing a big role. The defense and his future were of secondary importance to him.

The habeas corpus petition of 112 pages reads like a novel. The petition stressed my status as an adverse witness to both parties, with an entire section titled, "The Testimony of the Examining Psychiatrist Was Not Properly Developed." The reason for this assertion was simple: the judge's direct examination was limited, since he was not an advocate for Bundy.

The direct examination is critical if a party wishes to prevail. Bundy's case highlights the evidentiary value of adversary proceedings. Experts often assume that being declared an adverse witness to both parties is beneficial to the cause of justice. The opposite is true. The function of an expert's testimony is to present the complexity of the issues involved. That happens effectively in the give-and-take of the adversary process.

In April 1987 the U.S. Court of Appeals Eleventh Circuit issued an order that confirmed my initial position that Bundy's competency was questionable and should be judicially determined. The following is an excerpt from this opinion.

Bundy was convicted and sentenced to death by the Circuit Court of Columbia County, Florida, for the abduction and murder of twelve-year-old Kimberley Leach. On direct appeal, the Florida Supreme Court affirmed both the conviction and the sentence. . . . Bundy[that means Bundy's post-conviction attorney] then immediately filed an application for a stay of execution, a petition for a writ of habeas corpus, and an application for a certificate of probable cause with the United States District Court for the Middle District of Florida. The state, anticipating that Bundy would file a petition for a writ of habeas corpus, had previously filed the trial record with the district court. Having reviewed the trial record in advance, the district court dismissed, without a hearing, the petition and denied the application for a stay of execution and for a certificate of probable cause. This Court subsequently granted a certificate of probable cause and a stay of execution pending appeal. *Bundy v. Wainwright*, 805 F.2d 948 (11th Cir.1986). . . . Bundy initially contends that he was incompetent to stand trial and that he was denied a full and fair competency hearing. . . . A defendant is mentally incompetent to stand trial if he lacks a "sufficient present ability to consult with his lawyer with a reasonable degree of rational understanding" and if he lacks "a rational as well as factual understanding of the proceedings against him."

The district court dismissed this claim, finding that Bundy was not entitled to an evidentiary hearing because he had failed to present sufficient evidence raising a legitimate doubt as to his competence to stand trial. In making that finding, the district court first noted that a trial court in Leon County had found Bundy competent to stand trial. The district court then stated that Bundy's failure to raise this claim at trial in this case was "highly significant" and that "[i]t would be 'a perversion of the judicial process' to allow petitioner to waive any challenge to his competence at trial and then permit a new trial on the grounds that he was not granted a hearing on his competence."

As I pointed out earlier in this chapter, I initiated the issue of competency but Ted Bundy acting as his own attorney decided not to pursue this issue and did not even recognize me as a witness. The U.S. Court of Appeals found competency to be a significant issue and declared:

However, our review of the record convinces us that the district court erred in concluding that Bundy was not entitled to an evidentiary hearing on this claim.

First, the district court erroneously relied on the finding of competency in the Leon County case because the record of the competency hearing in that case had not been filed with it. A state court's finding that a defendant was competent to stand trial is not entitled to a presumption of correctness unless the state court applied the correct legal standard for determining competency to stand trial and unless its conclusion that the defendant met that standard is supported by substantial evidence developed at a full and fair hearing. [citation omitted] Without the record of the competency hearing in the Leon County case before it, however, the district court could not have determined that the Leon County court applied the correct legal standard and that its conclusion was supported by substantial evidence. . . .

As indicated, the trial court in the Leon County case determined that Bundy was competent to stand trial. . . . Therefore, because trial counsel's failure to raise this claim gives rise to conflicting inferences, the district court attached too much weight to the failure to raise this claim at trial.

In contrast, the district court seemingly ignored strong indications of Bundy's incompetence to stand trial. After the sentencing jury recommended the death sentence, defense counsel offered to the court the report of Dr. Tanay. The trial court in the Leon County case appointed Dr. Tanay, a clinical psychiatrist, to examine Bundy. Dr. Tanay interviewed Bundy and defense counsel in the Leon County case and examined Bundy's behavior during police interrogations and in the courtroom. As a result, Dr. Tanay concluded that Bundy "lacks a rational understanding of what is facing him" and that he probably lacks "sufficient present ability to consult with his lawyers with a reasonable degree of rational understanding" and recommended that the court conduct an inquiry into Bundy's competency to stand trial. Such evidence—the uncontradicted opinion of a qualified psychiatrist directed expressly towards the relevant legal standard—is far more significant than defense counsel's failure to raise this claim at trial. The district court, however, failed even to mention Dr. Tanay's report. . . . Bundy's behavior throughout this prosecution reinforces Dr. Tanay's conclusion that Bundy lacked a rational understanding of the case against him and that Bundy could not rationally consult with counsel. We believe that the district court gave too little weight to that fact.

Furthermore, it is highly significant that both defense counsel and the state moved for a competency hearing in the Leon County case after Bundy refused to accept a joint plea offer. Bundy's behavior in rejecting that plea offer was central to the state's decision to request a competency hearing in the Leon County case. Because the joint plea agreement covered both this case and the Leon County case, the trial judge in this case attended the hearing where Bundy theatrically rejected the plea offer. Bundy's behavior at that hearing, atop his already suspect behavior, sufficed to question seriously his competency to stand trial in the Leon County case. It has the same effect here.

Finally, the district court erred in denying a hearing on the ground that, because Bundy did not raise this claim at trial, granting him a hearing now would be a "perversion of justice." A defendant cannot waive his right not to stand trial if he is incompetent. [citation omitted] Thus, a defendant can challenge his competency to stand trial for the first time in his initial habeas petition and, if he presents facts raising a legitimate doubt as to his competency to stand trial, he is entitled to an evidentiary hearing in the district court. [citation omitted]. . . .

We do not suggest in any way, however, that Bundy was incompetent to stand trial. That determination can be made only after a full and fair evidentiary hearing. We hold simply that the district court's finding that Bundy failed to present evidence sufficient to warrant an evidentiary hearing on his competency to stand trial is clearly erroneous.

Accordingly, we REMAND this case to the district court for the limited purpose of conducting an evidentiary hearing into Bundy's competency to stand trial.

Bundy sabotaged all of the efforts to save his life. Occasionally his manipulative behavior was even humorous. One day I received a telephone call regarding Bundy's refusal to be transported from Tallahassee to Orlando. He refused to sit in the back of a squad car because it had no seatbelts. Bundy was to attend a hearing in the U.S. District Court designed to set aside his execution.

In the last week before the execution, Coleman and Nelson still hoped to save Bundy's life. Bundy argued that confessing his crimes and promising to help find the bodies would delay the execution indefinitely. The lawyers made it clear to him that this would defeat their efforts to save his life. He seemed persuaded. The lawyers drove to Orlando, but the following day they read a newspaper headline that Bundy had confessed.

Bundy's ultimate theatrical performance occurred just before his execution. On January 24, 1989, he summoned the missionary, James Dobson, and confessed all of his crimes to him. Bundy attributed his sexual sadism to the influence of pornographic literature. This was music to the ears of this evangelical psychologist crusading against pornography.

Bundy's execution was reminiscent of the medieval festivities that accompanied putting heretics to death. A huge crowd gathered outside the prison in Starke, Florida, to celebrate the event. On later occasions when I visited Starke Prison to examine inmates of that terrible institution, I couldn't help but recall the television spectacle that preceded Bundy's execution.

For me, the conclusion of the case came in October 1989, when I organized a panel of all the legal participants in the Ted Bundy case at the annual meeting of the American Academy of Law and Psychiatry in Washington, D.C.. The night before, we met in my hotel room and exchanged our personal experiences with the case. The common thread was that no matter what we tried to do, Bundy upstaged us. Minerva remembered that I told him that if he came close to achieving his objectives in the case, Bundy would do something to sabotage it. Bundy's masochism, in combination with his malignant narcissism, would prevail. Ultimately, Bundy's pathological need for immediate gratification led him to the electric chair.

In the final analysis, Ted Bundy achieved quasi victory. His execution, in spite of a decision by an appellate court that he was incompetent to represent himself, leaves a troubling legacy for the criminal justice system. Ted Bundy's execution will not have a deterrent value upon other sadistic psychopathic serial killers. Society gained nothing in return for the enormous efforts expended in prosecuting Ted Bundy. The system enabled a psychopath to play his game at the taxpayers expense for ten long years.

In contrast, the Cincinnati serial killer known as "Angel of Death" was not given a similar opportunity, because the prosecutor was interested more in the pragmatic results and not in publicity.

NOTES

1. Hervey Cleckley, M.D., *The Mask of Sanity*, rev. ed. (New York: New American Library, 1982).

2. Letter from Michael Minerva to author, March 23, 1979.

3. "The violence of antisocial behavior must be differentiated from violence due to psychiatric disorders defined by Diagnostic Statistical Manual (DSM-IV.) Physical violence is associated with a number of psychiatric disorders and varies in severity, frequency, and nature, depending on the psychopathology of the specific disorder and the environmental context of the specific incident. For some psychiatric disorders violent behavior is part of the diagnostic criteria listed in DSM-IV, such as intermittent explosive disorder, antisocial personality disorder, borderline personality disorder, and conduct disorder." *Kaplan and*

Sadock's Comprehensive Textbook of Psychiatry, 7th ed. (Philadelphia: Lippin-cott Williams & Wilkins, 1999).

4. Wilmer, Cutler, and Pickering LLC has since merged with Hale and Dorr LLC to become Wilmer Hale in 2004. Wilmer Hale has over 1,000 lawyers. They continue to have a record of outstanding pro bono work, for which their firm has won many awards.

5. This chapter was written before the passage of health care legislation in March 2010.

Emanuel Tanay is inducted into the College of Psychiatry, whose membership is limited to 400. 1988.

7

INNOCENT AND ON DEATH ROW

Sterling Spann

In February 1996, Diana Holt, a staff attorney at the Post-Conviction Defender Organization of South Carolina, contacted me about the case of Sterling Spann, a man convicted in 1981 of raping and murdering Melva Neill, an eighty-two-year-old woman. Ms. Holt was an intense young woman whose determination to free an innocent man languishing on death row was apparent even on the phone.

On September 16, 1981, in the town of Clover, South Carolina, Melva Neill's body was discovered in her bathtub. She had been raped, tortured, and killed in what was obviously a sadistic sexual homicide. An anonymous female tipster called the local police station and said simply, "Sterling Spann killed that lady." Sterling Spann was a young black male from a law-abiding, church-going family. His mother was a teacher and all of his brothers and sisters had gone to college. Spann had once done yard work for the victim and lived a few blocks from her home. The police found Spann carrying a coin in his pocket that had belonged to Neill; Spann claimed that he got the coin from a stranger named "Cool Breeze." Spann maintained his innocence, but he was charged with the murder.

The defense lawyers who represented Spann were convinced that they would secure acquittal since there was virtually no evidence to their knowledge to connect Spann to the crime. However, at the last minute the prosecution produced an expert who testified about a fingerprint found on a sheet of paper on the bed of the victim. Although it wasn't recognized at the time, that evidence was highly suspicious.

It was discovered by the nephew of the victim after the crime scene had been cleared. It was supposedly found on the bed, and yet it was not in the photograph of the crime scene. The piece of paper was not crinkled—it was in pristine condition. I have encountered planting of evidence by police on a number of occasions designed to prove that a suspect is the perpetrator, and that is what I believe happened in this case.

Spann did not take the witness stand because his lawyers were concerned that he would have to tell the story about the coin which was, according to them, not believable (even though it was true). Ultimately, Spann was convicted and sentenced to death

Believing that Spann had been unjustly convicted, Holt asked me to examine Sterling Spann and William "Johnny" Hullett. Hullett was serving a life sentence for the sadistic murder of sixty-nine-year-old Bessie Kate Alexander—a killing with striking similarities to that of Melva Neill. Both took place in Clover, which has a population of about four thousand people and is located in York County, South Carolina. Sadistic sexual murder is rare, therefore it was unlikely that this small community had two sadistic murderers; it seemed more reasonable to assume that Hullett also perpetrated the murder of Neill. The mode of operation and the choice of victims were identical.

By 1996, fifteen years after Neill's murder, the lawyers defending Spann had recognized similarities between four local murders. Even before I examined Hullett and Spann, I hypothesized, based upon the material that Holt had provided, that Hullett had perpetrated all four of the sadistic sexual killings, three of which had occurred within four months and all of which had taken place within a seven-mile radius. The evidence against Spann was negligible, and much of it was of dubious validity. For example, Holt went to heroic lengths to locate the stranger whom Spann called "Cool Breeze." She found him under a bridge: he was homeless and admitted giving the coin to Spann. We know now that Johnny Hullett, the real perpetrator, arranged the planting of the coin.

On February 29, 1996, I sent a report to Holt detailing my interviews with Hullett and Spann. I had interviewed Hullett at the Perry Correctional Institution in South Carolina. He was cheerful and superficially helpful, though he repeatedly lied to me. In this he reminded me of Ted Bundy, though he did not have Ted's intelligence.

I did not confront him with some of the information I had that contradicted his stories, but from time to time I did let him know that I was aware of it. This did not make him change his approach. He denied ever having had any psychiatric difficulties. When asked why he went to see a psychiatrist, his answer was, "My family doctor sent me." Whatever happened of adverse nature in his life was always somebody else's fault; his confession in regard to killing Mrs. Alexander was made up by the investigating officers. Abuse of his wife or children was dismissed as made-up stories. He loves his brother. The fact that his brother testified against him and is responsible for the fact that Johnny "unjustly" serves a life term in prison does not change the fact that Johnny loves his brother. He found nothing inconsistent in his accusations that his brother was the perpetrator of sadistic murders. The concept of inconsistency does not exist in Johnny's mental makeup.

From a purely descriptive standpoint, Johnny showed no overt psychopathology. He appeared of average normal intelligence. There was no abnormality of mood. He remained cheerful and pleasant throughout the interview.

The clinical picture presented by this individual is consistent with the diagnosis of Personality Disorder, antisocial type. He is manipulative and information provided by him should not be considered reliable. He has engaged, by his own admission, in many activities which provided grounds for arrest, even though he has been arrested on only a few occasions.

Historical information from family members, including his wife, indicates that he has a propensity to violence and sexual sadism. He has confessed to participating in the sadistic sexual murder of an elderly woman [Mrs. Bessie Alexander].

I left the interview with Hullett convinced that he was a sadistic sexual serial killer. I had interviewed Sterling Spann about a week earlier, on February 18, at the Broadriver Correctional Institution outside of Columbia, South Carolina. At that point Spann had been on death row for about fifteen years. In my letter to Holt, who was trying to free Spann, I reported the following.

The demeanor and attitude of this man was out of place in the setting of Death Row. He was calm, self-assured, friendly, and gently outgoing. A sense of communication developed with him rather quickly. He was quick to smile and occasionally broke out in sincere laughter. In my long experience of interviewing people who have been incarcerated for an extended period of time, I have never encountered an individual who presented such a well-integrated personality. His ability to cope is impressive. He has adapted remarkably well to the difficult circumstances of his incarceration and death sentence. He has attained a mature adult outlook on life in spite of the fact that almost all of his adult years have been spent on Death Row. He made an excellent adjustment to the prison setting. It was obvious that he is respected by guards and fellow inmates who often seek his counsel. . . .

Based upon careful consideration of his history and observations I made during the interview, I am of the opinion that this individual does not suffer from a personality disorder. He certainly does not have any overt psychopathology.

I reviewed with Sterling the circumstances of his arrest and trial and reached the opinion that it is exceedingly unlikely that he was the perpetrator of the sexual sadistic homicide of elderly Mrs. Harry Neill, who was found nude in a partially filled bathtub, strangled to death, with her genitalia mutilated by a blunt instrument, possibly a broom handle.

Having interviewed both Spann, whom Holt believed was innocent and had been unjustly imprisoned for fifteen years, and Hullett, whom Holt suspected had murdered Mrs. Neill, my professional opinion corroborated Holt's beliefs in this case. I concluded in my report that

the homicides of Mrs. Mary Ring, Mrs. Harry Neill, and Mrs. Bessie Alexander were most likely committed by the same individual. All three homicides represented typical sadistic sexual murders. This type of homicide is very rare. I consider it significant that all three homicides took place within a 7-mile radius within four months. Furthermore, it is a legally established fact that Mr. Hullett has been found guilty of one of these homicides, namely that of Mrs. Alexander. It is significant that after Sterling [Spann]'s arrest and before his trial, another similar homicide (that of Mrs. Alexander) has occurred. Subsequent to the arrest of Mr. Hullett for the killing of Mrs. Alexander, no additional homicides took place. There is considerable evidence, including the confession of Mr. Hullett, that he was the perpetrator of the sadistic sexual murder of Mrs. Alexander. It has been recognized by the police investigating the homicide of Mrs. Neill that the homicide of Mrs. Alexander was most likely perpetrated by the same person. In fact, suspicion was expressed that Sterling escaped from incarceration and perpetrated the murder of Mrs. Alexander [obviously this was a far-fetched theory]. . . . It is my professional opinion that it is unlikely that Sterling Spann is the perpetrator of the sexual murder of Mrs. Melva Neill. It is my opinion that Mrs. Neill was killed by a serial killer.

I subsequently received a copy of a letter written by Johnny Hullett to another inmate dated March 9, 1995. The letter was typical for a sadist. Hullett contemplates raping, humiliating, and possibly even torturing a woman named Carolyn. He assures his friend, "yes she will enjoy everything we do to her." This is a typical notion of a sadist—that the victim enjoys being humiliated and tormented.

The fact that Hullett sexually abused his daughter, Candy Lynn Hullett, from age six to age thirteen or fourteen, is certainly relevant to his sadistic personality. In March 1996, Candy Lynn Hullett (by then in her twenties) gave an affidavit in which she said, "When I was a little girl, my father sexually abused me. The first time I recall him sexually abusing me, I was six years old. Many times he would sexually abuse me for hours at a time. My father used to beat me and my brother, William Johnny Hullett, Jr. My father would punch me and my brother in our faces. My father would beat us with electrical cords. Sometimes he would beat us so bad with electrical cords [that] we would bleed."

A diligent investigation at the time of the York County murders would have revealed Johnny Hullett's history, which any forensic psychiatrist should have been able to connect to the sadistic sexual murders of elderly women.

I recommended to the defense team, which consisted of Holt and John H. Blume, that they retain the services of Dr. Werner Spitz, a well-known forensic pathologist and my neighbor in Grosse Pointe, Michigan. Spitz reviewed the autopsy reports and found that all three of the women were killed in a similar and unusual manner. The lawyers used my report and that of Spitz as the basis for a request for a new trial under the legal principle of "newly discovered evidence." Spitz and I then traveled to York, South Carolina, where we testified before a local judge who predictably rejected the motion because it was not "timely."

The South Carolina Supreme Court subsequently granted a new trial, and Spann was freed. Sterling wrote me a letter expressing his gratitude for my work. He described the call from his lawyer: "It was early one morning, my attorney called me and she was crying. I kept saying 'What's wrong what's wrong?' His lawyer was crying . . . because he had won!" After eighteen years on death row, Spann, now thirty-six years old, was back in court hearing he had won—not exoneration, but a new trial.[1]

Spann remained free for three years. He and all of us expected that his long nightmare was over, that justice had finally prevailed. But a new prosecutor, Tommy Pope, decided to charge him with the murder one more time. He aggressively—and very publicly—asserted Spann's guilt. Pope also alleged misconduct by the defense team of John Blume and Diana Holt.[2]

In February 2002, Spann's lawyer Blume advised me that the prosecution had retained forensic psychiatrist Dr. Park Dietz to examine Spann. Dietz was supposed to conduct a three-day-long video examination of Spann. This was an unusual role for Dietz, since no insanity defense was being raised on Spann's behalf. Furthermore, the length of the proposed examination was unheard of and qualified as harassment. Considering that Dietz charges $600 per hour, if he examined a defendant for eight hours a day for three days, his charges would be in excess of $14,000 for the examination time alone. An indigent defendant represented by a public defender could never afford an equivalent expenditure. I had charged the public defender something in the neighborhood of $150 an hour.

Blume quite correctly objected to the proposed marathon evaluation. The prosecutor argued that, in the event that Dietz was precluded from examining Spann, I should not be able to mention in my testimony that I examined Spann. Although legally reasonable, this would have been tactically detrimental. I argued my persuasiveness would be diminished by an inability to rely upon my clinical examination.

Furthermore, I did not believe that the prosecution could benefit significantly from Dietz's examination. Their quest to once more convict Spann for a crime he did not commit was apparent. I believed that the prosecution's efforts and expense would backfire.

The issue became moot. The prosecutor offered Sterling a short sentence and parole if he agreed to an Alford plea.[3] In an Alford plea, the criminal defendant does not admit the act but admits that the prosecution could prove the charge. The court then pronounces the defendant guilty.

During these negotiations, Spann's beloved sister was killed in an automobile accident, which led to a depressive episode on the part of Spann. In this frame of mind, he decided to accept the plea offer. As part of the deal, Spann was promised an almost immediate parole hearing. Sterling Spann, who had been found innocent, returned to prison on the assumption that the parole board would send him back to his wife and family at his very first hearing. At this point he had served almost twenty years in prison and now he held a job and resumed a normal life during the three years before he took that Alford plea. Unfortunately for Spann, the sentencing judge did not honor the plea agreement and sentenced Spann to life in prison.[4] Thus Spann was once again in the same predicament in which I had originally found him.

Three years later, after considerable legal efforts on his behalf and extensive publity about this flagrant injustice, Spann was released. A televised interview with me on NBC's *Dateline* gave rise to additional television and newspaper coverage. A Connecticut couple, Diane and Neil Mellen, heard my *Dateline* interview and hired an investigator who interviewed me and did other work on the case. They gave Spann legal support for his parole hearing. The details of the new prosecutorial efforts are lengthy and could be the subject of an additional chapter.

The Spann-Hullett story exemplifies the failure to sufficiently involve experienced forensic psychiatrists in the investigative and adjudicatory processes. One cannot expect a small police department or the average criminal lawyer to be familiar with sadistic sexual psychopaths, who, fortunately, are quite rare. This is where a forensic psychiatrist can be an important resource. The next chapter, which deals with the case of Dr. Sam Sheppard, exemplifies the same problem.

NOTES

1. *Dateline* NBC/Crime reports.
2. *Dateline* NBC/Crime reports.
3. *North Carolina v. Alford*, 400 U.S. 25 (1970), was a case in which the Supreme Court of the United States affirmed on a 5-3 vote that there are no constitutional barriers to prevent a judge from accepting a guilty plea from a defendant who wants to plead guilty while still protesting his innocence.
4. Bryan H. Ward, "A Plea Best Not Taken: Why Criminal Defendants Should Avoid the *Alford* Plea," 68 *Missouri Law Review* 913 (Fall 2003).

8

THE SAM
SHEPPARD SAGA

The Sam Sheppard case gives us a window into the dysfunctional state of the U.S. criminal justice system. The initial investigatory phase was reminiscent of the Keystone Cops, the trial was conducted, in the words of the Supreme Court, in a "carnival atmosphere," and the Ohio appellate process failed miserably to deal with an obvious miscarriage of justice. Politics played a significant role in the Sheppard trial and continued to exercise influence during the post-trial period. It took federal courts to restore a semblance of justice in this case. By that time the life of Sam Sheppard had been destroyed and irreparable damage inflicted upon his family and community.

In 1954, Sam Sheppard was a young, successful osteopathic physician in Bay Village, a fashionable suburb of Cleveland. Sheppard's father and two brothers were also osteopaths, and together they operated Bay View Hospital. Sam and his wife, Marilyn, had a beautiful lakeside home and a seven-year-old son, Samuel Reese, whom they affectionately called "Chip." The couple was expecting a second child.

During the evening of July 3, Sam and Marilyn Sheppard were watching television with another couple, the Aherns, at the Sheppard residence. Sam was called to the hospital on an emergency case; when he returned home he rejoined the group and promptly fell asleep on a daybed. Sam Sheppard was still asleep when the Aherns left at 12:30 A.M. on July 4, 1954.

Sometime later that morning, Marilyn Sheppard was bludgeoned to death in her bed. Sam Sheppard recalled later that he was awakened on the daybed when he heard his wife call his name. When he ran to her side, an intruder struck him on the head and he lost consciousness. After regaining consciousness, Sheppard saw his attacker flee toward the lake. He pursued his attacker down the steps to the lake, where Sheppard was evidently knocked out again. He awoke floating in the lake after an unknown length of time. His clothing was torn and he had suffered significant injuries, including a fractured cervical vertebra, a life-threatening injury.

Sheppard returned to his wife's bedside and discovered that she was dead. At 5:45 A.M. Sam called neighbor Spencer Houk, who was also the mayor of Bay Village, who rushed to the Sheppard residence with his wife. They found Sam Sheppard in shock. The Houks called the police, and an ambulance took Sheppard to the hospital.

Marilyn Sheppard had been beaten to death with a blunt weapon. She had thirty-five wounds, including fifteen on the head and face, which was so disfigured that she was barely recognizable. Her pajamas had been moved to expose her genitalia and breasts and her legs were spread open. She had obviously been sexually abused. The mattress was soaked with blood, which was also spattered on the walls. The crime scene was typical for a sadistic sexual killer. It takes a psychopath to engage in sadistic sexual murder. A psychopath has a typical life history, there is even evidence that psychopaths have specific brain pathology. Adrian Raine, D.Phil., chair of the criminology department at the University of Pennsylvania and his coworkers reported that the prefrontal cortex was significantly smaller in violent, antisocial men than in controls (*Psychiatric News*, March 3, 2000).

Dr. Sheppard, a law-abiding and well-to-do surgeon, cooperated fully with the investigation. This is a common mistake made by innocent people who are unaware of the dangers of interacting with police. Against his lawyer's advice, Sheppard spoke freely to the police, who subjected Sheppard to psychological torture under the guise of investigation. Dr. Samuel Gerber, the coroner, interrogated Sheppard as soon as he arrived at the hospital to be treated for his serious cervical spine injuries. On the Friday after he was discharged from the hospital, Sheppard was again interrogated from 8:00 A.M. until 5:30 P.M. Sheppard was offered many inducements to confess, with the implication that he could get off on the insanity defense or get away with a manslaughter verdict.

The Marilyn Sheppard killing was the first homicide that the Bay Village Police Department had investigated in a long time. A competent homicide investigation is often beyond the capacity of a small suburban police department. They simply don't have the resources or the experience. It's not uncommon for the police or prosecution to focus too early on a single suspect and ignore evidence that doesn't support their theory of the crime. In this case, the police firmly believed that Sheppard was the killer, and they did not pursue other obvious leads that indicated the presence of a suspicious person in the neighborhood. Witnesses noticed a suspicious man in the neighborhood early on July 4 who fit Sheppard's description of the intruder; neighbor Leo Staviski reported that he observed a man standing close to a tree in the vicinity of the Sheppard home. Richard and Betty Knitter reported to the police that on July 4 they saw a man in the vicinity of the cemetery, the first lot west of the Sheppard home, between 3:30 A.M. and 4:00 A.M. Contrary to the law, this information was not shared with the defense.

Throughout July, headlines and comments by the prosecution and the police suggested that the husband was the killer. On July 30, a front-page *Cleveland Press* headline asked, "Why Isn't Sam Sheppard in Jail?"[1] At 10:00 P.M. that very same night, police arrested Sheppard and charged him with his wife's murder. The prosecution had no evidence to support this most serious charge, and grand-jury foreman Bert Winston complained that the members of the jury were under tremendous pressure. However on August 16, a judge found no evidence supporting the charge and released Sheppard on bail.

Shortly afterward, Sheppard was arrested once again. The three-day inquest that followed, conducted by pathologist Gerber, resembled an inquisition more than an inquiry into the cause and mode of death. This time, the prosecution felt they had enough evidence to convict Sheppard.

On October 18, 1954, Sheppard's trial for first-degree murder began. William Corrigan, a solo practitioner whose primary practice was labor law, was Sheppard's defense lawyer. He was assisted by his son, who had just finished law school. It is typical for naive defendants to retain lawyers they know and trust instead of lawyers who are competent criminal trial lawyers. Having a labor lawyer defend a man charged with first-degree murder is similar to having a general practitioner perform brain surgery.

There was compelling evidence that Sheppard was not the perpetrator of his wife's homicide; one could even argue that there was great evidence pointing to Richard Eberling, the Sheppards's window washer. But not until twelve years after Sheppard's 1954 conviction did another jury find him not guilty—after the Supreme Court of the United States issued a scathing condemnation of the 1954 trial's "carnival atmosphere."

The critical question was what happened between the departure of the Sheppards's neighbors and Marilyn Sheppard's death. In the 1954 trial, the prosecution team gave two possible explanations. Sheppard woke from the daybed, went upstairs, quarreled with his wife, went into a rage, and killed her. This claim assumes an impulsive homicide. The police speculated that Sheppard had injured himself to make it appear that he had fought with an intruder and then washed Marilyn's blood off his clothes in the lake.

Physical evidence contradicted this view. Gerber consulted a neurologist who said that Sheppard's injuries could not possibly be self-inflicted. An independent examiner later confirmed the neck (cervical vertebra) fracture as well as other injuries observed upon Sheppard's admission to the hospital. In the 1954 trial, nurse Anna Franz testified that Sheppard's "feet were all shriveled up, as if they had been in water a long time." Dr. Gervase Flick, a radiologist, testified that an x-ray of Sheppard revealed a probable fracture of his second cervical vertebra. Dr. Clifford Foster told jurors he found swelling at the base of Sam's skull. Dr. Charles Elkins testified that the neck spasms he detected when he examined Sam could not be faked but were the result of a real and significant injury.

This evidence did not prevent prosecutor John Mahon from telling the jury, "A reasonable interpretation of the state's evidence will point the finger of guilt at Sam Sheppard." He said that the evidence would show that "this defendant and Marilyn were quarreling about the activities of Dr. Sam Sheppard with other women" and that "that is the reason she was killed."[2] However, no such evidence was ever produced. Furthermore, the autopsy results were not consistent with a rage killing.

The jury found the prosecution's case compelling; on December 21, 1954, Sam Sheppard was convicted of second-degree murder. He was sentenced to life in prison.

Sheppard served ten years of his life sentence, with several unsuccessful appeals, before F. Lee Bailey took on his case and helped Sheppard win a hearing before the Supreme Court. Sheppard's conviction was overturned and he was granted a new trial, which took place in 1966. This trial ended in a verdict of not guilty, and twelve years after his wife's murder Sam Sheppard was finally a free man. Sheppard attempted to move on with his life, but he was a destroyed man. He married Ariane Tebbenjohanns, a German pen pal, just three days after his release but they divorced about six months before Sheppard died in 1970 of liver failure, likely the result of the alcoholism he developed after his release.

A SON FIGHTS TO CLEAR HIS FATHER'S NAME

For the Sheppards's surviving child, Samuel Reese "Chip" Sheppard, his mother's death and his father's wrongful imprisonment had immense consequences. Not only had he lost his parents, but starting on January 7, 1955, little more than two weeks after the 1954 jury found Sheppard guilty, Chip had begun to lose his extended family as well. On that day Sam Sheppard's mother, Chip's grandmother, committed suicide by shooting herself. Shortly thereafter, Sam Sheppard's father died of a hemorrhagic gastric ulcer. In February 1963, Thomas Reese, Marilyn Sheppard's father, committed suicide with a shotgun. As a result of these tragedies, Chip grew up in his uncles' homes, living first with Richard and Dorothy Sheppard and later with Steve and Betty Sheppard and their two daughters.

Although Sam Sheppard had died in 1970, Chip still wished to clear his father's name. In late 1991, he retained Terry Gilbert, a prominent Cleveland attorney who filed a civil lawsuit against the Cuyahoga County for the wrongful imprisonment of his father. Sheppard's acquittal, according to the prosecutor, meant that there was a reasonable doubt about his guilt; it did not prove his innocence. Thus Sam Sheppard was posthumously being tried for killing his wife. Gilbert faced the task of proving Sheppard's innocence, a higher standard than reasonable doubt about guilt.

Gilbert retained me as an expert on the psychology of homicide and supplied me with a mountain of documents about the case, including information about the crime scene and the events of July 1954. Based on my review of the transcripts of the original trial and all of the related documents, I prepared a lengthy report detailing the gross miscarriage of justice in the investigation and the original trial. In my opinion the wrong man was charged and convicted of the sadistic murder of Mrs. Sheppard. I had no doubt that Sam Sheppard did not kill his wife.

The nearly forty-year span between 1955 and the wrongful imprisonment case brought to light new information. Several revealing "discoveries" can be attributed to a police report written during the original homicide investigation in 1954 but not disclosed until 1993. The report indicated that the Sheppard home may have been broken into on the night of the murder. While the prosecution had argued during the original trial that there was no indication of a break-in, the police report clearly notes that fresh tool marks were found on a basement door.

Buried deep within a vault of evidence at the Cuyahoga County Coroner's Office was another report with more interesting evidence that had never been disclosed to the defense. The report told of a dented metal flashlight found on a Lake Erie beach thirteen months after the homicide, several yards from the Sheppards' house. The flashlight was described as a three-battery Eveready flashlight, about a foot long, with pieces of its red paint chipped off and the glass broken. This report was significant given that chips of red enamel paint were found on the floor underneath Marilyn Sheppard's bed.

By the time this report surfaced, no testing could be conducted to determine whether the paint from the flashlight matched that found under the bed. But among the documents I reviewed in this case was a 1955 report by Paul Kirk, an eminent criminologist and criminalistics professor at the University of California, Berkeley. After the 1954 verdict, Kirk conducted an investigation of the Sheppard crime scene and reviewed all of the physical evidence. Upon examination of the crime scene and the wounds inflicted upon Marilyn Sheppard in 1955, Kirk described the weapon as "most likely a flashlight." He also determined that red paint at the crime scene was a commercial lacquer used to paint hardware. Kirk's report contained additional compelling findings, including the following.

1. A large spot of blood was found in the murder bedroom that matched neither Sam's nor Marilyn's blood type, indicating the

    presence of a third person in the bedroom at the time of the murder.

2. Two pieces of teeth were found on Marilyn Sheppard's bed that matched two of her upper front teeth. Since there were no injuries to Marilyn Sheppard's lower face, Kirk determined that the teeth were broken when she bit someone (presumably her attacker) and that these marks would have been noticeable on her attacker. Sam Sheppard had no bite marks on his body.

3. Based on the blood stains on the wall, the position of Marilyn Sheppard's body, and the backswing of the killer's blows, the murderer had to be left-handed. Sam Sheppard was right-handed.

4. The crime started as a sex attack, not a murder. This was supported by the fact that Marilyn Sheppard's pajama pants had blood accumulated at the bottom, showing definitively that they had been pulled down before the murder.[3]

None of this information was available to the defense during the first trial; police and prosecutors either missed or concealed it. The defense was not given access to the crime scene at all.

This physical evidence contradicted a spousal homicide. Most spousal homicides occur in an impulsive manner in a rage state, but this victim was not killed in an impulsive way; physical evidence showed a sadistic murder involving sexual abuse and that prolonged, elaborate torture caused Marilyn Sheppard's death.

As I reviewed the documents pertaining to the case, I was struck by the fact that the prosecution argued that Sheppard's motive was his desire to pursue a relationship with another woman. They also speculated that Marilyn Sheppard was pregnant by another man, and therefore Sheppard decided to kill her. Yet neither of these speculations is consistent with the psychology of homicidal behavior or the facts of the case. The prosecution claimed that Sheppard acted in a state of rage, which was inconsistent with the crime scene that was typical for sadistic sexual murder.

Clearly Samuel Gerber, the coroner, believed Sheppard was the perpetrator from the moment he entered the investigation. I'm amazed by the fact that Gerber both interrogated and medically examined Sheppard as soon as Sheppard arrived at the hospital. A coroner's job is to determine the cause and manner of death, not to conduct a criminal investigation. Sheppard testified that during the investigation, Gerber "permitted" him to take his medical bag from his house in order to continue his work at Bay View Hospital. Thus, Gerber seems to have been the chief investigator making decisions about the crime scene. He played a central role in the formulation of the theories of homicide but he had no knowledge about the psychology of homicide. His basic premises were that wives are killed by husbands.

Gerber was the county coroner and a general practitioner, yet he fancied himself not only a forensic pathologist but also a latter-day Sherlock Holmes. Upon entering the Sheppard residence, he told the detectives, "It looks like Sheppard did it. Go get his confession." His comment was overheard by Dr. H. Max Don, who testified under oath to hearing this statement during the 1954 trial. Gerber was convinced of Sheppard's guilt before any evidence was gathered.

The police suspected the true perpetrator (Richard Eberling, the window washer) early in the investigation, but ended up going along with Gerber's guess. The police were under intense pressure to deliver evidence confirming Sheppard's guilt, and they did so by commission and omission. Even early on, inconsistencies in the police and coroner's investigations emerged. The postmortem examination by a respected forensic pathologist placed Marilyn Sheppard's time of death around 5:00 A.M., but Gerber claimed that she was killed around 3:00 A.M., putting a greater amount of time between her homicide and Sam Sheppard's 5:45 A.M. phone call to Houk. In the Gerber version, Sheppard killed his wife around 3:00 A.M. and was busy staging a crime scene and inflicting injuries upon himself until he finally called Houk at 5:45 A.M.

Another example of the incompetent investigation was the handling of the trail of blood discovered on the screened-in porch, which was not subjected to blood-typing. It was obvious that it did not come from Sam Sheppard, who had no bleeding wounds, and could not have dripped from a murder weapon because it would have coagulated by the time it traveled there from the Sheppards' upstairs bedroom. The blood most likely came from the real perpetrator when he chased Sam Sheppard down to the lake after a physical confrontation in the bedroom. (The window washer Eberling, anticipating this evidence, volunteered that he had bled in the Sheppard house.)

The position of Marilyn Sheppard's body left no doubt that she was sexually abused and the mutilation of her face was characteristic of sadistic murder. The Sheppards's seven-year-old son, who was sleeping in the next room, was not awakened by the assault, so we can infer that Marilyn Sheppard was somehow silenced during the attack. I made this inference during my cross-examination by the prosecutor.

It takes just 20 to 30 seconds to cause unconsciousness by asphyxiation, a minute to cause brain damage, and three to four minutes of continuous asphyxiation to cause death. This medical knowledge was the basis for my opinion that the victim had been sleeping and was prevented from screaming when she fought for her life. A knowledgeable observer should have concluded that much in July 1954.

Nothing in Sam Sheppard's history made such sexually sadistic behavior likely. The prosecution tried to show that he had a history of violence, but they could only produce a single witness (Tom Weigle) who testified that Sheppard sternly reprimanded his little son when the youngster hit his mother.

Let me once again stress that the real villain in the Sheppard story is coroner Samuel Gerber, who instructed detectives to arrest Sheppard before the investigation got under way. This is a familiar pattern to me, one that I call "deductive investigation." It starts with the assumption that a suspect is guilty; what follows is a search for evidence to prove that assumption. While Sheppard was recovering from his injuries in the hospital, under the terrible trauma of having lost his pregnant wife to a gruesome murder, Gerber and his team were plotting how to entrap him in a confession. Unlike many other innocent defendants, Sheppard refused to give a false confession, even under enormous pressure. Yet before long, the public accepted his culpability as a foregone conclusion.

We know now that the window washer, Eberling, was almost certainly Marilyn Sheppard's murderer. The police suspected a connection between Eberling and Mrs. Sheppard's murder, but the prosecutor and Gerber declared this revelation insignificant because they were determined to convict Sheppard. The instruction to disregard any potential connection between Eberling's blood and the murder is referred to in the police report. Had the police pursued this link, Sheppard might have never been arrested, charged, and convicted; at the very least, he would have been released from prison before the 1966 Supreme Court decision that reversed his 1954 conviction. Eberling would have gone to jail long before his 1989 conviction, and Eberling's final victim, Ethel Durkin, would not have been brutally murdered in 1984.

In contrast to the attention surrounding Sheppard, Eberling was hardly acknowledged by the press. Even when it was revealed that he murdered Ethel Durkin in the 1980s and was a suspect in a number of other killings of women, he received little attention in Cleveland papers, even though Eberling had cleaned the Sheppards's windows just two days before Marilyn Sheppard's murder and admitted to leaving traces of his blood in the house.[4]

In 1959, when Eberling was arrested for larceny, he volunteered that he was in the Sheppard house two days before Marilyn Sheppard's murder and had bled throughout the house. He then described stealing Marilyn Sheppard's rings from Dr. Richard Sheppard's (Sam Sheppard's brother's) home, where they were stored after her death: "Opening one box, I noticed Marilyn Sheppard's cocktail or dinner ring and what I believed to be her engagement ring. I picked them up and put them in my pocket and walked off with them. I had seen this one dinner ring earlier in Dr. Sam Sheppard's home setting up on Marilyn's dressing table . . . I did not pick it up. I just noticed it, and for that reason, I knew it was Marilyn's ring."

Subsequent to the exhumation of Marilyn Sheppard's body in 1999, Eberling published a message on the Internet accompanied by a picture of himself. In the picture he appears to be in his late twenties with a dark bushy hairstyle—obviously a wig. We should remember here that Sheppard said he was attacked by a bushy-haired man, and others, too, observed such an individual in the neighborhood of the Sheppard home. Eberling's publication of this photo was a provocative challenge to the police. Thus, Eberling called attention to himself at various stages and connected himself to the murder of Marilyn Sheppard. This type of game-playing with police is typical for serial killers. I have encountered this with other psychopaths, including Ted Bundy.

Eberling assumed that he might be charged with Marilyn Sheppard's homicide once his blood had been identified at the scene. What he did not anticipate was the incompetence and bias of the police who failed to type-test the blood. Blood typing has been a standard testing procedure since the 1930s. The failure to do so in this case may have been deliberate.

The manipulation of evidence by Gerber and the police was flagrant, and I've seen this kind of thing many times before. Once a firm belief exists that the suspect is the perpetrator, all that remains is to build a case against him. Among other things, the investigators ignored the drop of blood in the bedroom that didn't match Sam or Marilyn Sheppard, they proposed a timeline of events that didn't fit the autopsy findings, and they failed to take fingerprints from most of the house.

The prosecution claimed that the house had been wiped clean of fingerprints; thus police incompetence was transformed into evidence that Sheppard was a deliberate, skillful criminal. A newspaper article printed during the trial proclaimed the killer to be "brilliant,"[5] and Gerber was quoted as saying that the fact that the murderer eliminated evidence proved he was someone "with very high intelligence, familiarity with surroundings, and full knowledge of police investigative techniques."[6] Dr. Sheppard was portrayed to be not only a competent osteopathic neurosurgeon but also a master criminal.

In the Sheppard case, Gerber and the prosecutorial team resorted to what the law calls "character evidence." Marilyn was glorified and Sam was demonized. Gerber declared her "a model wife" who had no enemies—the implication being that Sam Sheppard was the only person with a motive to kill her. In reality, Marilyn Sheppard was no stranger to extramarital affairs. The police discovered her infidelity, but that information never reached the news media. During my cross-examination in the 1999 Sheppard civil case, the prosecutor asked me whether infidelity was a motive for murder. I answered the question with a question, asking whether it was a motive for Marilyn to kill Sam. Only years later did I discover that Sheppard had used virtually the same phrase when talking to his lawyer in 1954.

While Gerber's conduct was possibly illegal, the Bay Village Police Department deserves a share of the blame for this miscarriage of justice. In Bay Village, an affluent suburb of Cleveland, there was little crime. Patrick Murphy, former police commissioner in several American cities, once wrote that many communities are policed by untrained individuals who are really nothing more than guards.[7] The Bay Village Police Department's botched investigation may also be blamed on the fragmentation of the American system of policing; one of the major recommendations made in 1967 by the President's Commission on Law Enforcement and Administration of Justice was the coordination and consolidation of police services.

The press also shares in the blame for Sheppard's trial and conviction. In the six months surrounding Sheppard's first trial, the *Cleveland Press* printed 399 articles about the case, an early example of the kind of media frenzy that surrounds high profile cases today. One could argue that next to coroner Samuel Gerber, the most critical figure in the Sheppard saga was Lee B. Seltzer, who was editor of the *Cleveland Press*, then the city's most prominent newspaper, from 1928 until he retired in 1966. Called the "crusading Seltzer," he was a kingmaker who launched the careers of several important politicians. Seltzer played a significant role in the life of Cleveland and was associated with many city improvements, including the municipal zoo, parks, and a beautiful lakefront. He even declined an appointment to the U.S. Senate because he could not leave the city he loved.[8]

Good works aside, Seltzer exploited Marilyn Sheppard's death to increase the circulation of his newspaper. In 1956, Seltzer published an autobiography in which he speaks of the press using "all its editorial artillery" to bring about Sheppard's prosecution. In fact, it was Seltzer himself who authored the front page editorial titled "Why Isn't Sam Sheppard In Jail?" that led to Sheppard's second arrest.[9] We condemn propaganda that generates hate for political reasons, but propaganda that develops bias in order to sell newspapers is for some reason tolerated.

Ten years later, U.S. District Judge Weinman in an appellate decision criticized media involvement in the court process: "The papers kept running pictures of Trial Judge Edward Blythin (who was up for re-election) and gave him pointed advice on how to conduct the trial." Blythin, wrote Weinman, should have ordered a change of venue; instead, he handed over most of the courtroom to the press. "If ever there was a trial by newspapers," he said, "this was a perfect example."[10]

THE CIVIL TRIAL

The fact that Sheppard was found not guilty according to Ohio criminal law did not mean that he was innocent for the purposes of civil law. Consequently, for damages to be collected by the Sheppard's estate, Sam Sheppard's innocence had to be established.

From a layman's perspective, it seems reasonable that a man who has been found not guilty in a court of law would be considered innocent—after all, at the time of the original 1954 trial, the jury was not given the option to find Sheppard guilty, not guilty, or innocent. The categorical proposition was "guilty" or "not guilty." The 1966 retrial established that there was no evidence to link Sheppard to his wife's murder and resulted in a "not guilty" verdict. If, after over forty years, no additional evidence had emerged to cast a shadow of doubt over the 1966 not-guilty verdict, it seems bizarre that Sheppard remained a suspect who needed to have his "innocence" established.

This issue was confusing to me even though I had been involved with hundreds of cases before being hired to work on this one. In 2007, as I started writing this manuscript, I wrote to Terry Gilbert requesting clarification of why Sheppard had to be declared innocent. Gilbert responded as follows.

> In the American legal system there is no such thing as a verdict of innocence in criminal cases. The result is either guilty or not guilty. 'Not guilty' means that the State has not met its burden of proving guilt beyond a reasonable doubt.
>
> Some states such as Ohio have enacted legislation to remedy wrongful imprisonments. This did not exist in Ohio until 1986. A declaration of innocence can be accomplished by a civil action in which the claimant has the burden of proving by a preponderance of the evidence that he is innocent. While this makes little sense, it is the legal framework we have to work with.
>
> In other words, to receive compensation from the state, there would have to be an imprisonment for a conviction, a successful appeal, a later dismissal or acquittal of the charge(s), and then the wrongfully imprisoned would have to prove that he is innocent (which is what we were trying to do in Sheppard through the Estate). At that point he is entitled to compensation.[11]

This reminds me of Orwellian double-speak. The sole purpose of the legislation enacted by the State of Ohio in 1986 is to deprive wrongfully convicted individuals of civil remedy, which is available for any other harm inflicted upon a citizen. This legislation inflicts additional harm upon a person whom the state already has unjustly abused—it puts them in a moral no-man's-land between "not guilty" and "innocent." Thus, it provides quasi-immunity for the state and does little to discourage prosecutorial and police misconduct.

Because of this strange legislation, Samuel Reese Sheppard could not file a civil action against the county for wrongful imprisonment. Instead, the Estate of Sam Sheppard first had to convince a jury that Sheppard was innocent. The fact that what amounts to a third "trial" had to be conducted in a civil proceeding leaves little doubt that fiscal considerations were at play. The need to establish Sheppard's "innocence" was a legal ploy to shield the county government from responsibility for having inflicted damages on Sam Sheppard and his family.

I spent two years working with Gilbert on the Sheppard civil case before the trial began. Throughout this time, the prosecution campaigned to keep me off the witness stand. As an experienced trial lawyer, Gilbert understood that public opinion plays a significant role in such cases. He facilitated the production of a PBS presentation on the Sheppard case. Cynthia Cooper, who coauthored *Mockery of Justice* with Samuel Reese Sheppard, came to Grosse Pointe with a television crew to interview me. A year or so later, Marian Marzynski, a well-known filmmaker and a friend of mine, came to Detroit with a crew to interview me again. There was little doubt that my contributions would play a significant role in the PBS documentary on the Sheppard case.

Shortly before the documentary was to air, I received a conference call from Gilbert and Marzynski, both of whom had just become aware that the prosecution claimed to have devastating information from a professor of psychiatry—information that would expose me as an unethical expert and disqualify me from testifying. I was told that this professor had written a letter describing various unethical practices in which I had allegedly engaged. I told Gilbert and Marzynski that this claim had been made previously, but that the mysterious professor and his letter had never seen the light of day; such claims have been made many times over the years, without any evidence. My reassurances did carry some weight with Gilbert and Marzynski, but the head producer at PBS decided to remove me from the documentary. Thus, the prosecution achieved a small victory. Their attempt to discredit me, however, was ultimately proved a sham created with collaboration of two forensic psychiatrists. Neither Gilbert nor I discovered who the culprits were until the day of the trial.

Shortly before the Sheppard trial was to begin, the prosecution conducted a lengthy discovery deposition of me. The young prosecutor came with a long list of questions to which he adhered for the entire three hours. He had a take-no-prisoners style. His questions were based upon my report, which was by then a few months old. It was written prior to my reviewing a great many documents, which I received after the report was written. The cross-examiner tried to keep me within the limits of my report, but my answers were more comprehensive than the questions. The result was that I was able to get on the record that I had a great deal more to say than the cross-examiner wanted to know. His objective was to impeach me, as if my report constituted my direct examination, but he discovered next to nothing because he limited himself to what he already knew—namely, the content of my report. He fought a good fight on the wrong battlefield. The deposition got the prosecutors nowhere.

On January 20, 2000, Gilbert called me. He told me he was planning to put me on the stand as the trial's last witness. I asked him what his order of witnesses was, and he told me that his first witness would be Samuel Reese Sheppard. Gilbert planned to present all testimony dealing with physical evidence next, laying the foundation for my testimony. Some of the country's most outstanding forensic scientists had evaluated the evidence and concluded that Sheppard could not have committed the murder and that Eberling was most likely the killer, so there was merit to Gilbert's approach. I told him he was doing exactly the opposite of what I would recommend. I considered it a major blunder to begin with Sheppard's son.

I could hear him gulp at the other end of the telephone line: Gilbert is an experienced attorney and does not often hear such comments from expert witnesses. I said, "You are throwing away your advantage of going first by putting on a witness who will be readily cross-examined and who will become a vehicle for the prosecutors to argue their case. You have powerful witnesses and are not using them when they can do you the most good. It is easier to persuade than to dissuade."

I argued that he was putting the cart in front of the horse by focusing on physical evidence. The prosecution's case against Sheppard in two prior trials was almost completely psychological in nature. I told Gilbert: "You are a plaintiff legally, but you are a defendant factually." Theoretically, the county and the prosecution were defending themselves against the charge of wrongful imprisonment. As a practical matter, Sam Sheppard was posthumously facing a third trial for the murder of his wife.

Gilbert agreed that the prosecution's case was built on psychological inferences and on the fact that Sheppard was in the house when his wife was killed. The prosecution also asserted that Sheppard had a motive: he was sexually involved with another woman. These "arguments" made little sense, but they were the basis for the 1954 guilty verdict.

I challenged Gilbert to name a single piece of physical evidence that tied Sheppard to the homicide. He could not name one. I then said, "Let the prosecution present physical evidence and then you can rebut it. Don't try to rebut an argument that has not been made. If the prosecution's case is based upon psychological inferences, then I am your most important witness."

Gilbert accepted my reasoning and said that he would not make Sheppard's son the first witness. We agreed that F. Lee Bailey, the defense lawyer in the 1966 case, would be the first witness; I would testify shortly thereafter. I was not happy about that, since I did not think that Bailey would make a good witness. Most lawyers do poorly on the witness stand. They also have little credibility with the jury as a result of lawyer-bashing.

On the day of the trial, the county's lawyers once again filed an elaborate motion to exclude my testimony. Then, just before I was to take the witness stand, they tried to prevent me from testifying by using the so-called letter of a professor accusing me of ethical violation. According to the prosecution, the letter was from "a Michigan professor" who wrote that "ethical complaints have been filed against Tanay for diagnosing people without examining them, and he, himself, has initiated complaints against peers for simple differences in clinical opinions in forensic cases." None that was true.

Gilbert demanded to see the basis for the accusations against me. We retreated to his office to examine the "evidence." To my astonishment, we discovered that psychiatrist Phillip Resnick was the source of the letter. He solicited it from Denise Koson, another psychiatrist who provided fabricated information. In a hearing before the judge, I testified under oath that these claims were false. After the Sheppard trial, Koson, when requested, declared in a written statement:

Dear Dr. Tanay:

I was mortified to learn of a letter apparently written years ago and the adverse impact you have suffered in your practice, especially in light of some of the language you cited. I apologize profusely and unreservedly and undertake never to repeat such language or comments orally or in writing to anyone, in any forum, public or private. I recant, retract and utterly disavow such comments as baseless and totally without merit. Specifically, I affirm:

1. That I have no personal knowledge of your filing ethical complaints against any other psychiatrists;

2. That I have no personal knowledge of ethical complaints having been filed against you;

3 That I have no personal knowledge that you charge exorbitant fees for testimony.

Resnick at first tried hide behind Koson and claimed that neither he nor Koson had the letter. When Resnick realized that he would face an ethics complaint and a civil lawsuit, he apologized in writing. I did not file an ethics complaint or file a lawsuit for defamation because that would ruin Resnick's career as a forensic psychiatrist. I have an aversion to vindictiveness.

Gilbert told me that in twenty-five years of practice, he had never seen such vigorous and "dirty" efforts to win a case. However, the prosecutors' behavior in this case was not new to me. Lawyers commonly try to exclude, by any means necessary, the testimony of a witness who damages their case.[12]

When I arrived in court, ready finally to testify, the prosecution handed Gilbert a thick document detailing why the judge should not permit me to testify, and if he did, what kind of limitations should be imposed. Gilbert said, "That's what happens every day. They've got six lawyers doing nothing but thinking up memos that put roadblocks in our way." A series of legal skirmishes followed. The prosecution argued that if I testified before the jury I would usurp the jury's functions. I knew that the objective was to eliminate or limit my testimony, and I tried to neutralize these arguments. According to law, an expert witness should not address the "ultimate issue"—in this case, guilt or innocence. However, an expert's function is to assist the jury in reaching a verdict. The notion that one can testify that the defendant could not have been the perpetrator without also "addressing the ultimate issue" is a legal fiction.

During this hearing, I was aware that the press was watching. I stressed that in my opinion Sheppard could not be guilty of murdering his wife, and that all evidence pointed to Eberling. While the judge asked me questions, I commented on Eberling's many confessions that had been disregarded. Finally, around 12:30 P.M., the judge said he had to step out for a few minutes and would come back with a decision. (I was told that the judge had a clerk with whom he often consulted before making his decisions.) After a short time, he returned to ask me a few more questions; he then returned to his chambers.

When the judge returned, he asked me to leave the room and announced to the lawyers what the rules would be for my testimony. When Gilbert and the other lawyers emerged, they looked glum. The judge had determined that my testimony about Eberling and Sheppard was character testimony, and therefore inadmissible. I testified during the hearing that what the prosecutors called "character testimony" should have been admissible since it was an element of the crime attributed to Sheppard—namely, that he was a sadistic sexual murderer. The judge listened to me but he accepted the legal ploy that any references to the personality of the principal figures would be character testimony and therefore not admissible. This was quite a victory for the prosecution and severely limited the usefulness of my testimony.

On our way to Gilbert's office we talked about what to do next. At this point it was clear that my views carried considerable weight and would determine our next move. I struggled with a number of ideas. I realized that our countless hours of preparation in reviewing the voluminous case records had been a waste of time, as we would not be permitted to use them. We had to regroup quickly. I concluded that if we tried to present my testimony as we had prepared it, it would be inadequate because most of the time would be spent on legal arguments. I said, "They have castrated us and we have to accept it." I proposed that we limit ourselves to purely educational testimony that would be relatively immune to objections. We would never mention Sam Sheppard or Richard Eberling. I would talk in theoretical terms, but it would be obvious that I was discussing the case at hand.

My direct testimony went beautifully. Gilbert is an excellent lawyer and the two of us made a good team. I was permitted to go in front of the blackboard and address the jury on the psychology of homicide and discuss the different varieties of homicides. Some observers later said, "You could hear a pin drop in the courtroom throughout the presentation." There was not a single objection. In the process, I conveyed most of the points that we wanted to make about Eberling and Sheppard, without ever using their names. I talked in this fashion for about an hour and a half.

Prosecutor Steve Dever, who by all previous indications was supposed to destroy me on cross-examination, approached me with great politeness, even deference. I readily agreed with most of his preliminary questions. However, later on, I was able to reiterate my main points even more effectively than on direct, because Dever was opening doors and I began quoting from the record. This was possible because the cross-examiner brought up Sheppard and Eberling by name, allowing me to apply my direct testimony about the psychology of homicide specifically to Sheppard and Eberling.

I also brought up something that, to my surprise, no one else had previously discussed in court—namely, that the assailant must have muffled Marilyn Sheppard's ability to scream. This would explain why the little boy who was sleeping next door never awoke and why Sam Sheppard did not respond sooner. I also had an opportunity to discuss rape and how sadistic rapists are surprised when victims fight back. I did not use Eberling's name, but it was apparent whom I had in mind.

Dever insisted that Sheppard could have slipped into an altered state of consciousness and killed his wife in a state of rage. I know from experience that a lawyer wants to finish on a high note, so I knew that the cross-examination was coming to an end. I turned to the jury and said in an emotional voice that only a monster could have done this. I hit the lectern and said, "Blow after blow without coming to his senses! No, that's not spousal homicide. A husband could not do it. A normal person could not do it, no matter what kind of rage. Only a monster could do it!" The courtroom was silent. Dever said quietly, "No more questions."

In the hallway after my testimony I was surrounded by students from a nearby college criminal justice class who congratulated me for my impressive performance on the witness stand. Even Mason, the elected prosecutor, shook my hand and said, "Job well done." I gave him credit for being a gracious opponent. I had thought he would be angry with me because during my testimony I had observed that he was making faces, which I called to the court's attention and the judge said such behavior was not acceptable; but good lawyers don't hold grudges if you beat them fair and square.

Subsequent to my testimony, the prosecution filed a brief that requested the court's permission to introduce rebuttal testimony. They used my opinions about spousal homicide as a basis for arguing that Sheppard's affair with Susan Hayes precipitated an explosive episode in which he killed his wife. The logic of this argument escapes me, and it is clearly a misapplication of my opinions on spousal homicide.

In my opinion, the crime scene contradicted a rage homicide and was consistent with extreme sadistic behavior. Sheppard could not have produced such a sadistic crime scene and could not have inflicted his spinal injuries upon himself. Forensic experts had disproved the prosecution's theory in all three trials. Nonetheless, the prosecution argued that in my book *The Murderers*[13] I referred to the "three-day syndrome" typical of explosive rage-type homicides. The prosecution believed that the syndrome matched the Sheppard situation. This was a distortion of my testimony. I use the term "three-day syndrome" to describe a sadomasochistic relationship's escalation of tension to some provocative episode. If the tension persists for three days without resolution, an explosive discharge of aggression often occurs. For "three-day syndrome" to apply, the homicide is generally a rage-type event. As indicated, the Sheppard crime scene was not consistent with a rage reaction but with the sadistic, prolonged, torturous activity of a sexual psychopath.

My testimony in the Sheppard posthumous retrial was standard fare for such cases. The prosecutor nevertheless argued that my forensic psychiatric testimony be excluded. At the same time, the prosecution introduced the report of a "profiler" to address issues that are traditionally the domain of forensic psychiatrists. Imagine that a forensic pathologist gave testimony on the cause of death. Now imagine that the rebuttal witness was an undertaker. An equivalent situation occurs when a forensic psychiatrist, one recognized as a national authority on the psychology of homicide, is rebutted by a retired FBI agent profiler. The Cuyahoga County Prosecutor's office had hired former FBI profiler Gregg McCrary as an expert witness to rebut my testimony. Profiling is a method of generating characteristics of possible perpetrators (suspects) based upon the crime itself and the crime-scene evidence. Profiling is an investigative technique.When someone fits a profile, it's possible that they are guilty. But mere possibility has no probative value. The degree of probability is critical. The National Institute of Justice has reported that 26 percent of primary suspects who underwent DNA tests were found to have been erroneously accused or convicted.[14] In a 2007 *New Yorker* article, best-selling author Malcolm Gladwell compared criminal profilers to astrologists and psychics. He cited a study by the British Home Office that "analyzed 184 crimes, to see how many times profilers led to the arrest of a criminal." The profile worked in five of the cases. That's just 2.7 percent.

In his testimony, McCrary argued that Marilyn Sheppard had been a low-risk victim, which made her a likely victim of domestic violence. This statement makes no sense. While it may or may not be statistically correct, it has no relevance when we are dealing with a population of one.

McCrary also testified that "facial battery and head trauma is uncommon for sadistic homicide and very common in domestic homicide. . . . Blunt force trauma is very rare in sadistic homicides."[15] Having examined hundreds of spousal homicides, I categorically state that this is contrary to my experience and to psychological principles. Sadistic murderers take pleasure in inflicting injuries, whereas domestic homicides are explosive discharges of aggression, most commonly perpetrated with a firearm (in the United States) or a knife (in Europe).

McCrary also argued that in high-risk environments offenders typically spend no more time than necessary to perpetrate the crime. He argued that offenders who remain for a longer time often have a legitimate reason for being at the scene and are therefore not worried about being interrupted or discovered. Marilyn Sheppard's killer, McCrary claimed, had spent an inordinate amount of time at this crime scene. In reality, sadistic sexual serial killers need time to gratify their morbid cravings.

Last but not least, McCrary claimed that the crime scene had been set up to appear as an intruder homicide. He claimed that the point of entry (in the basement) made no sense for this type of crime and that there was evidence of overkill, meaning more effort than was needed to do the job. In reality, sadistic-sexual psychopaths typically perpetrate crimes with a high degree of risk (see chapter 6 on Ted Bundy). However, McCrary concluded, "When you look at the case closely and distill it to its essence you can see that it's nothing more than a staged domestic homicide."

The very opposite was the case. The prosecution wanted us to believe that a law-abiding man known for his altruism killed his wife in a rage, tortured her, inflicted thirty-five wounds on her body, and disfigured her face—all in order to mislead investigators. Physically and psychologically, it would have been impossible for Sheppard to stage this crime scene. He suffered a well-documented concussion and fracture of his cervical vertebra. All of the earlier medical evidence that Sheppard's injuries could not have been self-inflicted were corroborated in the civil case by Dr. William F. Fallon, Jr., a consultant whose qualifications included being fellow of the American College of Surgery and director of Metro Health Medical Center. Fallon issued a report dated July 29, 1999, based on his review of the extensive records of Sheppard's injuries when he was treated at Bay View Hospital between July 4 and July 8, 1954. Fallon concluded, "The pattern, distribution, and nature of wounds are all such that it would be impossible to characterize these as being self-inflicted, intentional, or having been sustained in a fall." Furthermore, the sadistic mutilation of Marilyn Sheppard's body and the evidence of sexual assault were inconsistent with any type of perpetrator but a sadistic serial killer.

McCrary had no qualifications that entitled him to offer opinions on the psychology of homicide. In fact, he had performed no work in this case that would justify such opinions even if he were qualified to do so. His testimony should not have been admitted, and once he did testify, his testimony should have been stricken. The testimony by a team of the country's most experienced and respected forensic scientists (almost all of whom worked pro bono) demonstrated persuasively that Dr. Sheppard did not kill his wife, but our efforts were in vain. The jury took very little time to rule in favor of the county, which means that in the eyes of the court Dr. Sheppard was not guilty and not innocent. I was disappointed that the opinions of America's leading forensic scientists and conclusive evidence was ignored by the jury. However, I have enough experience with the power of propaganda not to be surprised by this injustice.

NOTES

1. *Cleveland Press,* July 30, 1954.
2. Trial transcript in my possession.
3. Kirk's report, in my possession.
4. I was scheduled to interview Eberling in prison, but the day before the scheduled visit he died. I rely here on documents about his history, his tape-recorded telephone call from June 28, 1998, and a videotape of his interview with a reporter. Among these documents is a report dated March 19, 1995, by a private firm retained by Terry Gilbert, the lawyer for the estate of Sam Sheppard in the 1996 civil trial. Gilbert retained the firm AMSEC Loss Control Services, Inc., of Middlebrook, Virginia, which produced a 200-plus-page report documenting evidence that Eberling was the serial killer who killed Marilyn Sheppard.
5. *Cleveland Press,* July 20, 1954.
6. *Cleveland Press,* July 21, 1954.
7. Patrick V. Murphy and Thomas Plate, *Commissioner: A View from the Top of American Law Enforcement* (New York: Simon & Schuster, 1977).

8. Louis B. Seltzer, *The Years Were Good* (Cleveland: World Pub. Co, 1956), 265.

9. *Cleveland Press*, July 30, 1954.

10. *Time* Magazine, July 24, 1964.

11. Personal communication with Terry Gilbert, September 8, 2007.

12. After the Sheppard trial, the originator of the false information wrote to me to express his mortification, retracted his lies, and promised never to spread these lies. And when the psychiatrist realized that he would face an ethics complaint and a civil lawsuit, he retreated and profusely apologized in writing. He openly said to me, in the presence of others, how much he appreciated my not pursuing action against him.

13. Emanuel Tanay, M.D., with Lucy Freeman, *The Murderers* (New York: Bobbs-Merrill Company, 1976).

14. Reported by innocenceproject.org, accessed 1/15/2010.

15. Jack P. DeSario and William D. Mason, *Dr. Sam Sheppard on Trial* (Kent, Ohio: Kent State University Press, 2003), 291.

Michigan Attorney General Frank Kelly chats with Emanuel Tanay before giving the keynote address at a banquet in Tanay's honor. 1998.

9

THE LEGACY OF
THE JOHN HINCKLEY,
JR., VERDICT

Most homicide perpetrators whose state of mind would justify an uncontested insanity verdict end up being charged with first-degree murder, and the prosecution usually prevails. Getting a conviction on a lesser offense (such as second-degree murder or manslaughter) is the goal in most insanity defense cases. Here is an example.

A grossly psychotic Michigan man named Bartley Dobben, age twenty-six, worked in a foundry even though he had been diagnosed as a schizophrenic who suffered religious visions and had a history of bizarre behavior. In 1989, he, his wife, and their two sons, Bartley Joel, two years old, and Peter David, fifteen months old, were traveling to a family Thanksgiving dinner. Dobben insisted that they stop by his workplace, the Cannon-Muskegon Corporation foundry. He took his two boys into the foundry with him and later returned without the children. His wife asked about the children and was told that the father had placed his sons, as a sacrifice to God, into a red-hot foundry ladle. He explained that he was saving them from hell.

Dobben was charged with first-degree murder and his defense lawyer asked me to examine the defendant who was obviously criminally not responsible. Even the Michigan Forensic Center, a state agency, found Dobben insane. I informed the lawyer that this was one of the rare cases known among lawyers as a "walk through." It turned out that, contrary to established practice, an ambitious prosecutor was claiming that Dobben was sane. The prosecution retained the services of Dr. Abe Halpern, past President of American Academy of Psychiatry and Law and a close friend of mine. His testimony was dominated by ideological antagonism to the insanity defense. Clinically, Dr. Halpern's testimony was not plausible, however it appealed to the biases of the jurors. The result was a miscarriage of justice and a misuse of psychiatry.

THE INSANITY DEFENSE

The insanity defense consists of a psychiatric component called "severe mental illness" and a legal component called " legal test," which asks whether the defendant knew right from wrong. The term "not guilty by reason of insanity," unlike the British term "guilty but mentally ill," is counterintuitive. A defendant pleading not guilty by reason of insanity does not deny committing the homicide; on the contrary, he admits it. The prosecutor, as the moving party, proves that the defendant is factually "guilty" of the homicide; the defense lawyer faces the difficult task of un-ringing the bell by asserting that the defendant is now "not guilty by reason of insanity."

In the United States during the 1960s, many states adopted the American Legal Institute Test (ALI-Test) for legal insanity. Under this test, "a person is not responsible for criminal conduct if, at the time of such conduct, as a result of mental disease or defect, he lacks substantial capacity either to appreciate the criminality of his conduct or to conform his conduct to the requirements of the law."

The Hinckley case (which I will examine later) resulted in a return, in many states, to the ancient McNaghten test formulated in 1843 in England. According the McNaghten rule, the accused is judged legally insane if he could not distinguish right from wrong at the time when he committed the crime.

The law presumes that adults have the mental capacity to make moral decisions. A severe mental illness or organic brain damage destroys this capacity. The psychiatric contribution to the legal decision on the issue of criminal responsibility is the determination of whether the defendant suffers a severe mental illness. Mental illness is a matter of fact; knowing right from wrong is a matter of moral values. Mental illness is an impairment of the ability to deal with reality. The ability to make moral judgments presumes being in touch with reality.

Wrongfulness, like beauty, is in the eyes of the beholder. Wrongfulness cannot be observed or quantified. The ambiguity of the term makes arbitrary judgments inevitable. I will give an example from a case I discuss in detail later. In the second trial of Andrea Yates, Dr. Michael Welner testified on behalf of the prosecution. He gave as one of the reasons that Andrea Yates knew right from wrong the fact that she called the police after she drowned her five children to save them from Satan. Does this prove knowledge of wrongfulness or the opposite? A defendant who calls the police, it could be argued, does not believe that he or she did something wrong. The judgment that a defendant knows the difference between right and wrong is inherently arbitrary.

To prevail with a first-degree murder charge, the prosecution must prove premeditation, voluntary action, and a sound mind. A person who is severely mentally ill is unable to assume the role of defendant when the crime involves a state of mind known in the law as *mens rea*, or "bad mind."

At the various stages of the proceedings of a criminal trial, the law asks not only whether the defendant was severely mentally ill but also whether he could pass the legal "test." The capacity to know right from wrong is a question to which there is no empirical answer and therefore it is an invitation to arbitrary decision making. In most insanity defense trials there is the appearance that all the elements of a crime, including the defendant being of sound mind, have been satisfied if this so-called test is answered in the affirmative. I have no difficultly testifying that a severely psychotic individual is unable to stand trial because he has insufficient mental ability to assist in his defense due to his severe psychosis. In order for me to testify that a person is able to stand trial, or is criminally responsible, I have to conclude that he does not suffer from severe psychotic illness. Whenever I have testified for the prosecution against an insanity defense, the defendant was not a severely psychotic person.

Psychotics who commit crimes, such as Andrea Yates, have little in common with sane and deliberate killers. Paradoxically, a psychotic or emotionally disturbed killer is more likely to be convicted of murder in this country than is a hit man. A professional criminal is difficult to apprehend. Once in custody, the case against him is circumstantial, for he will have left little incriminating evidence.

Today the insanity defense, like the care of the mentally ill, is as a practical matter an endangered species. In the 1970s, deinstitutionalization resulted in a shift of the care of schizophrenics from the dismantled state hospital system to outpatient clinics, which have few resources to manage severe psychotic illness.[1] The current practice is to hospitalize an acutely psychotic individual and then discharge him or her after a short hospital stay. This approach is not based on science but on politics. In this system, many severely mentally ill persons will, sooner or later, violate some law and be incarcerated. As a result, our nation's jails have become the default institutions for our mentally ill.[2]

The Associated Press reported on September 6, 2008, that approximately "50 large centers for mentally disabled people have closed nationwide over the past 20 years," and "fewer than 60 state-operated institutions that care for more than 200 residents remain open in the U.S." Researchers from the University of Minnesota noted that "the number of mentally disabled adults living in large institutions has declined over the past 30 years from 150,000 to 37,000." I recall the time when the nationwide population of mental institutions was 600,000.

Even though the insanity defense can theoretically be asserted in a variety of crimes, it is most often introduced when the charge is first-degree murder. In our society, first-degree murder is punishable by the death penalty or life imprisonment without parole. In the hundreds of insanity-defense cases in which I have testified, I do not recall a single case in which the charge was less than first-degree murder. I know innocent defendants who, faced with the charge of first-degree murder in a death-penalty state, accepted the offer to plead guilty to manslaughter.

The insanity defense is commonly perceived as a fraudulent tactic. Defense lawyers who assert the insanity defense are usually doing it for the first time in their careers and are often ineffective. Many of these lawyers do not exclusively practice criminal law and may have very limited trial experience. Compounding this situation is the fact that most psychiatric experts generally have little experience with the insanity defense. Forensic psychiatry is popular among psychiatrists as an academic subject, but few have sufficient practical experience. Psychiatrists with a real understanding of homicidal behavior and legal intricacies are rare.

In other Western countries, mitigating and extenuating circumstances are taken into account more consistently. French juries were first empowered to consider undefined extenuating circumstances in 1832. Anything that could mitigate punishment became admissible and could affect the verdict. This is still the case in most European countries. But American juries are kept uninformed about the past and future of the accused. The jury sees the defendant primarily as the perpetrator of a "murder."

The insanity defense is essential to justice because some homicides are committed by severely mentally ill individuals. Some homicides are impulsive acts by otherwise law-abiding citizens who enter a dissociative state. The real issue in such cases is not whether the crime was committed but whether the perpetrator will spend his or her life confined to a prison because the prosecutor and or a judge finds it necessary to prove that he or she is tough on crime.

The attacks on insanity have a long tradition and lead to practical elimination of this defense.[3] The result is that American prisons hold increasing numbers of psychotics. The U.S. Department of Justice issued a release on this topic on September 6, 2006, entitled, "Study Finds More Than Half of All Prison and Jail Inmates Have Mental Health Problems."

Fifty-four percent of local jail inmates had symptoms of mania, 30 percent major depression, and 24 percent psychotic disorder, such as delusions or hallucinations. Forty-three percent of state prisoners had symptoms of mania, 23 percent major depression, and 15 percent psychotic disorder. Thirty-five percent of federal prisoners had symptoms of mania, 16 percent major depression, and 10 percent psychotic disorder. Female inmates had higher rates of mental health problems than male inmates—in state prisons, 73 percent of females and 55 percent of males; in federal prisons, 61 percent of females and 44 percent of males; and in local jails, 75 percent of females and 63 percent of males.

This situation is cruel for the mentally ill prisoners, highly stressful for the non–mentally ill prisoners, and very expensive to maintain. The cost of keeping a mentally ill person in prison is far higher than was the cost of keeping him or her in our now-defunct state hospital system.

The much-maligned state hospital system served us well until it fell victim to propaganda. In 1953, in an Illinois State Hospital I encountered a memorable patient who had been civilly committed after demonstrating his "dangerousness" by amputating his own testicles and penis. I asked this patient, who had been at Elgin State Hospital for twenty-some years what brought him to the hospital, he answered, "I came to get my mind straightened out and found a place where living is possible." This is the essence of the old concept of asylum, the need for which has not been eliminated by the ever-elusive cure for schizophrenia. Elgin State Hospital (which had six thousand patients) no longer exists. My next employment as a psychiatrist was at Ypsilanti State Hospital, which also been eliminated. The hospital grounds are now occupied by the Huron Valley Correctional Institution (a prison). So, where did all the patients go?

THE TRIAL OF JOHN HINCKLEY, JR.

On March 30, 1981, John Hinckley, Jr., shot President Ronald Reagan. Press Secretary James Brady, Police Officer Thomas Delahanty, and Secret Service Agent Timothy J. McCarthy were severely wounded in the attack. Hinckley's reason for this attack was his psychotic preoccupation with the actress Jodie Foster. He was trying to impress her with "the greatest love offering in the history of the world": attempting to kill President Reagan. Hinckley was not deterred by the presence of police officers, which would have qualified him for the insanity defense under the old English law.[4]

The trial of John Hinckley, Jr., was a watershed event in the evolution of attitudes on the insanity defense in the United States. After Hinckley was found legally insane the news media promoted the idea that the Hinckley verdict was a miscarriage of justice. There are two criteria that can be used to evaluate any trial: the validity of the claims made by the adversaries and the observance of the legal process.

The validity of claims is uncertain, since we are dealing with a complex interplay of facts regarding the interpretation of the legal standards for legal insanity. However there is no doubt that the Hinckley trial paid deference to the legal process. The participants were respectful of each other. The judge, the prosecutor, the defense lawyer, and the experts for the defense recognized that each of them had a legitimate argument to present to the jury. Dr. Park Dietz, the lead expert for the prosecution, was the sole exception: he trivialized Hinckley's illness and implied that the defense subverted the legal process by coaching the defendant.

After the Hinckley trial, politically motivated legislators all over the country enacted strict restrictions designed to prevent "abuse" of the insanity defense. Idaho, Kansas, Montana, and Utah have abolished the insanity defense altogether. Before the Hinckley verdict, the insanity defense had been used in less than 2 percent of all felony cases and was unsuccessful in almost 75 percent of the trials in which it was used. The Hinckley verdict transformed the insanity defense into a theoretical concept. The Federal Rules of Evidence were drastically modified. Rule 704(b) states:

> The purpose of this amendment is to eliminate the confusing spectacle of competing expert witnesses testifying to directly contradictory conclusions as to the ultimate legal issue to be found by the trier of fact. Under this proposal, expert psychiatric testimony would be limited to presenting and explaining their diagnoses, such as whether the defendant had a severe mental disease or defect and what the characteristics of such a disease or defect, if any, may have been. The basis for this limitation on expert testimony in insanity cases is ably stated by the American Psychiatric Association:
>
> > [It] is clear that psychiatrists are experts in medicine, not the law. As such, it is clear that the psychiatrist's first obligation and expertise in the courtroom is to "do psychiatry," i.e., to present medical information and opinion about the defendant's mental state and motivation and to explain in detail the reason for his medical-psychiatric conclusions. When, however, "ultimate issue" questions are formulated by the law and put to the expert witness who must then say "yea" or "nay," then the expert witness is required to make a leap in logic. He no longer addresses himself to medical concepts but instead must infer or intuit what is in fact unspeakable, namely, the probable relationship between medical concepts and legal or moral constructs such as free will. These impermissible leaps in logic made by expert witnesses confuse the jury. . . . Juries thus find themselves listening to conclusory and seemingly contradictory psychiatric testimony that defendants are either "sane" or "insane" or that they do or do not meet the relevant legal test for insanity. This state of affairs does considerable injustice to psychiatry and, we believe, possibly to criminal defendants. In fact, in many criminal insanity trials both prosecution and defense psychiatrists do agree about the nature and even the extent of mental disorder exhibited by the defendant at the time of the act.[5]

Contradictory opinions are part and parcel of the adversary system. Appellate judges more often than not arrive at contradictory conclusions. Scientific conferences are frequently dominated by contradictory views. None of these diverse opinions are considered to be a "confusing spectacle." The American Psychiatric Association spoke of "injustice to psychiatry"; what they really meant was public opinion of psychiatry.

The Hinckley verdict was a triumph of justice. The evidence was overwhelming that he suffered from severe mental illness. The jury had little choice but to follow the instructions of the trial judge. The *New York Times* reported on May 2, 1982, that "Judge Barrington D. Parker ruled today that to convict John W. Hinckley Jr. of shooting President Reagan and three other men, prosecutors must prove beyond a reasonable doubt that he was sane at the time of the shootings, on March 30, 1981." It would have been a mockery of justice if Hinckley had been found sane beyond reasonable doubt. Let us look at the facts of this case.

HINCKLEY'S BACKGROUND AND CRIME

John Warnock Hinckley, Jr., was born in Ardmore, Oklahoma, on May 29, 1955. He was the youngest of the three children of John W. Hinckley, Sr., a successful and wealthy chairman and president of the Vanderbilt Energy Corporation. JoAnn Moore Hinckley was a home-maker and loving mother. Hinckley's history is a classic example of the development of schizophrenia. He was withdrawn for most of his life, and during seven years of college he accomplished nothing. His fellow classmates rarely saw him in the company of others. In December 1979, Hinckley took a photograph of himself holding a gun to his temple. He played Russian roulette twice in November and once in December of the same year.

Hinckley's delusional obsession with Foster began when he saw the 1976 film *Taxi Driver*. The movie features psychotic cabbie Travis Bickle (played by Robert De Niro), who has problems relating to people in general and to women in particular. Bickle is interested in Betsy, who works for a presidential candidate. Bickel is unable to attract her attention and decides to assassinate the presidential candidate so that he may win Betsy's admiration. Since he is unable to get close enough to the candidate to kill him, he shifts his homicidal target. In an effort to rescue a young prostitute (played by Foster) from her depraved life-style, Bickle shoots the young prostitute's pimp and other inhabitants of the brothel where she is working. In the film, the psychotic killer is not prosecuted but celebrated as a hero. Hinckley saw the movie at least fifteen times and bought the soundtrack to the film and listened to it for hours.

Hinckley was not exacting about which famous man he had to kill to gain the love of Jodie Foster or bring about his own death.[6] Hinckley had stalked President Jimmy Carter. On October 2, 1980, he went to one of Carter's reelection campaign appearances but left his three guns and two rifles in his hotel room. When Hinckley went to Nashville during another Carter campaign stop, he was arrested when airport security officials found handguns in his suitcases; the arsenal was confiscated. Hinckley was fined $62.50 and sent on his way. Soon after, Hinckley bought two more handguns.

Hinckley's parents were concerned with his increasingly bizarre behavior. In the fall of 1980, they arranged a consultation with John Hopper, MD, a psychiatrist practicing in Evergreen, Colorado. Dr. Hopper met with Hinckley several times over the course of four months.

Dr. Hopper failed to recognize Hinckley's schizophrenia and treated him with biofeedback, a treatment used to help patients cope with stress. Dr. Hopper also prescribed Valium, a common tranquilizer. In February 1981, Dr. Hopper persuaded Hinckley's parents to force their son to leave home in order to make him less dependent. He advised them to get tough. Hinckley's father testified during his son's trial that following Dr. Hopper's advice to "kick John out" was "the greatest mistake of my life." I was retained as an expert on the issue of Hopper's malpractice, and I relate that story later in this chapter.

It is typical for schizophrenic patients to undertake aimless travels, so Hopper's recommendation actually accommodated Hinckley's pathological needs. Hinckley went to Washington, where President-elect Ronald Reagan was at the time; to New York, where John Lennon had just been assassinated; and to New Haven, Connecticut, where Jodie Foster attended college. While in New York, Hinckley contemplated killing himself in front of the Dakota Hotel on the exact spot where Lennon had been shot.

On New Year's Eve of 1980, three months before his attempt to kill President Reagan, Hinckley recorded a very disturbed monologue in which he spoke of not really wanting "to hurt" Jodie Foster, his fears about losing his sanity, and the likelihood of "suicide city" if he failed to win Foster's love.

> John Lennon is dead. The world is over. Forget it. It's just gonna be insanity, if I even make it through the first few days. . . . I still regret having to go on with 1981. . . . I don't know why people wanna live. John Lennon is dead. . . . I still think—I still think about Jodie all the time. That's all I think about really. That, and John Lennon's death. They were sorta

binded together. I hate New Haven with a mortal passion. I've been up there many times, not stalking her, really, but just looking after her. I was going to take her away for a while there, but I don't know. I am so sick I can't even do that. . . . It'll be total suicide city. I mean, I couldn't care less. Jodie is the only thing that matters now. Anything I might do in 1981 would be solely for Jodie Foster's sake.

My obsession is Jodie Foster. I've gotta, I've gotta find her and talk to her some way in person or something. That's all I want her to know, is that I love her. I don't want to hurt her. I think I'd rather just see her not, not on earth, than being with other guys. I wouldn't want to stay here on earth without her.[7]

In the recorded monologue, Hinckley assured Foster that he was not a "dangerous person." On the one hand, he wanted to win her love; on the other hand, he was uncertain about whether or not he would harm her. In my view, Foster was in great danger. In May 1980, Hinckley read in a newspaper that Foster had entered Yale University. He promptly enrolled in a Yale writing course in order to be near her and attempted to establish contact with her, leaving letters and poems in her mailbox. He managed to have two telephone conversations with Jodie, during which he assured her that he was not a "dangerous person." Hinckley continued to be preoccupied with his delusional idea that by assassinating a president of the United States he would gain Foster's respect and love.

In February 1981, Hinckley flew to Hollywood. He stayed there for only a day and then traveled by bus to Washington, D.C., where he checked into the Park Central Hotel on March 29. The following day, Monday, March 30, Hinckley wrote a letter to Foster describing his plan to assassinate Reagan in order to impress her with this "historical deed":[8]

Dear Jodie,
There is a definite possibility that I will be killed in my attempt to get Reagan. It is for this very reason that I am writing you this letter now. As you well know by now I love you very much. . . .

I've got to do something now to make you understand, in no uncertain terms, that I am doing all of this for your sake! By sacrificing my freedom and possibly my life, I hope to change your mind about me. This letter is being written only an hour before I leave for the Hilton Hotel. Jodie, I'm asking you to please look into your heart and at least give me the chance, with this historical deed, to gain your respect and love. I love you forever.[9]

Hinckley took a cab to the Washington Hilton, where Reagan was to speak at a labor convention at 1:45 P.M. At 1:30 P.M., John Hinckley, Jr., shot Reagan and several people near him.

THE TRIAL

Testimony from expert witnesses during Hinckley's trial made it clear that he had suffered from schizophrenia. Defense expert Dr. William Carpenter, one of the most-cited schizophrenia researchers, testified that Hinckley suffered from schizophrenia. Carpenter had never testified in court before but gave very persuasive testimony in this case. He diagnosed Hinckley as suffering from "process schizophrenia," a pernicious form of this grave illness. Few psychiatrists would question this diagnosis. According to Carpenter, Hinckley identified with Travis Bickle and "picked up in largely automatic ways many [of his] attributes." Hinckley imitated Bickle's preference for army fatigue jackets and boots and developed a fascination with guns. Like Bickle, Hinckley started to drink peach brandy and began keeping a diary.[10]

Dr. David Bear, then an assistant professor of psychiatry at Harvard Medical School, agreed with Carpenter's diagnosis that Hinckley was psychotic. Roger M. Adelman, the senior prosecutor, noted in cross-examining Dr. Bear that Dr. Sally Johnson, a psychiatrist at the Federal Correctional Institution in Butner, N.C., had concluded after fifty-five interviews with the defendant that his preoccupation with Miss Foster was not a "delusion" because he realized "that a relationship was not likely to develop."[11] "I believe she was absolutely incorrect," Dr. Bear replied. Ernest Prelinger, a Yale psychologist, testified about the psychological testing that he performed on Hinckley. With an I.Q. of 113, Hinckley could be classified as "bright normal" on the intelligence scale, but on the Minnesota Multiphasic Personality Inventory (MMPI) Hinckley was near the peak of abnormality.

Dr. Park Dietz, the prosecution's expert, disagreed with Drs. Carpenter and Bear, describing Hinckley as a spoiled, lazy, self-concerned, manipulative, rich kid.

Dietz testified that Hinckley had not been "occupationally successful" and therefore "turned to high-publicity crime." He claimed that Hinckley was "in love with himself" and not obsessed with Foster at all, only infatuated. He also implied that Hinckley might be feigning insanity to avoid serving time in prison. The jury, made up mostly of poor African Americans, rejected Dietz's testimony that "Mr. Hinckley has not been psychotic at any time." Dietz claimed that the defense, as part of its strategy, had "coached" Hinckley on how to appear more disturbed than he was—a rather serious charge for which there was no evidence.

Dietz argued that Hinckley's ability to conform his behavior to norms in the past, including the fact that he hadn't drawn a gun in Dayton or Nashville, and that at Blair House in Washington, D.C., he hadn't shot, was evidence that Hinckley could have controlled himself again on March 30th outside the Hilton Hotel. "At no point has Mr. Hinckley stated to me that he had a compulsion or a drive to assassinate or to commit other crimes," Dietz testified.

Dietz also argued that Hinckley's ability to make other decisions on March 30, such as what to eat for breakfast and other personal decisions like taking a shower or buying a newspaper, showed that he was not mentally ill. "He was not a man incapable on that day of making decisions about his life, about which of these relatively minor things to do. He deliberated and made a decision to survey the scene at the Hilton Hotel. There was no voice commanding him to do that. There was no drive within him pushing him to do that." Dietz pointed to Hinckley's hiding his weapon from people he encountered at the hotel and on his way to the scene of the shooting and his willingness to wait until he had a clear shot of the president as further evidence of Hinckley's sanity. "A man driven, a man out of control, would not have the capacity to wait at that moment for the best shot."[12]

In my view, Dietz's examples illustrated the severity of Hinckley's mental illness, not the lack thereof. The fact that Hinckley did some things that normal people do, like take a shower, did not make him sane. Hinckley was an obviously mentally ill defendant engaged in an act driven by his delusions. Hinckley's delusional behavior and testimony of an authority on schizophrenia established the diagnosis beyond doubt. On June 21, 1982, after seven weeks of testimony and three days of deliberation, a jury found Hinckley "not guilty by reason of insanity."

This verdict has stood the test of time; Hinckley's schizophrenia has persisted, and more than a quarter-century later he is still confined to

St. Elizabeth's Hospital in Washington, D.C., a federal institution for mentally ill people who have been "acquitted by reason of insanity" or are unable to stand trial because of mental illness.

THE APPROPRIATENESS OF THE VERDICT

After Hinckley's shooting spree at the Hilton, James Brady and others who were injured sued Hopper for medical malpractice.[13] I was retained by the lawyer representing the plaintiffs in this lawsuit as an expert witness, and I reviewed a great many documents dealing with the case.

Medical malpractice is the failure of a physician to follow the accepted standards of practice resulting in harm to the patient. The standard of care is usually established by expert testimony, and I was prepared to give such testimony. In my opinion Hinckley was in need of admission to a psychiatric hospital, where he would have received antipsychotic medication. However, Dr. Hopper prescribed a tranquilizer because he failed to recognize that his patient was a paranoid schizophrenic. The combination of wrong diagnosis and inappropriate treatment constituted gross negligence. There was no malpractice trial in the Hinckley case because the appellate court ruled that the plaintiffs did not have a cause of action as a matter of law. I presume that if the parents had filed a malpractice lawsuit on behalf of their son a cause of action would exist. Contrary to the propaganda promulgated by the insurance industry, most actual medical malpractice does not lead to litigation.

Since there was no malpractice lawsuit we have to rely upon the information developed during the criminal trial of John Hinckley. During Hinckley's insanity trial both parents had testified about John's psychiatric treatment. His mother, Jo Ann Hinckley, testified on direct examination:

> John seemed to be going downhill, downhill, downhill and becoming more withdrawn, more antisocial, more depressed, and more down on himself. He was just discouraged and we were just terribly worried about him. . . . We didn't know what was wrong, but we knew something wasn't right. . . . We wanted John to be self-supporting, to be a happy child, to

stand on his own two feet. . . . The harder we tried to push him from us, the harder he tried to stay. . . . Dr. Hopper strongly advised us not to do it [to institutionalize John]. He talked us out of it. . . . Dr. Hopper said, "No, don't do it. It will really make a cripple out of John if you put him in an institution."[14]

Describing dropping John off at the Denver Airport, three days before the shootings, Jo Ann Hinckley testified:

I broke down for the first time and gave him some money of my own. I just couldn't stand to see him go off without any money. . . . John got out of the car and I couldn't even look at him. He said, "Well, Mom, I want to thank you for everything you've done for me." I said, "You're very welcome" and I said it so coldly . . . and then I drove off and that was the last I saw of John. . . . On March 30, I received a telephone call. It was a reporter from the Washington Post. He said, "Mrs. Hinckley, do you have your television set on? . . . Did you know your son John Hinckley is the man they have identified as shooting the President?"

Hinckley's father, Jack Hinckley, testified on direct examination that he met John at the Denver Airport on March 7, 1981, and informed him of the family's decision to cut off his financial support.

I prayed all the way [to the airport] that we were doing the right thing. . . . He was in very bad shape. He needed a shave. He was wiped out. He could hardly walk from the plane. We sat down and I told him how disappointed I was in him. How he had let us down, how he had not followed the plan [for independence] we had all agreed on. He had left us no choice but to not take him back in the house again, but force him to go on his own. So that's what I did. I took him to his car which was parked at the airport. It was an old car and the radiator leaked. And I put some antifreeze in it and we got the car started. And I had a couple of hundred dollars with me that I had brought from the house. And I gave that to him and I suggested that he go to the YMCA. He said he didn't want to do that. I said, "Okay, you are on your own. Do whatever you want to do." In looking back on that, I'm sure it was the greatest mistake in my life. We forced him out at a time when he just couldn't cope. I am the cause of John's tragedy. I wish to God I could trade places with him right now.

The testimony of Drs. Carpenter and Bear during the insanity trial established that Hinckley was psychotic and suffering from a malignant form of schizophrenia. As I pointed out above, Dr. Hopper departed from the standard of practice by his wrong diagnosis and his failure to provide appropriate treatment.

REACTIONS TO THE HINCKLEY VERDICT

No one complained about the procedural aspects of the Hinckley trial. The defense presented a persuasive, scientifically valid claim that Hinckley was schizophrenic and engaged in homicidal behavior based upon his delusional ideas. The jury applied the law to the factual situation in a reasonable and consistent manner. And yet the verdict that Hinckley was insane outraged many Americans. An ABC News poll taken the day after the verdict showed that 83 percent of those polled thought "justice was not done" in the Hinckley case. Interestingly, the American Psychiatric Association and the American Medical Association also joined the chorus of the detractors, crying for "reform"—a code word for the abolition of the insanity defense. This seems like a strange position for an organization of psychiatric professionals, but the organization believed that so-called battles of experts reflected poorly on psychiatry. The jury from the Hinckley case was even subpoenaed and grilled by a U.S. Senate commission.

Dr. Alan Stone, professor of law and psychiatry at Harvard Law School and a past president of the American Psychiatric Association, was the featured luncheon speaker at the annual meeting of the American Academy of Psychiatry and Law in October 1982. I was among the large audience of forensic psychiatrists who listened carefully and took notes as Stone told us that what we do has no scientific, clinical, or moral justification. He prefaced his address by stating that the Hinckley trial left American forensic psychiatry wounded and in need of encouragement, "but I come from the ivory tower to shoot the wounded." Stone lived up to his aggressive metaphor. He proudly proclaimed, "I am not a forensic psychiatrist." Ethical considerations had kept him out of the courtroom. "Psychiatrists are immediately over the ethical boundary when they enter the courtroom," Stone declared. Stone was critical of practitioners, "traveling around the country, testifying in insanity defense cases." Sitting there listening to the lecture, I wondered whether it was ethical to teach what is unethical to do. Nowhere in his lecture did he raise any question about his life's work of being the theoretician and teacher of forensic psychiatry. One wonders why it is more honorable to travel around the country teaching about the insanity defense than advising or testifying in actual insanity defense cases. Stone said,

> Let me state what I think the ethical boundaries problems are. First there is the basic boundary question: does psychiatry have anything true to say that the court should listen to? Second, there is the risk that one will go too far and twist the rules of justice and fairness to help the patient. Third, there is the opposite risk that one will deceive the patient in order to serve justice and fairness. Fourth, there is the danger that one will prostitute the profession, as one is ultimately seduced by the power of the adversarial system and assaulted by it.

Psychiatry obviously has something to say to the courts. Psychiatry, like any other profession, may be called upon to assist the legal fact finders in their decision making. Stone's second question also has no validity. No forensic psychiatrist should testify on behalf of a patient he or she has personally treated. In my fifty years of practicing forensic psychiatry I have never done so.

Stone has likened psychiatrists who testify for and against a defense of insanity to "clowns performing in a three-ring circus." In his book *Law, Psychiatry and Morality*, he comments on the Hinckley trial.

> The trial of John Hinckley was a bleak experience for American psychiatry, and the verdict shook public confidence in the American Criminal Justice System. Criticism went in two directions: outrage against the law and outrage against psychiatry. . . . But neither the law nor psychiatry had recognized that Hinckley was dangerous. There had been no protection for the public, and now there was to be no punishment for Hinckley. Indeed, given the judicial interpretation of the statutes governing the subsequent confinement of persons found not guilty by reason of insanity, there was real possibility that Hinckley might regain his freedom.[15]

The opinion that a defendant is not criminally responsible consists of three propositions: 1) the defendant committed a crime, 2) the defendant is severely mentally ill, and 3) the defendant is criminally not responsible. Usually, the dispute is about the legal interpretation of the legal test of insanity. In the Hinckley case, the claim that he was not severely mentally ill was indefensible. It was a tactical error on the part of the prosecution to deny that Hinckley was severely mentally ill. The prosecution's chances of prevailing would have been much better if they had tried to refute that he was legally insane, that is, to dispute that he met the criteria to be deemed legally insane rather than arguing that he was not mentally ill. It is easier to argue about an abstract legal "test" of sanity than against the reality of an obvious case of schizophrenia.

The *New York Times* (June 27, 1982) asked Senator Arlen Specter, a Pennsylvania Republican, and Alan Dershowitz, a professor at the Harvard Law School, whether from "the perspective of the jury's verdict and the law the jury was told it must apply" they thought justice had been done. Specter answered, "I think justice was not done. If the Hinckley standard is available to all those accused of acts of violence, I would say that upward of 70 percent could provide as good an insanity defense—based on my experience as district attorney for Philadelphia, where we handled some 250,000 cases during my eight years of office." Dershowitz answered, "I believe that justice was done. Justice is a process, not a particular result. In this case, the process included an independent jury given a great deal of information from a wide variety of sources, presented by an excellent team of defense attorneys."

Since the Hinckley case, the insanity defense has become rare due to adverse publicity and legislative obstacles.

For some time I have been reluctant to accept insanity defense cases because they are a futile undertaking. Since the outcome is predictable, I feel that charging a fee for an evaluation and testimony in an insanity defense case is like taking money under false pretenses. Here is an illustrative example.

On August 3, 2007, I was contacted by Michele Orlando, whose husband, Anthony LaCalamita III, was charged with shooting up the offices of the accounting firm where he had been employed for one year. She told me that on April 9, 2007, her husband went to Gordon Advisors with the intention of killing his former employers (he had been fired). In the process a much-beloved sixty-two-year-old receptionist was killed and two senior partners were severely injured. Anthony had been mentally abnormal for a long time. Michele and Anthony had met more than ten years ago when he had been studying for the priesthood in Baltimore. They had fallen in love, he had left the seminary, and they were married shortly thereafter. Throughout his marriage Anthony "suffered from sex addiction," including his compulsive use of prostitutes on a twice-a-week basis, and on a number of occasions Anthony had attempted suicide.

After being fired from Gordon Advisors, Anthony decided to kill some people at the firm and applied for a handgun. He was denied a permit because he had been involuntarily hospitalized by his psychiatrist following a homicidal episode involving a pimp. Once Anthony was denied the handgun permit, he purchased a long gun (rifle or shotgun) and proceeded in broad daylight carrying the unconcealed gun into the office where the shooting occurred.

When Michele called me, she emphasized that money was no object because Anthony's well-to-do parents would pay my bill. I told Michele that regardless of whom she retained, the outcome would most likely be conviction for first-degree murder and a life sentence without parole. I told her that I did not wish to become an expert for her, since in this case it would feel like taking money under false pretenses. She eventually did find an expert who charged $30,000 for his preparation and testimony in support of the insanity defense.

As I had predicted, Anthony LaCalamita III was found guilty of first-degree murder and assault with intent to murder. He was sentenced to the mandatory life in prison without possibility of parole.

The insanity defense debate is focused on the divergence of expert witness testimony. The near uniformity of outcome is conveniently overlooked. The prosecution wins about every time. The near elimination of the insanity defense violates our sense of justice. The practical consequence is the overrepresentation of psychotics in the American prison system. As long as psychotics exist there will be psychotics who kill for delusional reasons.

NOTES

1. *Care in the Community: Illusion or Reality* (Chichester, England, and New York: John Wiley & Sons, 1997).

2. E. Fuller Torey, ed. *Criminalizing the Seriously Mentally Ill: The Abuse of Jails as Mental Hospitals*, a joint report of the National Alliance for the Mentally Ill and Public Citizen's Health Research Group (Darby, PA: Diane Publishing, 1998).

3. *Attacks on the Insanity Defense: Biological Psychiatry and New Perspectives on Criminal Behavior* by C.R. Jeffery in collaboration with Rolando V. del Carmen and James D. White (Springfield, IL: Thomas, 1985).

4. The "policeman at the elbow test" was the criterion for insanity in medieval England. The jury had to decide if the defendant would have committed the crime even if there had been a policeman standing at his elbow.

5. U.S. House of Representatives, Committee on the Judiciary. *Federal Rules of Evidence.* Washington, D.C.: Government Printing Office, 2009.

6. Suicide-by-police, or police-assisted suicide is relatively common. M. E. Wolfgang, "Suicide by Means of Victim-Precipitated Homicide," *Journal of Clinical and Experimental Psychopathology and Quarterly Review of Psychiatry and Neurology* 20 (October–December 1959): 335–49.

7. Trial transcript in my possession.

8. Lee Harvey Oswald wrote a similar letter to Marina Oswald before he embarked on the assassination attempt of General Walker and President John Kennedy.

9. www.law.umkc.edu/faculty/projects/ftrials/hinckley/letter.htm.

10. Transcript of testimony is in my possession.

11. *New York Times,* May 24, 1982.

12. Transcript of testimony is in my possession.

13. The case of *Brady v. Hopper,* 570 F. Supp. 1333 (D. Colo. 1983), aff'd, 751 F. 2d 329 (10th Cir. 1984). The U.S. District Court held that because Hinckley never threatened anybody, Dr. Hopper could not have known that Hinckley was dangerous or warned Brady and the others of the danger.

14. Transcript of testimony is in my possession.

15. Alan Stone, *Law, Psychiatry, and Morality: Essays and Analysis* (Arlington, VA: American Psychiatric Press, 1984), 77.

10

JACK RUBY AND LEE HARVEY OSWALD

The Homicidal Spectrum

Within a forty-eight-hour period in November 1963, three men were killed in Dallas: first, President John F. Kennedy; next, Police Officer J. D. Tippett; and finally, Lee Harvey Oswald, who was shot by Jack Ruby as he was being transported from police headquarters to the county jail. Millions of people watched on television as Ruby shot Oswald.

These three homicides represent a wide range of the homicidal spectrum. President Kennedy was assassinated by a marginal individual, Oswald, who suffered from a personality disorder.[1] Oswald's behavior had more to do with his pathology than with his politics. He was bent on killing somebody: he had tried to kill the right-wing Birch Society leader General Edwin Walker only months before he killed the liberal President Kennedy. Oswald had killed Officer Tippett while trying to escape apprehension; this homicide was situational. Jack Ruby, in contrast, killed Lee Harvey Oswald in an impulsive manner, in a situation made possible by the incompetence of the Dallas Police Department that I will describe in more detail below.

The prevailing mythology following the assassination was that Ruby was part of a conspiracy, involving Fidel Castro, to kill Kennedy and that his group had recruited Oswald to assassinate President Kennedy. According to this scenario, Ruby killed Oswald to silence him as a witness to the plot. The conspiracy theories multiplied with the passage of time. Americans needed to believe that a man of John F. Kennedy's stature was the victim of an international conspiracy. At the very least, they insisted, Kennedy was the victim of the vengeful Mafia as it sought revenge for Attorney General Robert Kennedy's moves against them. The notion that a "nobody" like Oswald, using a $12 rifle, could rob the country of a national leader was intolerable. Ruby's assassination of Oswald rubbed salt in the wound by preventing Oswald from being brought to justice.

Jack Ruby's trial is emblematic of the failed collaboration of psychiatry and law and the ineffectiveness of defense lawyers faced with mentally ill clients. Ruby's original lawyer was Melvin Belli, an outstanding civil lawyer who had no understanding of the psychology of homicide. Belli based his claim that Ruby was insane on the fact that Ruby allegedly suffered from an epilepsy variant. Belli rejected the advice of a leading forensic psychiatrist, Dr. Manfred Guttmacher, who said that Ruby was a chronically depressed man given to explosive rages and impulsive acts.

Belli did an inadequate job defending his client because he tried to function as his own psychiatric expert; and Dr. Guttmacher failed Ruby by not refusing to testify when the lawyer failed to accept his opinion. A jury of Dallas citizens deliberated for just two hours and nineteen minutes and found Ruby to be sane and guilty of capital murder. Ruby was sentenced to die in the electric chair.

Ruby's lawyers appealed, and in October 1966 an appellate court overturned the conviction on the grounds that Ruby's lawyers' request for a change of venue in the original trial should have been granted because Ruby could not have received a fair trial in Dallas. Ruby died before his second trial, slated to begin in February 1967, got underway; in December 1966 he was hospitalized and diagnosed with cancer in his lungs, liver, and brain, and he died in January 1967.

After Ruby's conviction was reversed, I was retained as the forensic psychiatric expert for the defense. I reviewed extensive records that dealt with Ruby's past, I had access to the transcript of the former trial, and I spent a day in San Francisco with Melvin Belli. I interviewed at length Ruby's siblings; his brother Earl and sister Eva were particularly good sources of information. I conducted a psychiatric interview of Jack Ruby lasting three hours at the Dallas County Jail. After I examined Ruby, I became convinced that, contrary to the prevailing view, Ruby was not involved in a conspiracy to kill Oswald or President Kennedy. Ruby's personality, his state of mind after Kennedy's assassination, and the timeline of his shooting of Oswald made a planned act highly improbable. Furthermore, Ruby's psychological makeup and social habits made it unlikely that anyone would ever trust him with a conspiratorial plan.

Following Kennedy's assassination, Ruby became depressed. He was the only Dallas nightclub operator who closed his establishment to commemorate the death of President Kennedy. All three siblings of Ruby told me that Jack became depressed subsequent to the assassination. I interviewed a number of Ruby's friends all of whom confirmed Jack's strong emotional reaction to the death of his beloved president. My extensive tape-recorded examination of Jack Ruby in Dallas County Jail revealed a clinical picture that established severe paranoid schizophrenia. In my interview Jack Ruby insisted that he precipitated a Holocaust of American Jews. He suffered from delusions and hallucinations.

Documents made available to me by the lawyers, which included transcripts of the trial, establish a timeline of Ruby's movements on the morning of Oswald's shooting suggestive of an impulsive act. Oswald's transfer from the Dallas Police Department Headquarters to the county jail was to take place at 10:00 A.M. What took place in the basement of the Dallas Police Headquarters left no doubt in my mind that Ruby's shooting of Oswald was an impulsive act. Around 9:00 A.M., Ruby's cleaning lady, Elnora Pitts, called him—as she usually did before coming over—and woke him up. His roommate, George Senator, recalled that Ruby got out of bed at about 9:30 A.M.[2]

At 10:19 A.M., Karen Carlin, a stripper who worked for Ruby at his nightclub, called him at home. Ruby had cancelled her performances at the nightclub, and she needed money. He agreed to send Carlin money by Western Union. Ruby arrived at Western Union, located around the corner from police headquarters, sometime after 11 A.M. There was another customer ahead of him; Ruby did not seem to be in a hurry. His receipt for the money that he sent to Carlin was stamped 11:17 A.M., a full hour and 17 minutes after Oswald's scheduled transfer from police headquarters. Given Ruby's movements in the moments leading up to Oswald's shooting, one would have to assume that the police and Ruby were coordinating their movements by walkie-talkies if this had been a planned shooting.

Oswald was scheduled to exit police headquarters through the basement entrance, which opened into an alleyway spanning the length of the building, with entrance points on both Main Street and Commerce

Street (the two roads ran parallel). Shortly before the Oswald transfer, Police Chief Curey had the brilliant idea that Oswald should be transferred in a "money wagon," but the armored truck could not fit through the basement entrance. Instead, it was parked at the Commerce Street ramp, blocking the exit. A police officer named Roy Vaughn was guarding the basement entrance on Main Street. Lieutenant R.S. Pierce backed his police cruiser out of the basement entrance on Main Street. To help Pierce get the cruiser out of the basement entrance, Officer Vaughn stepped into the middle of Main Street to stop traffic. At this point Ruby, who happened to be walking back from the Western Union to his car, was attracted by a crowd gathering outside the basement entrance of police headquarters. He walked down the ramp. Video footage recorded him entering the basement. At 11:21 A.M., the elevator door opened and Oswald, handcuffed to two detectives, emerged. At that moment Ruby shot Oswald with the gun that he habitually carried everywhere (except, as he mentioned during an interview with me, to synagogue). Ruby was in front of the elevator door no more than thirty seconds before the shooting. Such coordination would have been hard to achieve even with a meticulously planned conspiracy between Ruby and a dozen members of the Dallas Police Department. All signs point to a coincidence, albeit a tragic one.[3]

Adding to the evidence that the shooting was unplanned is the fact that when Ruby left his apartment around 11:00 A.M., he had brought along his dog, Sheba. Ruby's sister, Eva Grant, told me that Jack would have never taken the dog with him had he planned to kill Oswald—"He loved that dog," she said. In my report, I elaborated upon Ruby's attachment to Sheba. I find it interesting that Bill Alexander, the prosecutor who drew up the indictment and argued the case, told investigative journalist Gerald Posner years later, "People that didn't know Jack will never understand this, but Ruby would never have taken that dog with him and left it in the car if he knew he was going to shoot Oswald and end up in jail. He would have made sure that that dog was at home with Senator and was well taken care of."[4]

When I examined Ruby in June 1964, I found him to be suffering from one of mankind's most malignant diseases: paranoid schizophrenia, complete with delusions and hallucinations. I concluded from the examination and his history that this condition had been obvious since February 1963.

Other psychiatrists diagnosed Ruby as psychotic both before and after my examination. In April 1964, Ruby was examined by the highly respected Dr. Louis West, professor and chairman of the Psychiatry Department at the University of Oklahoma, who found him to be overtly psychotic and in need of treatment. On April 23, 1964, psychiatrist Dr. William Beavers, an assistant professor at the University of Texas Southwestern Medical School in Dallas, arrived at the same diagnosis. He spent two hours with Ruby and reported "Recommendation: If this patient were without criminal charges, it would be my opinion that there should be immediate psychiatric hospitalization and close observation because of the possibility of suicidal attempt. In addition to chemical therapeutic agents, antidepressant drugs and phenothiazines were indicated."[5]

In May of 1964, Judge Joe Brown, the trial and sentencing judge who had presided when Ruby was convicted in March 1964, appointed a sanity commission consisting of Dr. Robert Stubblefield, chairman of the Department of Psychiatry at the University of Texas Southwest Medical School, and Dr. John Holbrook, a forensic psychiatrist from the community, and Dr. Beavers. The purpose of the commission was to determine whether Ruby required admission to a psychiatric hospital because of his psychotic illness at the time of examination. This is not to be confused with the state of mind of the defendant at the time of the crime.

These three psychiatrists told the judge that Ruby was psychotic and should receive treatment. Judge Brown pressured them to change their opinions before they wrote their report. It was a unanimous opinion of the court-appointed psychiatrists, who had no connection to the defense, that Ruby should be admitted to Rusk State Hospital. Judge Brown ruled nevertheless that Ruby should remain in jail. Ruby's need for psychiatric treatment was not purely a psychiatric issue; it required a finding by a jury acting in response to determination made by a court-appointed sanity commission.

The criminal proceedings, on the other hand, dealt with the state of mind of Ruby at the time when he killed Oswald. The criminal jury had to determine whether Ruby planned the homicide, in which case it was first-degree murder, or whether it was an impulsive act, which would require a lesser charge like second-degree murder. He could also be found not guilty by reason of insanity, in which case he would be sent to a psychiatric state hospital. In my opinion there was overwhelming evidence Ruby's shooting of Oswald was not premeditated.

I interviewed Jack Ruby at length and spent many hours with his siblings. Ruby was born in Chicago in 1911 to a family of Jewish immigrants from Eastern Poland. Throughout his early childhood, the family lived in what Jack described as a "rough neighborhood." He was one of eight children, four boys and four girls. His father was a carpenter by trade and an alcoholic, which was practically unknown among Jews at the time.[6] Ruby's father spent two decades in the Russian army, beginning at a young age, until his successful escape. His children recalled their father best as he appeared in a photograph sitting on a horse with a big sword in his hand and a wearing a long mustache. Jack and his siblings claimed that their father was a member of the famous Kossack outfit.[7]

Throughout Jack's early years, there was considerable violence between his parents and the children seem to have been neglected and permitted to wander freely around Chicago.

When I interviewed Ruby's siblings, Bea Grant (Jack's sister) recalled that her mother had acted strangely for many years—but in those years, few people thought in terms of psychiatric illness. Throughout Jack's infancy, his mother was delusional. She believed that a fishbone was stuck in her throat and insisted upon a doctor's examination every few weeks. During my interview with the family in June 1964, they indicated that reports about Jack's past psychiatric examinations existed. They also claimed that although the FBI uncovered this prior to the first trial and communicated it to the prosecution, the interviews were never revealed to the defense. A report about the Jack Ruby family, from the Institute for Juvenile Research in Chicago going back to 1922, was known to the prosecution. This information would have been of great value to the defense and relevant to the insanity plea, but it was withheld by the prosecution.

In 1921, the family was completely disrupted by the separation of the psychotic mother from the alcoholic father, and the court transferred the custody of the children to a Jewish social agency. Jack and his siblings recalled vividly the family's disintegration and their subsequent life on farms and in foster homes. All of the children except two were separated from one another; Jack lived first on a farm and then in a number of foster homes where he encountered anti-Semitism.

In young adulthood, the children reunited the family around their mother. The siblings had been working, and they rented an apartment and took her in. They had a semblance of a family life, but attempts to reunite their parents failed; the parents continued to fight whenever they were in proximity. Ruby's father would occasionally come to the apartment drunk and create a disturbance. It was at this time that the mother was committed to Elgin State Hospital; she remained there until her death.

Throughout his life, Ruby was intensely preoccupied with being a Jew and with the persecution of Jews. Even as a child, he had fought for "the Jewish cause." His given name was Jacob Rubenstein, which he changed to Jack Leon Ruby in 1947 as part of his obsession with anti-Semitism. He sought out people and situations where Jews were insulted and criticized. He lent money to Christians, not expecting repayment, because he "wanted to show them that Jews can be generous." He engaged in physical fights "to show . . . that Jews are not cowards."[8] He owned a nightclub called Carousel, and in the nightclub any allusion to Jews, including any jokes of the so-called Jewish variety, were strictly prohibited. If a master of ceremonies or an entertainer transgressed this rule, he was usually fired. Yet at the same time, Ruby associated mostly with non-Jews and kept himself in situations where he would have to continue to "fight for his cause." He emphasized to me that although he was mostly among non-Jews, he was proud of being a Jew and he would always let the non-Jews know that he was a Jew. He had a strange affection for Dallas, yet considered it to be the hotbed of anti-Semitism. In his delusional ideas, Dallas was the "Auschwitz of America." One of his explanations for killing Oswald was, "I wanted to show Gentiles that a Jew can love them," referring to his love of Kennedy.

Ruby told me of various episodes wherein one person had insulted another and he had protected the victim. He broke up fights by pulling his pistol; he followed a man who was following a young waitress and then rescued her at gunpoint. Ruby was hungry for approval and yet unable to form lasting relationships; to my knowledge he did not have a single friend. He had many business acquaintances, including people for whom he would do all kinds of favors, but there was no one with whom he was more deeply involved. For example, newspaper accounts often referred to Bill Senator, Jack's roommate, as a close friend. But the relationship was just another attempt at earning an outsider's approval.

Senator was out of a job and unable to pay his rent, so Ruby invited him to stay in his apartment for as long as he wanted.

Between 1953 and 1963, Ruby had a close relationship with a young woman he called his girlfriend and fiancée. They broke up early in 1963. Ruby stated that she broke up with him "because I had been using her and I was mean to her." When asked to explain this, he referred to his inability to decide to get married. He was always concerned that he didn't have enough to offer her (such as financial security) and he thought of himself as unattractive and overweight.

Prior to Kennedy's assassination, Jack Ruby was suffering from a paranoid personality with episodes of depression. It is my opinion that at the time he shot Oswald, Ruby was suffering from a dissociative reaction that rendered him incapable of consciously controlling his actions.[9] The paranoid schizophrenia became manifest in Ruby later, following the torments of his trial and conviction.

Ruby had already been diagnosed as psychotic when he was interviewed in June 1964 at the Dade County Jail by Chief Justice Earl Warren, chairman of the Special Presidential Commission for the Investigation of the Assassination of President Kennedy. Chief Justice Warren, Representative Gerald R. Ford of Michigan, and other commission members went to Dallas and met with Ruby. Ruby begged Warren several times to take him to Washington, D.C., because he feared for his life and those of his family members, claiming among other things that "a whole new form of government is going to take over this country, and I know I won't live to see you another time." Ruby said he wanted to convince President Lyndon B. Johnson that he was not part of any conspiracy to kill Kennedy. Warren refused Ruby's request and told him that the commission would have no way of protecting him since it had no police powers.

Conducting such an interview without prior consultation with a psychiatrist disregarded basic medical considerations; fortunately the transcript shows that Chief Justice Warren handled the interview with skill and sensitivity. No such sensitivity was shown by U.S. District Judge Davidson when Ruby was permitted to testify on his own behalf on March 19, 1965. Ruby was not accompanied by an attorney of his own choice, even though five psychiatrists had by then diagnosed him as psychotic. The judge put Ruby's irrelevant, incoherent ravings on display, permitting him to ramble agitatedly while members of the press and the courtroom audience watched the pathetic scene.

In March 1965, Ruby conducted a brief televised news conference in which he stated that "everything pertaining to what's happening has never come to the surface. The world will never know the true facts of what occurred, my motives. The people who had so much to gain, and had such an ulterior motive for putting me in the position I'm in, will never let the true facts come above board to the world." What many viewers took to be proof of a conspiracy surrounding the assassination of President Kennedy and the shooting of Oswald, were really just the rantings of a paranoid, deluded mind.

I am certain that Ruby's murder trial precipitated his psychotic illness. In their book *The Trial of Jack Ruby*, John Kaplan and Jon Waltz corroborate my belief:

> Although Oswald may have died, undisturbed, with whatever illusion led him to his deed, Jack Ruby, before a crowded courtroom and the press of the world, was stripped of both his self-respect and his illusions. He heard himself analyzed by his psychiatrists as a latent homosexual with a compulsive desire to be liked and respected, described by his own lawyer as the village clown, damningly quoted—untruthfully, he felt—by members of the police department in whose reflected prestige he had been happy to bask, and was forced to sit as a passive witness while the attorneys, the judge and the jury fought over and decided his fate.[10]

There is no reason in law or humanity that Ruby could not have been excused from the courtroom during some of these episodes. His apparent mental deterioration following the trial may have resulted not so much from his death sentence as from the trial's torment. Jack Ruby suffered from schizotypal personality disorder throughout his life. This condition made him particularly vulnerable to the stress of the trial.

In June 1966, the long-postponed hearing on Jack Ruby's sanity took place.[11] The prosecution introduced four guards from the jail as witnesses to show that Ruby was sane. They testified that he had played gin rummy with them, occasionally cheating, and that he had read and discussed sports—and therefore must be sane. As on previous occasions, Ruby behaved bizarrely. He did not cooperate with his attorney and "was hollering throughout the time that he was not insane and was very anxious to be found sane," according to Sol Dann, one of the attorneys involved in the case.[12] Ruby also shouted, "Never at any time since I was convicted have I done anything to make anybody believe I was of unsound mind."

John Callahan, the Dallas County Jail physician, also reported on Ruby's behavior during this hearing:

> Jack, who was opposed to the sanity motion to begin with, was bitter. "They are trying to make me out as crazy, and it just won't work." At other times he ranted about Nazis prowling the country in search of more Jews for their furnaces, and maintained that the Jewish people were slated for total extinction. At the proceedings, though his lawyers stood mute, Jack did not. In a loud and insistent voice, he proclaimed that he was sane and wanted nobody to doubt it. His lengthy speech was angrily defensive, but apparently the jurists weren't harkening to the old saying about lunatics never believing they are. Instead, they took him at his word and found him sane.[13]

One wonders why Ruby had to be present during proceedings that obviously agitated him. Had he been bleeding in a courtroom, he would have had medical care without concern over whether or not it was helping him legally. The psychiatric equivalent afforded him no such protection.

My motivation for becoming involved in the Ruby case after he had been sentenced to death was to secure treatment for a psychotic who was in acute need of hospitalization and psychiatric care. The lawyers, on the other hand, were preparing for a new trial during which the defense of insanity would be asserted on a more valid basis then it was the case during the first misguided trial. The lawyers viewed Ruby's psychotic behavior during the sanity trial as beneficial to the insanity defense in the new trial. Thus, the defense lawyers and I had somewhat different goals. They were focused on the forthcoming new trial, during which the insanity defense would be asserted. I certainly was supportive of this effort, but I was also interested in securing treatment for a severely mentally ill man tormented by delusions and hallucinations.

Melvin Belli, who represented Ruby in the first trial, recognized that his client was in need of psychiatric treatment. He told me that he sensed that "something was mentally wrong with Ruby." Even the prosecutor was reported in the *Dallas Morning News* as saying, "Although he [Ruby] is sane, there is no question that . . . [Ruby] has some neurotic tendencies that could be treated in the penitentiary."[14] But the judge repeatedly refused to hold a hearing.

After the conclusion of the first trial it became clear why Judge Brown was so reluctant to examine the question of Ruby's mental illness. In the spring of 1965, evidence surfaced that led to a hearing to disqualify Judge Brown from the Ruby case. By his own admission, in June 1964, the judge conceived the idea of writing a book on the Ruby trial and in July he signed a book contract with Holt, Rinehart, and Winston. This was an obvious breach of judicial ethics. The judge's behavior from that point was motivated primarily by his financial interest in the case, as Sol Dann, one of Ruby's attorneys, revealed in his description of the disqualification hearing. In his letter to me, Dann recalled:

It was most embarrassing for me as a lawyer to hear Judge Brown testify in reckless disregard of the truth, and to action contrary to judicial canons of ethics. In addition to the false, conflictive and evasive answers given by Judge Brown while under oath, he admitted that he presided over matters requiring his judicial discretion after he received $5,000 and entered into a contract to write his book on the trial while proceedings were still pending. He admitted that he publicly denied receipt of said money, and denied that he was writing a book because he wanted it to be kept secret; as he said, it leaked out. He admitted that he "recused" himself after a deposition was taken of the publisher that disclosed that negotiations began in the spring of 1964. Also, there was a letter on Judge Brown's stationery dated March 12, 1965, and signed by him, which states: "It perhaps is a good thing that it is not finished, because they have filed a motion to disqualify me on the ground of having pecuniary interest in the case. I can refute that by stating that there has been no book published or that I have not begun to write a book. We are coming along nicely. We have approximately 190 pages completed. . . . the Court of Criminal Appeals tossed the case back to me to determine Jack Ruby's sanity. . . . it is my opinion that they will never prove Ruby insane . . . but I do not want to put myself in the position of being disqualified."[15]

In other words, the judge believed that preventing a ruling on Ruby's mental illness would also prevent his own disqualification. Judge Brown also admitted that Clinton Murchison, Sr., of Dallas, Texas, had arranged his negotiations with the publisher. Murchison, a principal owner of the publishing firm, also arranged to pay the judge's expenses of over $1,000 for trips to La Jolla, California, and New York. On the basis of such condemning evidence, Judge Brown was disqualified from deciding the issue of sanity commission and Judge Holland was assigned to the case. To my knowledge, Judge Brown was not disciplined for his unethical behavior.

Once Judge Brown was removed there was the expectation that Judge Holland would accept the sanity commission recommendation and Ruby would be transferred to a hospital. The lawyers representing Ruby in the preparation of the re-trial on the charges related to killing Oswald were focused on legal issues and not on medical care of their client. When they concluded that the sanity hearing would not benefit Ruby's criminal defense they opposed the hearing dealing with his admission to a psychiatric hospital.

I was about to leave for Dallas in June 1966 to testify at a sanity hearing when Sol Dann and William Kunstler, a lawyer who had joined Ruby's team, told me the defense had decided to withdraw the petition for the sanity hearing. Elmer Gertz later explained at the 1970 American Academy of Forensic Sciences Annual Meeting that a finding of insanity would have stopped the progress of Ruby's appeal of the original verdict. The defense withdrew the petition for the hearing, the Texas Appeals Court was about to review the case, and according to Texas law, a person must be sane to file an appeal.

The defense submitted to the state court of criminal appeals a fifty-eight-page brief that dealt with the fact that Ruby had been denied due process of law because Judge Brown was planning to write a book. The defense contended that the conviction and subsequent proceedings were not valid. The question of Ruby's mental illness and its bearing on his ability to stand trial, as well as on his conviction, was not introduced into these defense arguments.

Upon reviewing the case, however, the Texas Appellate Court ordered that a jury be impaneled to "determine the question of appellant's present sanity or insanity." Judge Holland was "directed to [impanel an insanity commission] without further delay and to certify to this Court the result of such a hearing."[16] This order also specified that Joe Tonahill, an attorney who had been dismissed from representing Ruby at the family's request, should participate in the hearing. The prosecution was pleased because they believed this would impede the appeal's progress, and so they objected when the defense attempted to withdraw its petition for a sanity hearing.

As Gertz reports in his book, the defense was very disappointed by the order for a sanity hearing and filed a motion in the state court of appeals on May 20, 1966, to reverse it. When this motion was unsuccessful, the defense went even further to maintain the illusion that Ruby was not mentally ill: they petitioned the U.S. Supreme Court to cancel the hearing, stating that Tonahill was being forced on Ruby and his family. Their petition was denied. As a result, the defense group decided not to participate in the sanity hearing—and thus to forfeit the one course of action that could have secured medical help for Ruby. The defense even persuaded Eva Grant, Ruby's sister, to withdraw her petition for a sanity hearing, although her concern was certainly for Ruby the man, not Ruby the legal entity.

On June 13, 1966, the long-awaited sanity hearing took place with the prosecution attempting to prove Ruby's mental health by the testimony of laymen, the four jail guards who testified that he cheated at cards. After this hearing—in which Ruby participated fully and in a bizarre way—the jury found him sane, thus clearing the way for his execution as well as for his appeal, and depriving him of treatment for his psychosis. This is a true example of the injustice of justice. It is not surprising that all of this sounds confusing because in fact it is. It is also irrational.

In October 1966, the appellate court reversed Judge Brown's sentence of Ruby and ordered a new trial. Lawyers hailed the decision as a triumph of justice. Dann, Frank Angelo (editor of the *Detroit Free Press*), and I appeared on a hastily arranged television panel soon after this order came down. On that program, Sol Dann (my friend) and I disagreed strongly. He was understandably proud of the victory, which was in large part the result of his efforts. He emphasized that his concern was not for Ruby the man, but for principles of justice. I, on the other hand, considered it a pyrrhic victory, analogous to a "successful" operation in which the patient dies. My concern was for Ruby the man, who had suffered from an acute mental illness through two years of legal maneuvering without treatment. Ruby's psychiatric illness was not considered in the same spirit as physical illness.

As soon as Ruby showed physical symptoms of an illness, he was transferred to a hospital. No commissions were required; no hearings were held. It took only a doctor's diagnosis that Ruby was suffering from pneumonia, and then he was admitted on December 9, 1966, to Parkland Hospital in Dallas—the very hospital where Kennedy died. A day later, doctors realized that Ruby had cancer in his liver, lungs, and brain. He died in Parkland Hospital on January 3, 1967.

Ruby's lack of psychiatric treatment during his confinement and trial are not unique. Many other, more obscure defendants find themselves deprived of needed psychiatric care for months or years while their attorneys and the people on the opposing side deal meticulously with legal issues. In my many years of experience, I have often seen human lives crushed by the relentless legal machinery.

NOTES

1. D. A. Rothstein, "Presidential Assassination Syndrome," *Archives of General Psychiatry* 11, no. 3 (1964): 245–54.

2. The report of the President's Commission on the Assassination of President Kennedy, known unofficially as the Warren Commission, confirms these details.

3. In May 1966, the American Psychiatric Association held a panel on the JFK assassination during its annual convention. The participants were Karl Menninger, the "dean" of American psychiatry at that time; Robert Blakey, the chief counsel for the House Select Committee on Assassinations; and me. In my presentation I mentioned that Oswald was separated from his wife, Marina, and had visited her in Irving, Texas, the day before the assassination. I pointed out that had Marina agreed to Oswald's plea to sleep with him that Thursday, he might not have made it to Dallas the next day. Had Karen Carlin not called Ruby with a plea to wire money, he would never have been downtown to confront Oswald. And had Oswald's transfer not been running over an hour late, Ruby never would have been at the scene. When I returned from the podium to the panel table, Blakey whispered to me, "You mean to say, had Lee gotten laid that night, President Kennedy would have been alive?" "Very likely," I responded.

4. Gerald Posner, *Case Closed* (New York: Random House, 1993), 394.

5. On file with author.

6. According to the Yale Center of Alcohol Studies, alcoholism was virtually unknown among Jews in the past. "But when it comes to alcoholism, Jews are virtually out of the picture. First admissions (1929-31) per 100,000 of 'alcoholic psychotics' in New York state hospitals: Irish, 25.6; Scandinavian, 7.8; Italian, 4.8; English, 4.3; German, 3.8; Jewish, 0.5. This was reported in *Time* magazine on March 17, 1958." Yale Sociology Professor Charles R. Snyder in *Alcohol and the Jews* (Free Press, Yale Center of Alcohol Studies); http://www.time.com/time/magazine/article/0,9171,863183,00.html#ixzz0XiJ5F8Fv.

7. Jack recalls that when he was effective in any particular area, his father would refer to him affectionately as "my little Kossack," even though most Jews knew Kossacks for the atrocities they had perpetrated against them.

8. Documents on file with the author.

9. Dissociation is a disruption of normal mental functioning. Dissociation can be a response to trauma or overwhelming emotion. Many homicides described in the law as manslaughter are the result of dissociation. Dissociative reactions can affect any aspect of a person's functioning; commonly memory is affected.

10. John Kaplan and Jon R. Waltz, *The Trial of Jack Ruby* (New York: The Macmillan Co., 1965).

11. In Texas, the assigned judge decides whether a hearing will be held on the question of the defendant's mental illness, so in this case, Judge Brown, who had presided over Ruby's original trial and conviction, would make that decision. Brown resorted to an elaborate series of delays and refusals.

12. Personal communication with Sol Dann.

13. Report of Dr. Callahan on file with the author.

14. *Dallas Morning News*, November 5, 1965.

15. Letter on file with the author.

16. Transcript on file with the author.

*Emanuel Tanay testifies in the case of Harlan Drake in Owosso, Michigan.
2010.*

11

ANDREA YATES
Sanity Based on Insanity

A novelist creating a narrative of injustice couldn't improve on the
Andrea Yates story: a mother kills her five children based on a
delusion that drowning them will save them from Satan; she tells the
police that she wants to be executed by the state in order to kill the Satan within her; the Houston prosecutor cooperates and seeks the death
penalty; and the police and prosecution argue both that she is competent to stand trial and that she was sane at the time of the murders.

On June 20, 2001, just two weeks after her release from a psychiatric
ward, Andrea Yates drowned her five children in a bathtub and then
called 911 and asked for the police. Yates was taken to police headquarters, where detective Ed Mehl interrogated her. The detective and Yates
worked together easily because they had the same goals: detective Mehl
needed evidence to support a capital murder charge, and Yates wanted
to be executed.

Ultimately, the Yates case is one of the clearest cases of legal injustice that I have ever witnessed. A publicity-seeking prosecutor succeeded in having Yates found guilty of capital murder. A jury rejected
the insanity defense, despite Yates's history of severe psychosis. And
two forensic psychiatrists contributed to this gross miscarriage of justice, one by giving ineffective and confusing testimony and the other by
giving ethically questionable testimony.

Yates's conviction represents a failure of society on a great many
levels. We failed as a society to provide a sick woman with appropriate psychiatric care; we failed to protect five children from their

psychotic mother; and we failed to discipline an overzealous prosecutor, Kaylynn Williford, for tormenting a bereaved family by saying in an open courtroom, "The children had become a hindrance, and she wanted them gone." And organized psychiatry failed to chastise Dr. Park Dietz, a professor of psychiatry, for testifying under oath that this psychotic mother was legally sane when she drowned her five children.

ANDREA YATES'S MENTAL ILLNESS

In the two years prior to the tragedy, Yates's husband hospitalized her four times for mental illness. Documented evidence of her psychosis goes back to June 17, 1999, two years before she drowned her five children. Her first hospitalization took place after Yates attempted suicide with an overdose of Trazadone, an antidepressant drug. Doctors diagnosed her as severely depressed and prescribed more antidepressant medication. Consistent with the current fiscally oriented management of mental illness, they released her from the hospital a mere seven days later with a prescription for a month's supply of medication. Three weeks after her discharge, Yates again attempted to kill herself, this time with a knife; her husband struggled with her and prevented her from succeeding. Once again, he took her to a hospital, where she was diagnosed as having severe depression with psychotic features.

On May 4, 2001, Yates's husband insisted that she be hospitalized at Devereux Hospital. The hospital records describe a profoundly psychotic woman. On May 7, Dr. Mohammed Saeed, the treating psychiatrist, wrote in the chart that he was considering electroconvulsive therapy, a treatment of last resort. But shortly after Dr. Saeed made that entry in the chart, he discontinued Haldol, a potent antipsychotic drug. Even more surprising is the fact that Yates was discharged from Devereux Hospital on May 14, 2001—a mere seven days after she was considered a candidate for electroshock treatment. It seems likely that the decision-making process in this case was driven by insurance concerns rather than by clinical judgment.

Sixteen days after her antipsychotic medication was discontinued, Andrea Yates drowned her children because she believed that she was saving them from hell. When questioned about her actions, Andrea Yates spoke of drowning her children after feeding them breakfast as if she were a woman merely doing her household chores. The absence of despair and bereavement was a clear symptom of psychosis, but the prosecution interpreted it as proof that she was a cold-blooded killer.[1] It is hard to imagine a more profound breakdown than a mother who systematically drowns her five children and describes that process without emotion. The killing of five children by a mother is not a defect of conscience but a psychobiological derangement.[2] A sane mother cannot will herself to kill her children, nor can a mother will herself not to do so when her psychosis is driving her acts.[3] Only a psychotic mother would drown her five children. Recent neuroscience confirms that compassion is part of our biology.

THE PROSECUTION'S ETHICAL VIOLATIONS

The ultimate responsibility for a miscarriage of justice in a criminal case rests with the elected prosecutor. Had he been guided by a sense of justice and public interest, he would have chosen not to contest Yates's insanity plea. Yates would have spent the rest of her life in a psychiatric facility. Harris County, the Houston community, and Yates's family would have been spared the stress and expense of the ensuing legal process that extended over a number of years and cost taxpayers millions of dollars. In the long run, the outcome in an uncontested insanity plea and the outcome of the effort to have Yates convicted of capital murder would have been the same. However, had the prosecutor accepted an insanity plea, he would not have gained the publicity of a trial.

The act of drowning five children on the instructions of Satan cannot be construed as criminal homicide, to say nothing of capital murder. The Texas Penal Code section 19.01 (a) states: "A person commits criminal homicide if he intentionally, knowingly, recklessly, or with criminal negligence causes the death of an individual."

Assistant District Attorney Joseph Owmby suggested that Yates fabricated her story to win an insanity verdict. This was a flagrant attempt to bias the jury. In reality, Yates was assisting the prosecutor in convicting her of a capital murder because she wanted to be executed, as she told police immediately after her arrest.

The Texas Disciplinary Rules of Professional Conduct entitled "Special Responsibilities of a Prosecutor" states: "A prosecutor has the responsibility to see that justice is done, and not simply to be an advocate.

This responsibility carries with it a number of specific obligations."[4] The rule further requires that a prosecutor shall:

(a) refrain from prosecuting or threatening to prosecute a charge that the prosecutor knows is not supported by probable cause;
(b) refrain from conducting or assisting in a custodial interrogation of an accused unless the prosecutor has made reasonable efforts to be assured that the accused has been advised of any right to, and the procedure for obtaining, counsel and has been given reasonable opportunity to obtain counsel;
(c) not initiate or encourage efforts to obtain from an unrepresented accused a waiver of important pretrial, trial, or post-trial rights;
(d) make timely disclosure to the defense of all evidence or information known to the prosecutor that tends to negate the guilt of the accused or mitigates the offense, and in connection with sentencing, disclose to the defense and to the tribunal all unprivileged mitigating information known to the prosecutor, except when the prosecutor is relieved of this responsibility by a protective order of the tribunal; and
(e) exercise reasonable care to prevent persons employed or controlled by the prosecutor in a criminal case from making an extrajudicial statement that the prosecutor would be prohibited from making under Rule 3.07.

In *Berger v. United States,* the U.S. Supreme Court determined that it is the prosecutor's duty to refrain from improper methods calculated to produce a wrongful conviction. The court was also critical of prosecutors who focus on obtaining "the maximum penalty for violation." The *Berger* decision states the prosecutor "may prosecute with earnestness and vigor—indeed, he should do so. But, while he may strike hard blows, he is not at liberty to strike foul ones. It is as much his duty to refrain from improper methods calculated to produce a wrongful conviction as it is to use every legitimate means to bring about a just one."[5]

It is fair to say that the average jury, to a greater or lesser degree, has confidence that these obligations, which so plainly rest upon the prosecuting attorney, will be faithfully observed. Consequently, improper suggestions, insinuations, and especially assertions of personal knowledge are apt to carry much weight against the accused when they should properly carry none.

The prosecution in the Yates case violated a number of these ethical guidelines. Unfortunately, this is not unique to Texas. Our criminal justice system's handling of psychotic defendants often ranges from deplorable to barbaric. The law and forensic psychiatry are both demeaned when they treat a psychotic mother's drowning of her five children as a rational criminal act. The Yates case and the many other killings of children by psychotic mothers raise profound moral, legal, and psychiatric issues. Should we judge human behavior by its consequences and disregard the state of mind behind it? Should we have a criminal justice system that does not consider intent? Should we make no distinction between rational homicides committed by criminals and homicides committed by psychotics as the result of delusions?

In the Yates case, the prosecution even objected to the introduction of mitigating circumstances on the issue of the death penalty. By some far-fetched interpretation of the law, one could argue that the insanity defense in the Yates case could be contested. Yet, by no stretch of the imagination could one argue that she was malingering and that she was not a proper subject for mitigation. The Andrea Yates case symbolizes our society's failure to provide appropriate care for psychotics before they become violent.

WAS ANDREA YATES COMPETENT TO STAND TRIAL?

A defendant charged with a crime must be competent to stand trial. The U.S. Supreme Court formulated a test for competency to stand trial in *Dusky v. United States*. The *Dusky* decision declared that: "the proper test must be whether he [the defendant] has sufficient present ability to consult with his lawyer with a reasonable degree of rational understanding—and whether he has a rational as well as factual understanding of the proceedings against him. Constitutional law and the Due Process Clause of the Fourteenth Amendment prohibit the criminal prosecution of a defendant who is not competent to stand trial."[6] To argue that Yates was competent to assist her defense lawyers was absurd. Her illness made her an ally of the prosecution; let me repeat it was her psychotic goal to be executed.

The day after Yates drowned her five children, she was under the care of Dr. Melissa Ferguson, the Houston jail psychiatrist. Ferguson was the first psychiatrist to diagnose Yates's condition correctly and to treat her illness appropriately. She gave Yates a high dosage of the antipsychotic medication Haldol. Yates then entered a less-acute form of her psychosis. Yet she continued to wish for her own execution; even in that "improved" state, she was still in need of indefinite psychiatric hospitalization. Yates was not competent to stand trial on two counts: she had a psychotic wish to be executed, and therefore could not assist in her own defense, and she was also impaired by the high dosage of Haldol.

Some lawyers argue, and some judges agree, that medication can, at times, make a person competent to stand trial.[7] Even if one assumes that to be the case, this cannot be true for a person who has been on 15 milligrams of Haldol (Haloperidol) for an extended period of time. One to two milligrams is the normal initial dosage, followed by an upward adjustment as tolerated, until the desired effect is achieved or limiting side effects appear. Clinical experience has shown that it is seldom necessary to employ dosages greater than four to six milligrams daily. Larger doses affect mental function even as they alleviate psychotic symptoms.

The Supreme Court addressed this issue in *Riggins v. Nevada*, in which it concluded that "the forced administration of antipsychotic medication during Riggins' trial violated rights guaranteed by the Sixth and Fourteenth Amendments."[8] The opinion states in part:

> While the precise consequences of forcing Mellaril upon him cannot be shown from a trial transcript, the testimony of doctors who examined Riggins establishes the strong possibility that his defense was impaired. Mellaril's side effects may have impacted not only his outward appearance, but also his testimony's content, his ability to follow the proceedings, or the substance of his communication with counsel. Thus, even if the expert testimony presented at trial allowed jurors to assess Riggins' demeanor fairly, an unacceptable risk remained that forced medication compromised his trial rights.[9]

These concerns are even more applicable to the Yates case because Haldol is a more potent drug than Mellaril, and Yates's dosage of it was higher in relative terms. Furthermore, experts testified that her improvement was not adequate to render her able to stand trial.

The question here is whether it is permissible for the government to administer antipsychotic drugs involuntarily to a mentally ill criminal defendant in order to render that defendant competent to stand trial.

The administration of antipsychotic medication for this reason in a death-penalty case raises some serious questions. The Supreme Court dealt with this issue on various occasions. In *Sell v. United States*, decided June 16, 2003, the Supreme Court declared the forceful administration of antipsychotic drugs to be permissible under certain conditions. The majority opinion, written by Justice Stephen Breyer, states:

> These two cases, Harper and Riggins, indicate that the Constitution permits the Government involuntarily to administer antipsychotic drugs to a mentally ill defendant facing serious criminal charges in order to render that defendant competent to stand trial, but only if the treatment is medically appropriate, is substantially unlikely to have side effects that may undermine the fairness of the trial, and, taking account of less intrusive alternatives, is necessary significantly to further important governmental trial-related interests.[10]

This standard will permit involuntary administration of drugs solely for trial competence purposes in certain instances. But those instances may be rare. That is because the standard says or fairly implies the following: "First, a court must find that important governmental interests are at stake. The Government's interest in bringing to trial an individual accused of a serious crime is important. That is so whether the offense is a serious crime against the person or a serious crime against property. In both instances the Government seeks to protect through application of the criminal law the basic human need for security."

It is obvious that in Yates's case these conditions were not fulfilled. Given the dosage of medication, side effects were unavoidable. Important governmental interests did not exist, because whatever the outcome, Yates would be confined indefinitely to an institution. The security needs were better served by the old civil commitment laws.

Gerald Harris, a psychology professor at the University of Houston and an experienced clinical psychologist, examined Yates five days after she drowned her children. His testimony presented a convincing clinical picture of schizophrenia: her affect was flat and she was delusional and hallucinating. This was consistent on all four occasions when Harris interviewed Yates. He noted her improvement on the antipsychotic medication, and he testified that "it might be a few months before she was functioning well enough and able to understand the trial, but after seeing her today, I think another month should do, maybe even in one month, she might be able to do that. She's rapidly getting better." Harris recommended that Yates receive more treatment and be reevaluated in ninety days. He observed, "You are not going to defend yourself if you believe your death is getting rid of Satan."

Prosecutor Owmby declared, "Delusional or not, she believes she committed the crime."[11] This was not the law regarding competency to stand trial. Thus, Owmby took it upon himself to reinterpret existing law to suit his purpose.

THE JUDGE'S PROSECUTORIAL BIAS

When I became involved in this case, I was sent the complete Houston Police Department offense report, which included within it a variety of items, including a recording of and a transcript of the 911 call, statements by various witnesses who were interviewed proximal to the crime, the observations of the responding officers, and their accounting of the interviews of Andrea Yates by Sergeant Mehl, and the trial transcript.

After reading the transcript, it was clear to me that the judge had shown a strong bias toward the prosecution during the trial. She restricted the testimony of Dr. Ferguson, the jail psychiatrist, who was a neutral observer of Yates's condition.[12] She didn't allow her to elaborate on her assessment of Yates's competency to stand trial but instead demanded a "yes" or "no" answer from an expert, which makes no sense because it calls for leading questions on direct examination.[13] Judge Hill's prosecutorial bias was clearly evident when it came time for the prosecution's experts to testify; they were allowed to give full answers regarding their opinions and their sources for those opinions.

My review of the trial transcript showed that no defense witness was given such freedom of expression as that granted to the prosecution's expert witnesses.

Judges are often former prosecutors. Putting on black robes does not necessarily remove their prosecutorial bias. Judge Hill was a good example of this predisposition. Judge Hill and Prosecutor Owmby had a close personal relationship, as Judge Hill was Owmby's mentor in the days when they were both assistant prosecutors.

It was my distinct impression that Judge Hill was not even-handed in her rulings. This is apparent in the transcript and would likely have been even more evident as an attitude in the courtroom. A judge's attitude has a major influence upon the jury.

THE INSANITY DEFENSE AND ANDREA YATES

First-degree murder requires premeditation by a person of sound mind. A prosecutor has to prove all the elements of first-degree murder in order to gain a conviction.

A criminal defense lawyer whose client suffers from severe mental illness must get a competent expert evaluation. A psychiatrist who testifies that a defendant is not criminally responsible has an obligation to present testimony that is legally and psychiatrically valid, and to do so persuasively. The Texas Penal Code's definition of insanity, found in section 8.01, reads as follows: "It is an affirmative defense to prosecution that, at the time of the conduct charged, the actor, as a result of severe mental disease or defect, did not know that his conduct was wrong."

The expert for the defense, Phillip Resnick, MD, testified in the Andrea Yates trial that she was legally insane. The expert for the prosecution, Park Dietz, MD, testified that Yates was sane. Dietz and Resnick both had impressive credentials. Both men had been presidents of American Academy of Psychiatry and the Law (AAPL), the professional association of forensic psychiatrists. Both teach forensic psychiatry and are role models for forensic psychiatrists in training. It is therefore essential to submit their testimony to a critical appraisal.

All of the experts in the Yates case agreed that Yates suffered from severe psychosis; even Dietz, the prosecution's expert, testified that Yates "had been psychotic for at least three years."[14] The experts made at least five different precise diagnoses, including postpartum depression, major depressive disorder, and schizophrenia. This would certainly confuse the jury. Even though I think that Yates suffered from schizophrenia, in a courtroom I would have limited myself to the diagnosis of psychosis. The type of psychosis is not an issue in the context of the insanity defense. A discussion about the precise nature of the psychosis inevitably confuses the jury because real or apparent contradictions arise when needless precision is pursued.

Precision and accuracy have an inverse relationship. In the treatment setting, precision is essential. Major depressive disorder calls for a different medical treatment protocol than schizophrenia. However, in relation to the insanity defense, the precise nature of the psychosis is irrelevant. Schizophrenia is more precise than psychosis, but in the context of the insanity defense, it is preferable to use the less-precise term because the level of certainty is greater. Some direct examiners ask for more precision than the circumstances of the case require. Some cross-examiners solicit excessive precision in order to prove inaccuracy. I have heard prosecutors argue to the jury that if the experts don't agree, then, "How could you, the jury, be certain?"

The *Houston Chronicle* reported that Dr. Saeed acknowledged that during Yates's first hospitalization, from March 31 until mid-April, he refused Yates's husband's request to put her on Haldol, the antipsychotic medication that Dr. Ferguson, the jail psychiatrist, later prescribed.[15] Saeed did agree to prescribe Haldol when Yates was hospitalized again at Devereux Hospital on May 4, after she told her mother-in-law that she had filled the bathtub because she "might need it." We can now see what she needed it for.

Saeed stated that on May 4: "We hospitalized her [again] because I thought filling the bathtub was an indication she might be suicidal." This was prescient, as Yates did in fact commit a suicide of sorts. Suicidal psychotic mothers quite often kill their children before they kill themselves. I have been involved in a number of such cases.

Yates was released from Devereux Hospital on May 14, 2001. Saeed examined Yates again on June 18, two days before she drowned her children, and claimed he saw no evidence of psychosis at that time. He did increase the dosage of one of Yates's antidepressant drugs.

Defense Attorney George Parnham asked Yates's husband why he sent his wife back to Saeed after what appeared to be unsuccessful treatment the first time. Mr. Yates responded, "I guess, at the time, I saw all psychiatrists as the same. They all have diplomas on the wall. It was my mistake." In reality, the patient, the husband, and the doctor were victims of our irrational health-care system. A chronically psychotic schizophrenic patient was treated as an outpatient. Yates was in need of indefinite psychiatric hospital care and should have been receiving antipsychotic medication. Her care was dominated not by clinical reality but by misguided civil-commitment laws and an insurance company's need for profits.

Mr. Yates testified that his wife spent ten days at Devereux Hospital and was discharged with many of the same symptoms for which she was admitted. He was alarmed by his wife's condition and asked the doctor three weeks later to keep his wife on Haldol. Saeed recommended that she be weaned from the drug. Mr. Yates said he and his wife returned to the hospital on June 18, but the doctor did not place her back on the antipsychotic drug. Two days later, Andrea Yates called her husband and told him to hurry home because something had happened to the children. He would soon discover that she had drowned them.

In the closing argument, the defense called attention to Saeed's negligent treatment of Yates. "Dr. Saeed basically testified before the Grand Jury that he saw no evidence of psychosis." The defense lawyer argued, "We all know why Dr. Saeed testified that way too, because Dr. Saeed takes her off the Haldol a few days before this drowning and Dr. Saeed ignores all of his own notes and every other note that we saw in the medical records that indicated she was psychotic and Dr. Saeed knows that he messed up big time. That's what Dr. Dietz bases his testimony on her not being psychotic on the 20th, you think about that."[16]

Dietz argued that this chronically psychotic woman happened to be not psychotic on the one day when she killed her children. Forensic psychiatric evaluation is an empirical undertaking. The process involves making observations based upon principles accepted by the psychiatric profession. Dietz shows a striking divergence from accepted psychiatric reasoning.

THE CAPITAL MURDER TRIAL OF ANDREA YATES

Once a defendant is declared competent to stand trial, the prosecution presents its evidence in support of the charge that has been filed against the defendant. In the Andrea Yates case, the charge was capital murder. To prove capital murder, the prosecution must provide evidence that the perpetrator undertook a voluntary criminal act. The jury in the Yates case was confronted with two propositions:

1. The prosecution claimed that the killings were the result of Yates's rational deliberation. In support of this claim, they offered the expert testimony of Dr. Park Dietz.
2. The defense claimed that Yates was insane when she drowned her five children and offered the expert testimony of Dr. Phillip Resnick.

Resnick and Dietz agreed that Andrea Yates had been psychotic for two years prior to the incident. Resnick believed that Yates killed her children due to delusional "altruistic" motives. Dietz claimed that Andrea

Yates's knowledge of the sinfulness and illegality of her behavior proved that she was legally sane.

The Yates case demonstrates the tactical advantages of the prosecution in cases where a mentally ill individual is charged with first-degree murder. Yates was extensively interrogated without an attorney, even though any layman could recognize that she was severely mentally ill. Another prosecutorial advantage was the composition of the jury. Prosecutor Owmby claimed that he had God on his side and prayed before seeking the death penalty; he referred to Yates's acts as a "sin." Yates's jury was "death-qualified," meaning it was a jury composed of people who were willing to impose a death sentence. The death-penalty charge was a deceptive ploy by the prosecution to gain a tactical advantage of having what is called a "hanging jury" (a term from the days when hanging was the preferred method of execution).

Eight of the twelve jurors were women, who, according to research, are inclined to "a legalistic, black-and-white interpretation of the law."[17] Two hundred and forty jurors were pre-screened. Creating a death-qualified jury was obviously a high priority for the prosecution. The prosecution may not have had "God on [their] side" as prosecutor Owmby claimed, but they had prejudice against the insanity defense in their corner and a judge whose favoritism for the prosecution was apparent to me throughout my reading of the trial transcript.

Owmby's opening statement did not challenge Yates's psychiatric illness. He told the jury, "After all, drugs like Effexor and Wellbutrin are not given for having just 'a little depression.' Andrea Yates had a mental illness."

Owmby knew from Resnick's public comments that altruism would be the theme of the defense expert's testimony. Owmby liked the term "altruistic," which doomed the insanity defense from the start. He concluded with the simple statement, "The evidence will show that, beyond a reasonable doubt, she is guilty of the murder of Noah, John, and Mary Yates."

Parnham, the defense lawyer, addressed the jury with a long and detailed opening statement. In the first few sentences, he made a promise that would be difficult to keep. He stated, "The question that we hope the evidence will answer is how does a mother, who has given birth, who has nurtured, who has protected, and who has loved the five children that she brought into this world, interrupt their lives."

Parnham showed a preference for euphemisms when speaking to the jury. His client did not "kill" the children—she "interrupted" their lives. He rarely used the words "insanity" or "psychosis." "Postpartum depression with psychotic features" was more to his liking.

Parnham did what many trial lawyers do in their opening statements: he outlined the whole case. In cases where scientific testimony plays a major role, as in this instance, I advise attorneys against this approach. When the lawyer tells the jury what the expert will say, it sounds as if the lawyer is the mastermind and the expert merely his mouthpiece. Parnham declared in the opening statement, "Our experts will testify that postpartum psychosis usually involves delusions regarding the infant. Unless mother and child are properly treated, mother and child are at great risk for harm. It is frequently associated with major depression with psychotic features, bi-polar disorder, schizophrenia, or schizodefective [sic] disorder."

The witnesses Parnham presented offered an array of diagnostic labels, including postpartum depression. As I mentioned earlier, the defense assumed an unnecessary burden of proving a specific diagnosis. All that was necessary was to establish the presence of severe mental illness required by Texas law as an element of legal insanity.

Without doubt, childbirth exacerbated Yates's chronic psychotic illness. However, the diagnosis of postpartum depression is not consistent with a history of years of bizarre delusions, hallucinations, and catatonic episodes. From a tactical perspective, the defense was ill-advised to argue for postpartum depression—a fairly common diagnosis, with which some of the women on the jury may have had experience. The standard psychiatric textbook by Kaplan and Sadock tells us that during the postpartum period, up to 85 percent of women experience some type of mood disturbance.[18] Ten to 15 percent of women are diagnosed with postpartum depression after delivery. However, it is unlikely that any of the jury members or their acquaintances killed their children because of postpartum depression.

The prosecution's first witness was Officer David Knapp, who was asked very typical questions about what happened when he arrived at the Yates's home following Andrea's 911 call. The next witness to testify was Dr. Melissa Ferguson, medical director of psychiatric services at the Harris County Jail. She presented a compelling picture of Yates's illness. Ferguson examined Yates one day after the tragedy and testified that Yates "believed that the children would be tormented and perish in the fires of hell unless they were killed." During the examination, Yates screamed at the doctor, "I was so stupid. Couldn't I have killed just one to fulfill the prophecy? Couldn't I have offered Mary?"

Ferguson further testified that Yates asked her for a razor to shave her head: "She told me she wanted a razor to see if the marks are still there. She referred to them as the marks of the beast and 666 [the anti-Christ]." Yates talked about then-Governor George W. Bush, saying she could not destroy Satan and that "Governor Bush would have to destroy Satan" by executing her. Ferguson told the jury, "In all the patients I've treated for major depression with psychotic features, she is one of the sickest patients I've ever seen."

DIRECT EXAMINATION OF DR. RESNICK

The questions asked by Mr. Parnham and the answers given by Dr. Resnick are in my opinion a primer on what one should not do on direct examination of an expert witness testifying in support of insanity defense. The qualifications segment of Resnick's direct examination was lengthy. He was asked about being the consultant to the U.S. attorney in the case of Theodore Kaczynski, the Unabomber. In this context, Parnham asked, "Are you familiar with the man, an individual—an expert by the name of Park Dietz?" Resnick replied that he was, that they had worked together on the Unabomber case. This was the first of the many references Parnham made to the expert for the prosecution during the direct testimony of the expert for the defense. In the first few pages of Resnick's testimony, Dietz was mentioned seven times. The defense lawyer considered Resnick's association with Dietz, the prosecution's expert, to be an asset, but in my opinion all he did was give more luster to Dietz's reputation. Parnham also repeatedly addressed Resnick, by mistake, as Dietz.

Lawyers often try to immunize their experts against cross-examination by what I call "preventive testimony." Many lawyers believe that they can steal the opposition's thunder by preemptive testimony. Preventive testimony, like preventive war, has unintended consequences. As I mentioned in the first part of this book, I welcome challenges during cross-examination, for they give me the opportunity to confront doubts that the jury may have in the jury room, where I would not be present to explain my reasoning.

Parnham, like many lawyers, anticipated cross-examination during the direct examination. He also asked mostly yes-or-no questions, which is counterproductive on direct examination. An expert, unlike a material witness, can rarely answer a significant question in an unqualified yes-or-no manner. The expert should have an opportunity to be persuasive on direct examination, which Parnham's approach did not allow. This yes-or-no approach amounts to the lawyer testifying and the expert confirming the lawyer's assertions.

Parnham also questioned Resnick concerning his work on malingering, or faking insanity.

Q. Are you familiar with the term malingering?

A. Yes, I am.

Q. And have you written articles and/or produced audio and videotapes relative to the term malingering and how that interacts with the process of the criminal law?

A. Yes. Whenever there is an insanity defense, juries often have some skepticism: is a person genuinely mentally ill or might they be faking? And the technical word for faking mental illness is called malingering, and that is an area that I have written a great deal about and teach courses in as to whether someone is generally mentally ill or may be putting it on to avoid being held responsible.

It is self-defeating for the defense expert to tell the jury that the defendant may be involved in "faking mental illness [that] is called malingering." Jurors need not be reminded of what they suspect and what the prosecution will argue or imply. Resnick's mention of teaching courses on detecting malingering likely made the jury believe that "faking mental illness" may be a widespread occurrence. In reality, it is exceedingly rare.

Parnham also asked questions about malingering and faking on direct examination of Dr. Harris during the trial on competency. In fact, Dietz would later testify on cross-examination that Yates was malingering in an imitation of an episode of *Law & Order* (a television show for which Dietz is a longtime consultant).

In reality, malingering is a spurious issue in insanity-defense cases. Michael Perlin of New York Law School writes, "There is virtually no evidence that feigned insanity has ever been a remotely significant problem of criminal procedure, even after more 'liberal' substantive insanity tests were adopted. A survey of the case law reveals no more than a handful of cases in which a defendant free of mental disorder 'bamboozled' a court or jury into a spurious insanity acquittal."[19] Perlin also notes that research on malingering among offenders indicates that most inmates feign sanity, not insanity, and that advances in detection of malingering can discern faking in over 90 percent of the cases when it does occur. Whatever the merits of arguments of malingering, they are absurd in connection with Yates, whom all experts agreed was unquestionably psychotic.

At the end of the direct examination, Parnham asked his only forensic expert the critical questions designed to lay a foundation for the insanity defense. However, some of Resnick's answers were inconsistent with the insanity defense. The prosecutor made good use of Resnick's mistakes later on.

Q. Did you form an opinion, Dr. Resnick, as to whether or not Andrea Pia Yates knew that it was wrong to drown her children on June the 20th?

A. Yes, I did form an opinion.

Q. What is that opinion, Doctor?

A. It's my opinion that with reasonable medical certainty, that even though Mrs. Yates knew that her acts were legally wrong, that she believed that her conduct was right in the circumstances. . . .

Q. Dr. Dietz [sic]—pardon me, Dr. Resnick, once again, I show you the affirmative defense definition and I ask you, Dr. Resnick, did Andrea Pia Yates on June the 20th, as a result of a severe mental disease or defect, know the difference between right and wrong?

A. How could anyone—

MR. OWMBY: Object.

THE COURT: Sustained.

A. The answer is that she does not know the difference between right and wrong because anyone facing—

MR. OWMBY: Object. Nonresponsive.

THE COURT: Sustained.

Nonresponsive? Although the expert hadn't actually answered yet, the judge agreed with the prosecution and so sustained an objection to a nonexistent answer, another sign of the judge's prosecutorial bias.

Q. (By Mr. Parnham) Why, Doctor, did she not know the difference between right and wrong?

A. Mrs. Yates did not know the difference between right and wrong because I don't think anyone could know the difference between right and wrong when faced with the psychotic dilemma of preserving your children in either eternal salvation by taking their lives or letting them go to hell as she perceived it. It was a cruel dilemma which turned upside down her sense of right and wrong.

Resnick's opinion was that Yates was insane, but his testimony supported the opposite view. A mother who makes "a choice" to take a criminal action for altruistic reasons is criminally responsible.

The expert for the defense told the jury that Yates had a "comprehensible motive" and that she knew her act "was legally wrong." Resnick's testimony that Yates made "the choice" to commit an "altruistic killing" dealt a mortal blow to the insanity defense.[20]

The prosecution argued that Yates was mentally ill and was motivated by a desire to "get rid of the children." The prosecution claimed that Yates had an evil motive. The defense claimed that her motive was "noble." For the purposes of the insanity defense, this is a distinction without difference.

Resnick was the star witness for the defense but his testimony was of more use to the prosecutor than the defendant. The testimony of an expert can be both truthful and incorrect. I think that Resnick believed what he was saying. However the law expected him to give forensic psychiatric testimony consistent with the insanity plea, the lawyer who retained him had the right to expect effective testimony, and Yates was entitled to a defense that made sense. Resnick's testimony was not consistent with the purpose for which it was intended.

It was in the prosecution's best interest to let Resnick's testimony stand even though they could have argued that his testimony was inadmissible under the *Daubert* criteria of expert testimony adopted by Texas. Resnick arrived at the correct opinion that Yates was legally insane, but his testimony was inconsistent with the defense. The worst was yet to come.

DR. RESNICK'S CROSS-EXAMINATION

During a cross-examination, an expert witness has to think like a chess player anticipating his opponent's next few moves. Albert Einstein famously said, "Imagination is more important than knowledge." Owmby manipulated Resnick, who didn't foresee the implications of his answers or the questions that Owmby was asking.

Q. Did you have a written report basically incorporating your opinion as to the legal insanity of Andrea Yates?

A. I developed written material, but Mr. Parnham never requested a written report. So, none was ever given to him.

Q. You have written material?

A. Right. In other words, I developed it in a format of a report, but it was never turned over as a signed document.

Q. And when you say you developed it in the format of a report, what do you mean by that?

A. I mean, I assumed a report would be requested. So, I organized my opinion in the form of a report and asked Mr. Parnham to let me know at what point I should give it to him. Additional material kept coming in which I, you know, reincorporated, but, eventually, Mr. Parnham indicated that it would not be necessary to turn over a report.

Through his answers Resnick informed the jury that the lawyer controls his actions, potentially casting doubt in the jury's mind about the independence of the expert witness's opinions and testimony. I never allow the lawyer to decide whether I will render a report. A report is part of my methodology and a condition for my testimony. Failure to render a report opens a Pandora's box of suspicions for the other side.

Owmby continued to press the point, even implying that not requesting a report might have been a defense strategy to withhold evidence from the prosecution.

Q. All right. And I would suppose it would be fair to call that the outline of a report?

A. Well, I would say it's more than that. It's really in the form of a report but never turned over at the request of the attorney. . . .

Q. And, obviously, it's not—there is no obligation for the defense to provide us with either a written report or even the summaries because, basically, you didn't do a written report. So, there was nothing to provide to us, even if there was a rule that required that. Would that be a fair statement?

A. Well, I'm not an expert on the law in Texas.

Q. You are not?

A. I'm not an expert in when reports are due. I just—the attorney either asks for a report or doesn't ask for a report.

Clearly "I'm not an expert on the law in Texas" is the wrong response from Resnick. A forensic expert should be knowledgeable about relevant legal issues, including whether reports are mandatory in a given jurisdiction. Failure to provide a report would disqualify the expert from testifying in Michigan. It is presumed that the expert will be familiar with basic requirements for the admissibility of his testimony.

More importantly, testimony has a great deal to do with control, and the prosecutor was in command of the situation. Owmby succeeded in putting Resnick on the defensive. Owmby used flattery, indicating that a Resnick was considered to be something of an expert on filicide (the killing of children by a parent), to lead Resnick into providing testimony that was extremely damaging to the insanity defense. Expert witnesses should be very wary of flattery when being cross-examined.

Q. Doctor, I think you would agree with me that there is no mystery that you were a logical person to be called in to work on a case like this?

A. I think that's fair.

Q. I mean, you have written articles from 1969, you've presented on this information over the course of those years and it seems that you would be fairly well-known as a person who has some authority in this field; is that right?

A. Yes.

Q. You also appeared on the ABC news program *Nightline* on June 21st, 2001, did you not?

A. My recollection is that I did, yes.

Q. And during that interview, you stated that based on what you had heard—I think you referred to it as the husband's statement—you didn't have explicit motive, you believed that Andrea Yates suffered from postpartum depression, you couldn't give a diagnostic evaluation, you couldn't comment, but you—but, broadly, you guessed she would fit into the category of an altruistic killer; is that correct?

Although no witness—particularly an expert witness—should be asked to "guess" on the stand, Resnick responds to the question. My response to such a comment would have been "I never guess when I testify under oath." I would also have asked the cross-examiner if he was reading from a transcript, and I would demand to see the transcript.

A. That's correct. If the husband's account was taken at face value, yes.

Q. And that was on June 21st, the day after the homicide occurred; is that right?

A. Yes.

Q. You also—do you remember when you talked to a representative of the *Houston Chronicle* around that June 21st, 22nd time?

A. Not in detail, but I'm commonly called by the media when this type of thing happens because of my writings.

Q. Right. Do you recall the story saying in the June 22nd, 2001, *Houston Chronicle* where you stated that, apparently, Andrea Yates did not attempt suicide after the children's death and that puts her in the minority of women in this altruistic category?

A. I don't recall phrasing it exactly like that, but that's correct. There are two subcategories of altruistic. One, where it's associated with a suicide, which is more common; and the other, where the mother kills to relieve the perceived suffering of her children; and she fit into that aspect of altruistic.

Q. And you suffered from what a lot of people suffer from the press from. You say something and then it's edited and put in the newspaper and they did not explain fully, I'm assuming, what you said to them, but you did place her on June 22nd—or at some conversation prior to June 22nd in the category of altruistic killer; is that right?

A. Yes.

Q. You also said in the *Nightline* interview on June 21st that she, meaning Andrea Yates, did what she perceived to be in the children's best interest by sending them to heaven or relieving them of some psychotically attributed symptoms. Do you remember saying something like that?

A. I don't recall specifically, but those would be the—that's, again, referring to them—referring to the two subcategories of altruistic filicide. And I don't recall if I was simply explaining those categories or referring to her case in particular.

Q. Well, let me see if this sounds like what you said: "That's right, I have no doubt that when all the facts come out, we are likely to hear that she honestly believed that she was doing her children a service rather than a disservice." That's what you said on *Nightline*?

A. Right and I think that's a fair statement, as in, when the facts come out what we are likely to hear . . . but I didn't know because the facts were not out at that time.

By reviewing the statements Resnick had made on ABC News's *Nightline* and in newspapers immediately following Yates's drowning of her children, Owmby was able to show the jury that Resnick had formed opinions about the case long before being hired by the defense, before reviewing any documents and examining Andrea Yates, which damaged his credibility. If the defense lawyer knew about Resnick's earlier statements, he should not have hired him.

Resnick's attempt to transform Yates's insanity into an act of altruism was neither persuasive nor psychiatrically valid. Resnick's testimony on direct examination about Yates's "cruel dilemma" gave the prosecutor an opportunity to emphasize the choices available to Yates (as if she were capable of making rational decisions).

Q. And by 'irresistible impulse,' would you explain what that means?

A. Yes. Some jurisdictions, but not Texas, say that in order to be found insane, one can either not know the wrongfulness of one's act or be unable to refrain from the act. And that inability to refrain is sometimes referred to as irresistible impulse, but in Texas, it is limited to knowledge of wrongfulness.

Q. So, when you stated on direct that Andrea Yates was faced with a dilemma— I believe you referred to it as a cruel dilemma—

A. Yes.

Q. —you did not mean to imply that she had no choice and had to do it because even if that were the case, she would not qualify under Section 801, would she? . . .

Q. I believe what we were talking about was—and we may have covered it—was the Durham Rule, a product of insanity. And what I kind of wanted to explore with you is, aren't you really saying that in your opinion that the—the delusions you claim that Andrea Yates was suffering from on June 20th, the dilemma that you claim that she was faced with on June 20th, is due to her mental illness and her actions were therefore a product of her mental illness. Aren't you saying that?

A. That's true, but that's not all I'm saying. I'm also saying that due to her mental illness, she thought her conduct was right.

Q. But she knew it was legally wrong?

A. That's correct.

Q. And she knew it was legally wrong—subjectively legally wrong. And by that, I mean, even from her standpoint, even in her delusion, she knew this conduct was legally wrong?

A. I agree.

With this type of testimony, under Texas law, the jury had little choice but to find Yates legally sane. The prosecutor could have argued that Resnick's classification of infanticide on direct examination was not generally accepted and therefore not admissible as a matter of law. The prosecutor shrewdly chose to rely instead upon this classification to undermine the insanity defense. His approach was tactically effective. The following exchange proves this point.

Q. I was about to ask you about subjective moral wrongfulness, but let me ask you this question instead. What you are actually telling this jury is that Andrea Yates believed that it was a higher moral good subjectively, based on her beliefs, to kill her children than to rely—than to follow the legal standard that she also knew?

A. That's not how I would phrase it. How I would phrase it is that Andrea Yates, in spite of knowing it was legally wrong, felt that considering her dilemma, what she perceived as right—you don't need to use the word morally right, but what she perceived as right in the context of her dilemma, was to take her children's life on earth to prevent them from eternal damnation.

Q. Right. There is no need to use the word morally right, but in the same explanation we are using the phrase legally right. So, we have to be talking about some other right, don't we?

Owmby correctly points out that Resnick and the prosecution are in substantial agreement, thus the defense expert was unwittingly acting as a witness for the prosecution. Once again his testimony is "contrary to the purpose for what is intended."

Resnick continues:

A. Well, I would say she's—it's a higher good or a lesser of negative consequences as to why she thought her conduct was right. . . .

Q. A person who is *delusionally altruistic* [emphasis mine] and says they are killing their children for that could also want to get revenge on a spouse, could they not?

A. I don't think that would go together. In other words, it would not be altruistic. If the goal is to hurt the spouse, that's not altruistic. They would be mutually exclusive.

Resnick has painted himself into a corner. If Yates killed her children for altruistic reasons, as he claimed, she could also kill them for selfish reasons. The prosecution's charge was that Yates killed her children because they were "unwanted," which was one of the categories in Resnick's classification of filicide. Experts should avoid the word "possible." What is possible is not probative, but the jury can misunderstand this as an affirmative answer to the prosecutor's assertion. I find it significant that Resnick did not object to the phrase "delusionally altruistic." One can be delusional or altruistic, but neither psychiatrically nor logically can one be "delusionally altruistic." But Resnick takes no notice of this fact as the cross-examination continues.

Q. Sending the children to heaven to get them away from a possibly controlling or domineering spouse and show him what you mean, show him how he hurt you would be altruistic. They are in a better place and the spouse is brought home to see what has happened?

A. Well, yes, you could have those elements, but the question is, what the primary motive is. Is it for the children's sake, which would make it altruistic, or is it to hurt the husband which would make it spouse revenge. So, there could only be one or the other in terms of the category.

Q. In terms of the category or the primary motive?

A. Yes.

Q. But, as you said, these categories are not mutually exclusive?

A. That's correct, but those two are.

Q. Isn't it possible for a chronically ill person, when they suffer from schizoaffective disorder, schizophrenia or depression, to kill children just because they feel overwhelmed and they can't see any other way for them out of this situation and the children will be in a better place anyway and kill those children just to get out of that overwhelming situation?

A. Well, when you say in a better place anyway, either the primary motive is the mother doesn't want the children or the primary motive is I want the children to be in a better place. And if the primary motive is to pursue the best interest of the children, it would be called altruistic. . . .

Q. You are saying that the cruel dilemma was a product of her delusion. That's not the law in Texas, is it?

A. I'm sorry, I think that you're mixing up legal criteria for insanity with the clinical facts of this case; and I can't answer the question the way it's asked because it's confusing.

Q. But you said that she knew right from wrong–

A. No, I never said that.

Q. –legally?

A. I said that she did know her act was legally wrong but believed her conduct was right when she drowned the children.

The cross-examination ended on a high note for the prosecution. Resnick's last statement would have been appropriate for an expert witness testifying against the insanity defense. With Resnick's testimony, the prosecutor could have rested his case and asked for a directed verdict in his favor. Resnick's testimony conflicted with his opinion that Yates was not criminally responsible. I mentioned earlier that forensic expert testimony has to be consistent with the purpose for which it was intended. The legal concept of "fitness for purpose" is a standard that must be met by someone who sells goods or services. The buyer informs the seller as to the purpose the goods or services are acquired. Resnick violated this principle repeatedly by his testimony.

Parnham, to my surprise, chose to redirect Resnick. The purpose of a redirect is "rehabilitation of the witness." I generally advise against it; redirect only calls the jury's attention one more time to whatever problems were created on cross-examination. An effective expert witness should not require a "do-over." Obviously there are exceptions—for example, when the cross-examiner has misstated the facts. However, Parnham went ahead with redirect without any valid reason to do so.

The redirect did not "rehabilitate" the witness; on the contrary it made a bad situation worse. Parnham tried to show that Resnick is an unbiased expert because after interviewing Susan Smith, another mother who drowned her two young chilgren, Resnick did not find her to be insane. Once again, the prosecutor did not object to this line of questioning, even though the cross-examination had not dealt with the subject of Smith. The rules of evidence require that the redirect be limited to issues raised on cross-examination, but the prosecutor saw the advantage of keeping quiet.

WITNESS FOR THE PROSECUTION

On the first day of his testimony in the Yates case, Park Dietz, MD, presented himself to the jury not only as a seeker of "truth" but also as someone whose views in the case had peer approval. The concept of peer review carries the implication of some organizational endorsement. Peer approval suggests that an independent body of professionals found another professional's written work to be within the standards and norms of their discipline. However, in this case, Dietz relied upon three colleagues whom he selected himself to review his report about the Yates case. Let us simply say—to be generous—that this is an unusual form of peer review.

Andrea Yates, according to the sworn testimony of Dietz, was legally sane because "She thought that killing the children was sinful. That's another piece of evidence that she knew it was wrong. If you know it's a sin, then you know it's wrong. Just as if you know Satan wants such things to happen or believe that, you know it's wrong."[21]

In the Yates case, Dietz "divided the offense into three phases: the pre-homicide phase, the homicide phase, and the post-homicide phase."[22] He selected video excerpts from his interviews with Yates to illustrate each phase and played them to the jury. His interviews are lengthy and he records them in their entirety. He was permitted to play to the jury portions of a video of an interview with Yates. I have never attempted or would agree to the playing of a video excerpt; I would consider that misleading and manipulative. Dietz was permitted to interpret for the jury the selected items. Here is an example.

> Well, the first point is that Mrs. Yates indicates that at that time before the homicide she had the idea of killing her children and she attributed the origin of that idea to Satan. So, of course, the idea comes from her mind, but she's mistakenly thinking Satan put it there. The fact that she regards it as coming from Satan is the first indication of her knowing that this is wrong. Because she recognizes even the idea of killing your children is an evil idea that comes from Satan. She doesn't think this is a good idea that comes from God. She thinks it's an evil idea that comes from Satan and she thought it was Satan who was somehow urging or encouraging or recommending that she do this. So she knows already it's a bad idea.[23]

Dietz emphasized that he did not consider Yates's ideas to be delusions. He minimized the severity of Yates's illness, and testified:

> Mrs. Yates blamed herself for improperly raising her children, who would therefore become a burden on society. She said that from the day of her arrest on. She's always acknowledged that. That's not delusional material; she's carrying it too far in being so guilt-ridden about it. That's because she's depressed, but it's true if she stays that depressed

and dysfunctional, she's not going to be an adequate mother. She can't adequately home school them. The children will become increasingly problematic and [sic] not going to be well disciplined. I mean, she's not wrong about that.[24]

The prosecutor asked Dietz whether Yates believed that the children were in danger from Satan. To this, Dietz responded with innuendo designed to cast doubt that Yates was delusional.

Well, I do expect people with delusions of imminent harm where somebody is going to get hurt, especially a loved one, to act as if that were true and to take steps to try to protect the one they love; and that can be calling the police, calling the FBI, calling a priest or a minister, pastor, sending the children away to a safe place. That doesn't involve killing them, take oneself away from the children, even suicide, but these are alternatives that are non-lethal to the children that, that I expect a person with that delusion to at least consider.[25]

Dietz implied that Yates's motivation for killing her children differed from those she presented after the homicides. The prosecutor then continues:

Q. All right. And next you have a question about whether she may have believed she was saving the children from torment. Would you explain what you mean by that?

A. Well, this is another one where I don't know for sure it's so. Mrs. Yates, after her arrest, talks about believing the children were in danger from Satan, believing they could be tormented by Satan, believing they could burn in hell. And as she tells me this, that she was thinking that before and during killing them, I'm inclined to believe her, I think she's trying to be forthcoming. At the same time, I have to be skeptical, both because that's my job and, also, because her behavior, as she kills them, doesn't do the things I would expect a mother with that belief to do.

Q. And what would that be, Doctor?

A. I would expect her to try to comfort the children, telling them they are going to be with Jesus or be with God, but she does not offer words of comfort to the children.[26]

Once again he expects rational behavior from a grossly psychotic person; the normal caretaking impulses of a mother were eliminated in Andrea Yates by her schizophrenia.

Dietz was permitted to go into considerable detail and testify in a narrative form; defense witnesses were not given this privilege by the judge. Owmby asked Dietz to explain the significance of the video excerpts E. and F. Dietz answered:

Those segments that were just played go right to the heart of the issue of her knowledge of wrongfulness. If one believes what she's saying in that interview was the way she believed and felt at the time, then this is complicated because there are factors weighing on each side. On the one hand, she knows that it's sinful and that, and she attributes the idea to Satan and she knows it's illegal, and she knows it will be judged as bad by society and by God, but on the other hand she believes that this saves the children from torment or from having their souls go to Satan. And that, therefore, it's the right thing for the children.[27]

Thus, Yates's delusional ideas about sin, Satan, and God are the foundation for the opinion of the expert for the prosecution that the defendant knew the difference between right and wrong and therefore is legally sane. From a legal perspective, behavior based on delusions cannot justify a first-degree murder charge. The last time delusions about Satan led to criminal charges was in the Salem witch trials in 1692.

THE CROSS-EXAMINATION OF DR. DIETZ

Dietz claimed that there is "a dramatic difference between everything we know about Andrea Yates up to and through June 20, 2001, and everything we know from June 21, 2001."[28] He repeatedly testified that the Satan notion appeared only after June 21st, saying that, "The day after the homicide was the first time she said Satan tormented her, and since then she's been consistent in saying she felt tormented by Satan."[29] This was an effort to pander to the tendency to view the insanity plea as "just an excuse." Yates offered no excuses, because her behavior, from her delusional perspective, was appropriate. In her view, she was protecting her children from Satan.

Parnham established that Dietz reviewed Yates's medical records, which showed that Yates suffered from severe schizophrenic illness. Dr. George Ringholz, a neurologist who also holds a Ph.D. in psychology, testified that Yates was schizophrenic. Even Dietz testified that Yates had been psychotic for two years. Dietz was also asked whether Yates's disease was schizophrenia, and he responded "It would be my judgment that that's the most likely, yes. . . ."

Nonetheless, during his testimony, Dietz presented a number of slides that supported his view that Yates was not insane under the Texas law. On cross-examination, the factual basis of these slides was questioned. Dietz's "findings"—the term implies the result of direct examination of the victim or some other records—was actually information related to him by the prosecutor, who in turn, relied upon information from Deputy Michael Stephens, who was eavesdropping on Ferguson, the jail psychiatrist. Stephens overheard Ferguson interviewing Yates in jail from his position outside the door of the examination room. For obvious reasons, it is a mockery of the rules of evidence to allow a jury to hear such testimony. It was hearsay of hearsay, based upon eavesdropping.

SANITY WITHIN INSANITY AND PARK DIETZ, MD

I found the conduct of Dr. Park Dietz particularly troublesome; his brilliance and standing within the forensic community gives him significant influence. In my mind his actions in this case raise ethical issues. Resnick and Dietz agreed that Yates had been psychotic for two years prior to the killing of her children and that she killed because of her delusions. Dietz claimed that Andrea Yates's knowledge of the sinfulness of her behavior proved that she was legally sane.

Sins are actions chosen by sane sinners; delusions are the involuntary ideas of sick human beings. Christian doctrine states that sin is the free and deliberate violation of God's law by thought, word, or action. St. Augustine writes, "There can be no sin that is not voluntary, the learned and the ignorant admit this evident truth."[30] A person deprived of reason cannot sin because he or she is without the power to choose. Willful intent is an essential element of sin and crime; therefore, Andrea Yates was not able to commit a sin or a crime because of her state of mind. Delusions can serve only as a basis for the diagnosis of psychosis; the use of delusions to prove sanity or insanity violates logic and ethics.

The test for the absence of criminal responsibility in Texas is the inability to know the difference between right and wrong as the result of "severe mental illness" at the time of the act. The defense claimed that Yates—as a result of being severely mentally ill—did not have the ability to know that it was wrong to drown her five children. In support of this claim, the defense produced testimony of Resnick that the killings were motivated by altruism. Delusional altruism opposed by delusional proof of sanity is breathtaking gobbledygook. A delusion is false by definition. In his classic book *General Psychopathology*, Karl Jaspers defined the three main criteria for a belief to be considered delusional: certainty, incorrigibility, and impossibility or falsity of content.[31] Yates certainly qualified as delusional by any standard known to psychiatry. If a lawyer informed a jury that sanity is determined by a delusion, he would be sanctioned for misleading the jury. Why should a psychiatrist be able to make such a disingenuous argument?

Dietz told *Time* magazine that the law "allows a psychotic person's own disordered thoughts to be used against them." Assuming that this is true, not everything that is acceptable as a legal argument can be used as scientific evidence or ethical medical testimony. Dr. Larry Faulkner, in his Presidential Address at the 30th Annual Meeting of the American Academy of Psychiatry and the Law (AAPL) on October 14, 1999, declared, "Forensic psychiatrists are physicians first, psychiatrists second, and only then forensic psychiatrists." What level of certainty does a physician need to tell a jury, a family, and a community that a psychotic mother who drowned her five children was sane and is a proper subject for a first-degree murder conviction? What level of confidence must an expert have if he knows that his opinion may result in an execution?

A forensic psychiatrist, like any physician, is bound by the ethics of consequentialism and the Hippocratic Oath. In the Yates case, Dietz debased the time-honored medical tradition of protecting the sick. His testimony implicitly supported the claim that Yates's actions were voluntary, as required for a capital-murder verdict. The standards of proof from the perspective of an expert witness must have some relationship to the magnitude of the consequences of the expert's testimony. A physician who testifies in support of a death-penalty verdict for a severely mentally ill woman violates medical ethics.

The *Standard Textbook of Psychiatry* by Kaplan and Sadock lists four core ethical principles that should govern the conduct of a psychiatrist: autonomy, nonmalefeasance, beneficence, and justice. Nonmalefeasance means that it is the psychiatrist's duty to avoid inflicting physical or emotional harm on the patient, or increasing the risk of such harm.

That principle is captured by the motto *primum non nocere*, or "first, do no harm." An adherence to medical ethics is essential if medicine is to view itself as an independent profession.

The law presumes that the expert's opinion is consistent with the prevailing views of a given science. This means that a critical audience of the expert's peers would accept his opinion. It is inconceivable to me that a group of psychiatrists would accept Dietz's reasoning. And yet there was no protest from organized forensic psychiatry. The defense lawyer should have argued that Dietz's testimony was inadmissible under the *Daubert* criteria of expert testimony adopted by Texas.

Psychiatrically, the question of knowledge of wrongfulness in this context is an oxymoron. Under the facts of the Yates case, the only way for the prosecution to overcome the defense's claim of insanity would be if they could establish malingering. Dietz did introduce the issue of malingering during Parnham's cross-examination; this, as we shall see, was his undoing. It was established after the verdict that this testimony was not accurate.

Dietz told *Time*, "Some of her psychotic symptoms—such as believing that cameras were planted in her cciling and TV characters were sending messages to her—were indisputable as much as two weeks prior to the death [of her children]."[32] This, in itself, precluded the claim that she was legally sane. On the same page, *Time* quotes Dietz as having told jurors that "there was no hallucination prior to the crime, and whatever she suffered was nothing more than 'obsessional obtrusive thoughts.'" I have never heard anyone describe the belief that cameras are planted in the ceiling and that TV characters are sending them messages as "obsessional obtrusive thoughts."

Let us assume that a psychiatrist, based upon clinical data, has an opinion that a defendant in a given jurisdiction does not qualify for the insanity defense. However, if his evaluation demonstrates that the charge of first-degree murder is inconsistent with the clinical reality, it would be unethical for the psychiatrist to support a first-degree murder charge by his testimony. In this case, the prosecution might change the charge from first-degree murder to a lesser offense more appropriate to the circumstances and state of mind of the perpetrator, in which case the psychiatrist might agree to testify.[33]

Dietz testified that his fees in the Yates case would exceed $50,000. But the *Houston Chronicle* reported on September 23, 2003, that at the time of that statement on March 9, 2002, he had already collected

$42,606. The reporter writes, "Maybe he didn't want the jury to know he would be getting six figures for testifying against Yates. Maybe he was concerned that these taxpaying jurors would question the credibility of any opinion that cost that much. Or maybe at that point he was still in the period of temporary insanity that caused him to invent a phony TV script. His final bill was $105,636.99."

A few jurors appeared on television after the trial and emphasized that Yates's supposed knowledge of wrongfulness was the deciding factor in their rejection of the insanity defense. Dietz was interviewed by a Charlottesville weekly called *The Hook* in December 2003. Reporter Willis Spaulding writes:

> Dietz is a prosecutor's dream because his method of forensic evaluation looks for a flaw in the internal logic of the defendant's purported madness, and in that way "proving" that the defendant is sane at least legally. For example, Andrea Yates was so concerned about Satan's influence on her children that she killed them. But believing in Satan implies believing that there's a difference between good and evil. Therefore, she was legally sane because she could distinguish right from wrong.[34]

In an April 23, 2002, interview with the *New York Times*, Dietz discussed his role in the Yates case. He said that the proper role of a forensic psychiatrist is to seek the truth, not to help a specific party in a case. He told the *Times*, "That's my core philosophical difference with both clinical psychiatry and the defense bar. And it's one of the reasons that I appear mostly for the prosecution."[35] The implication is that Dietz, unlike the rest of psychiatry, is not biased in favor of criminals. Dietz sounds more like a politician than a physician. I wonder how he reconciles seeking truth and using delusions to prove sanity. In reality, the expert's ethical obligation is to assist, within ethics and reality, the party that has retained him or her: that is the essence of the adversary system. By definition, the "truth" is unknown during the trial and will be determined by the jury. I find it disturbing that when Dietz presented the account of his testimony to a large AAPL audience no one rose to challenge him.

The prosecution's enormous effort to have Yates declared sane borders on the grotesque. The transcript of the proceedings consists of forty-eight volumes, with innumerable exhibits introduced. The cost of preparing the trial transcripts alone was $50,000. The prosecution won the bragging rights of having defeated one more insanity plea, but the last thing that Harris County needed was one more schizophrenic person in its jail system. In October 2006, *Psychiatric News* reported that 37 percent of inmates in the Harris County Jail were mentally ill.[36]

Judging from the total of $105,636.99 paid to Dietz by the prosecution for his services, one must assume that Dietz spent countless hours to arrive at the opinion that Yates was not insane. The question then arises of how long a psychiatrist might reasonably take to evaluate a defendant who is asserting an insanity defense. In my view, Dietz's fees for evaluation and testimony in the Yates case raise an ethical issue. A forensic psychiatric evaluation, unlike psychotherapy, is not an open-ended process. The *Comprehensive Textbook of Psychiatry* by Kaplan and Sadock states, "The initial psychiatric assessment usually lasts between 45 and 90 minutes, with the length of time agreed upon in advance. Sometimes additional time is necessary to complete the evaluation, in which case it is better to schedule an additional session."[37]

A forensic psychiatric evaluation does require a great deal more time than a routine diagnostic evaluation. Additional time is needed to review records, write reports, meet with attorneys, and prepare and give testimony. However, in the hundreds of homicide cases in which I have testified since the 1950s, I rarely needed more than four hours to interview a defendant; usually two hours was sufficient. Some of the civil cases in which my testimony played a role resulted in verdicts of millions of dollars. I believe that I am generally regarded as an effective expert witness, but regardless of who pays the bill, or how big the verdict was, it has never occurred to me to charge more than $350 per hour.

In the Bundy case, in which the defense retained me, it took me less than three hours to determine that Bundy was not insane. In the case of the Cincinnati Angel of Death, my videotaped interview lasted about two hours. I determined that there was no basis for the insanity defense. The prosecutor dropped the death-penalty charge and the defendant pled guilty. There was no trial.

ANDREA YATES A MALINGERER?

The prosecutor argued in his final argument that "these thoughts came to her, and she watches *Law & Order* regularly, she sees this program. There is a way out." On March 12, 2002, the jury found Andrea Yates guilty of two counts of capital murder. On March 18, 2002, after Yates's conviction and sentencing, the *Houston Chronicle* reported,

> Dr. Park Dietz had told the jury that an episode of the television drama "Law & Order" about a mother who drowned her children, and got off on insanity, aired before Yates killed her five children in the same manner. Prosecutors argued that [this episode] gave Yates an idea of how to get out of her marriage. The defense did not learn until two days after the guilty verdict that no such program was broadcast.[38]

On March 14, 2002, after Yates was convicted of murder but before the sentencing phase, Dietz informed the Harris County district attorney's office that he had given an incorrect answer during cross-examination. He said that after the *Law & Order* producers had conducted a search of the show's 269 episodes they told him that they could find none in which a woman with postpartum depression drowns her children in a bathtub. The appeals court agreed with Yates's defense, finding that "the State used Dr. Dietz's false testimony to suggest to the jury that [Yates] patterned her actions after that 'Law & Order' episode."[39] The appeals court set aside the verdict and ordered a new trial. The overzealous prosecutor and his expert wasted the taxpayers' money and tormented a sick women.

In an interview with *Psychiatric News*, Dietz expressed dismay at the "mischaracterizations" of his testimony and his correction of it flooded the popular press. He emphasized that he did not testify about "nonexistent episodes" of *Law & Order*, but after reading scores of scripts for the show as a paid consultant to the show and watching nearly 300 episodes, he "misremembered" and "confounded" details of some of the episodes.[40]

If we accept that Dietz "misremembered" and unintentionally misled the jury that Andrea Yates faked her illness based upon a television show in which a mother killed her children and was acquitted by reason of insanity, then we must ask why he gave this testimony during cross-examination. If he believed that Yates was faking insanity based upon a television episode, then this should have been part of his direct testimony.

Yates is not the first, nor will she be the last, psychotic woman to kill her children. The emphasis on punitive criminal justice distracts us from more fundamental and far-reaching questions, like why we neglect to care for psychotics before they grow violent. The Yates trial was a tragedy that could have contributed to the public understanding of psychotic illness and its relation to homicidal behavior. Instead, Resnick presented an unbelievable "altruistic infanticide" theory, while the prosecution's expert offered as rebuttal an equally far-fetched interpretation of delusion as proof of sanity. Rationality within irrationality (Resnick) and delusions that prove knowledge of wrongfulness (Dietz) are mirror images. Fiction writers could not get away with such ideas, yet these strange views have been admitted as expert testimony.

A JUDGE MAKES A DIFFERENCE

On May 10, 2003, in the small town of Tyler, Texas, Deanna Laney stoned to death her two sons, Joshua and Luke. The third son, Aaron, survived, but he suffered severe brain damage. On May 11, 2003, the *Tyler Morning Telegraph* reported:

> In a 911 call to Smith County early Saturday morning, Mrs. Laney told authorities she had just "bashed their [her children's] heads in with a rock" and that two of her sons were dead. Smith County Sheriff deputies arriving at the Arizona Drive residence in New Chapel Hill found Joshua Keith Laney, 8, and Luke Allen Laney, 6, dead in the yard, wearing only their underwear. Large rocks were found on top of their tiny bodies. Mrs. Laney, wearing blood-stained pajamas, told the first deputy on the scene "I had to" when he took her into custody, according to an arrest affidavit.[41]

Laney's homicidal behavior was more brutal than that of Andrea Yates. She believed that the day after the end of the world she and Yates would be the only two women who would remain alive.

Dietz was once again the expert for the prosecution and Resnick was the expert for the defense. A critical difference between the Laney case and the Yates case is that in the Laney case, Judge Cynthia Stevens-Kent, a scholarly jurist, appointed Dr. William H. Reid, a Texas forensic psychiatrist, to be her advisor. She appointed Reid after Resnick and Dietz were already involved in the case; I believe the judge wanted to prevent what had happened a year before in Houston with the Yates case. Judge Stevens-Kent asked Reid to evaluate the defendant and give his opinion regarding her sanity. In a report dated February 1, 2004, Reid stated that Laney was psychotic and that she had an irrational belief, caused by her severe mental disease, that God was instructing her to kill her sons, and that doing God's will, in this way, was both necessary and "right."

A Texas jury found Deanna Laney not guilty by reason of insanity in the stoning deaths of her two children and the mutilation of a third. There was no significant legal or psychiatric difference between the Laney and Yates cases; both were psychotic with religious delusions, and both had home-schooled their children because of their religious beliefs. Laney even said that she identified with Yates's conduct and that they were pursuing the same God-directed goals. Neither of their husbands was aware of the impending disaster. The prosecution and defense in both cases used the same psychiatrists, and both cases were tried in Texas under the same laws. The greatest surprise was the opinion of Dietz.

The *Tyler Morning Telegraph* reported on April 10, 2004, that First Assistant District Attorney Brett Harrison "was surprised [that] Dr. Park Dietz, a man known for evaluating such people as child-killers Andrea Yates and Susan Smith, 'Unabomber' Ted Kaczynski and serial killer Jeffrey Dahmer, who rarely finds defendants insane when hired by prosecutors, found Mrs. Laney insane."[42]

In 2004, Dietz and Resnick once again put on their retrospective presentations at the annual meeting of the AAPL. Judge Stevens-Kent and Reid were also on the panel. Dietz was the moderator; he introduced the subject by saying:

> Tonight, we will be talking about a serious topic and a difficult one. To the public, there was a superficial resemblance between two cases in Texas in the past couple of years. One being the case of Andrea Yates; the other being the case of Deanna Laney. In both instances, these women, who eventually killed their children, had a history of intense religiosity; they were very active in their churches and their lives revolved in many ways around fundamentalist religion. In both cases they were home schooling their children. In both cases they had lived for a time in a trailer and in both cases their crimes elicited the public outcry and yet there were different verdicts in the two cases, which have led to confusion for some and concern among others and some cause for reform. Last year we had a chance to talk about the Andrea Yates case, this year we're going to—two years ago we talked about the Andrea Yates. Tonight we're going to be talking about the Laney case and spend a few minutes comparing them.[43]

According to Dietz, Laney was convinced that she was killing her children at God's direction, but that was true only with the first two boys. When it came to Aaron, she began to have doubts. Dietz said:

> With respect to the key issue—a knowledge of wrongfulness—first, from the initial 911 call to all of the examinations done by everyone up to my exam, she consistently maintained that she had killed Luke and Joshua at the direction of God. She stated that she was attacking Aaron, the son who survived, at the direction of God, but by the time she made the 911 call, she doubted that this was actually God's will and thought she must have misinterpreted God. By the time Dr. Resnick saw her, which was within a week, she knew that it hadn't been God's will. I thought if there were one point that the prosecution might have wanted to differentiate in order to pursue a conviction on something—that it would be this issue of her distinguishing the attack on Aaron from the attack on the other two boys.

Once again, one would think that this whole line of reasoning would support Dietz's approach in the Yates case. Surprisingly, Dietz ascribes the unanimity of forensic psychiatric experts to the fact that the interviews were tape-recorded, not done "in secret." I am a proponent of videotaping and have, as I have pointed out, been the first forensic psychiatrist to videotape forensic interviews. But I do not believe that my colleagues who do not follow this procedure avoid videotaping in order to hide something.

The Texas law regarding insanity did not change in the few months between the two trials; therefore it is reasonable to ask what motivated Dietz to render a different opinion in the Laney case. One cannot help but wonder if Dietz had sensed a shift in the winds of public opinion and made a self-serving adjustment.

At the 2006 annual AAPL meeting I approached Resnick and told him that I was writing a book in which I would discuss his testimony in the Yates case. I informed him that I did not agree with his testimony and that I'd like to interview him. On October 26, 2006 we met in the lounge of the Marriott Hotel in Chicago, where the AAPL meeting was being held. I took notes while we talked. At the outset, I said that I did not understand his formulation of the insanity defense in the Andrea Yates case. I referred to his paper on "child murderers" and said that I did not understand the criteria for the categories he devised.

Resnick explained that the critical element was whether or not there was "understandable motive in the psychotic individual or if the motive was not comprehensible." About the Andrea Yates case he said, "She had a rational motive based upon a delusion." This made no sense to me. I consider rational behavior understandable, intelligible, and accepted by a community—but since this was not a debate, I did not contradict him. Resnick told me, "Park Dietz and I agreed that she [Yates] was severely mentally ill and that she knew that it was against the law what she did, but the contest was about the word 'wrongfulness.'" Yates believed that she was acting in the best interest of the children; therefore, she was doing the right thing, Resnick said.

I asked Resnick why the prosecutor did not object to this testimony. The prosecutor could have argued that his testimony did not meet the criteria for admissible testimony since it did not represent accepted psychiatric thinking. Resnick replied, "This is an interesting question," and I did not pursue the subject with him. The reason was understandable to me—the prosecutor had recognized Resnick's testimony as the gift to the prosecution that it was.

We also discussed Dr. Michael Welner, the expert retained by the prosecution in the second Yates trial, in which Yates's insanity defense was successful. Resnick said that he found Welner's testimony excessive. According to Resnick, Welner characterized Andrea Yates as selfish. Resnick showed me on his laptop a 150-page single-spaced report submitted by Welner that seemed to be quite harsh in relation to Yates. I did not take the time to read it in its entirety. Resnick said "there was uniform dislike" of Welner's testimony. This was an understatement. According to the *Houston Chronicle*, juror Gina Dickinson said, "After hearing and reading all the doctors' notes [referring to Dr. Ferguson, the jail psychiatrist] while she [Yates] was in the Harris County Jail, there is no way anyone could come to the conclusion that she was just selfish."[44]

The *Houston Chronicle* commented in the same article, in a section appropriately titled, "Are You Sitting Down?" about the fees paid to Dietz and Welner.

The mistake [the nonexistent *Law & Order* episode] may have dented Dietz's vaunted reputation, but it helped his pocketbook. He earned $37,000 more for his testimony in the second trial. But Dietz looks like a bargain compared with the new hired gun brought in by the DA's office for the second trial. Dr. Michael Welner and his consulting firm, the Forensic Panel, were paid a jaw-dropping $242,966.74 for work on the second Yates trial. At least Dietz's testimony worked with the jurors in the first trial but was overturned by an appeals court because of the mistake. Welner's testimony seems to have backfired with the second jury, which found Yates not guilty by reason of insanity. "Although Dr. Welner's qualifications were impressive, his presentation in court was not good," said juror Bobby Chism. "He came across as very aloof and self-serving."[45]

Returning to my interview with Resnick: when he spoke of "rationality within irrationality," I was reminded that he used this formulation during a presentation to the plenary session of AAPL. He discussed the notorious case of Charles McCoy, Jr., known as "The Columbus Sniper." Resnick was the expert for the prosecution and justified his testimony by stating that the grossly psychotic paranoid schizophrenic "showed rationality in his irrationality." All severely mentally ill people have some islands of rationality; therefore, virtually no psychotic could ever meet Resnick's criterion for legal insanity. The phrase "rationality within irrationality" in the context of a severely mentally ill person who has committed a homicide is neither true nor false, but empty. A basic question about an expert's formulation is its "explanatory adequacy." This is a concept introduced by the American linguist Noam Chomsky; it states that an explanation must be in accord with the accepted standards.

The only voice of rationality in the two-trial Yates drama was the *Houston Chronicle*. This newspaper's coverage of the Yates saga deserved a Pulitzer Prize. Unlike so many major newspapers in similar circumstances, the *Houston Chronicle* subjected the proceedings to critical appraisals. I credit the *Houston Chronicle* with the fact that Andrea Yates's second trial in 2006 resulted in finding this psychotic woman legally insane. The *Houston Chronicle*'s efforts dramatically changed public attitudes in the Houston community.

The Yates case is emblematic of our flawed system for treating chronic psychiatric illness. As noted earlier in this chapter, a schizophrenic mother of five children was hospitalized and discharged a few days later based not upon clinical criteria but upon insurance company standards. In the not-too-distant past patients like Andrea Yates were committed to a state hospital where they remained for as long as necessary. Yates gained appropriate care only after she drowned her five children and was subjected to two capital murder trials.

The Yates case also exposed the corruption of our criminal justice system by electoral politics. There was no uncertainty as to the fate of this sick woman after she made the 911 call to the police. It was obvious that she would be confined to an institution for the rest of her life. What followed was legal gamesmanship. A prosecutor guided by a sense of justice and public interest would not contest Yates's insanity plea.

Harris County spent millions of dollars to satisfy the pursuit of publicity by prosecutors. The United States is the only country in the world where judges and prosecutors are elected and have the insatiable need for publicity. The erroneous claim by the prosecution's expert, Dr. Dietz, that Andrea Yates patterned her behavior after a nonexistent television show was the reason the appeals court granted a new trial. This led to an even more expensive trial with more publicity. Once again the prosecutor could have chosen not to oppose the insanity plea. The second jury found Andrea Yates legally insane but the end result would have been the same without any trial.

NOTES

1. Psychosis has been defined as "[a] severe mental disorder characterized by gross impairment in reality testing, typically shown by delusions, hallucinations, disorganized speech, or disorganized or catatonic behavior." *American Psychiatric Glossary,* 7th ed. (Washington D.C.: American Psychiatric Press, 1994).

2. Marc D. Hauser, a Harvard biologist, argues in *Moral Minds* (New York: HarperCollins, 2006) that there is biological basis for moral judgments.

3. Frans de Waal, *Primates and Philosophers: How Morality Evolved.* Princeton, NJ: Princeton University Press, 2006.

4. Comment 1 to Rule 3.09.

5. *Berger v. United States*, 295 U.S. 78 (1935).

6. *Dusky v. United States*, 362 U.S. 402 (1960).

7. Administration of forcible medication to criminal defendants to restore their competency to stand trial is evolving law. See Michael Perlin, *Mental Disability Law,* § 14.09 (Charlottesville, VA: Michie Co., 1989 & 1997 supp).

8. *Riggins v. Nevada*, 504 U.S. 129 (1992).

9. *Riggins v. Nevada*, pp. 9–10.

10. *Sell v. United States*, 539 U.S. 166 (2003).

11. Yates trial transcript.

12. Andrea Yates trial transcript, vol. 10, p. 38.

13. Leading questions are allowed on cross-examination, but they are prohibited during the direct examination.

14. Yates trial transcript, p. 140.

15. *Houston Chronicle*, February 28, 2002.

16. Trial transcript.

17. *Inside the Juror: The Psychology of Juror Decision Making*, edited by Reid Hastie. (Cambridge: Cambridge University Press, 1994).

18. *Kaplan & Sadock's Comprehensive Textbook of Psychiatry* (Philadelphia: Lippincott Williams & Wilkins, 2000).

19. Michael Perlin, *The Jurisprudence of the Insanity Defense* (Durham, NC: Carolina Academic Press, 1994).

20. Doing "what was right" is not a basis for the insanity defense. The idea of altruistic infanticide was based upon a paper based on a review of psychiatric literature on parental homicide of children that Resnick wrote during his training as a resident in psychiatry at University Hospitals of Cleveland in 1969, "Murder of the Newborn: A Psychiatric Review of Neonaticide," *American Journal of Psychiatry* 126 (1970): 58-64. The use of the term *murder* was fairly consistent in his paper. I always object to lawyers' use of that term during my testimony. *Homicide* is the appropriate term before the jury renders a verdict.

21. Yates trial transcript, p. 90. In a 2002 paper I delivered at the meeting of the American Academy of Forensic Sciences, I said, "One is forced to conclude that Dr. Dietz would have a different opinion if the delusion referred not to Satan, but to God." I believed that I was taking Dietz's position to an absurd level, but before long, my fantasy became reality. Dietz testified in the Deanna Laney case that she was insane because she killed her children at the direction of *God* (not Satan).

22. Yates trial transcript, p. 83.

23. Yates trial transcript, p. 86.

24. Yates trial transcript, p. 91.

25. Yates trial transcript, pp. 93–94.

26. Yates trial transcript, pp. 105–6.

27. Yates trial transcript, pp. 107–8.

28. Yates trial transcript, p. 95.

29. Yates trial transcript, p. 92.

30. *St. Augustine Confessions*, Oxford World's Classics (Oxford: Oxford University Press, 1998).

31. Karl Jaspers, *General Psychopathology* (Chicago: University of Chicago Press, 1963).

32. "Interview: Dr. Park Dietz," *Time*, March 19, 2002.

33. A Philadelphia prosecutor retained me to examine a woman who had killed her stepfather, transported his body from Philadelphia to Florida, and buried it.

The homicide was a rage response to sexual advances by the stepfather, which the woman had endured during her adolescence. The man's disappearance remained a mystery for years. On her wedding night, the young woman told her husband about killing her stepfather. The husband believed that this was justifiable homicide and persuaded his wife to go with him to the police station and confess. She was extradited from Florida to Pennsylvania and was charged with first-degree murder. The insanity defense was asserted by her defense lawyer.

I examined the woman in jail and concluded that the insanity defense was not justified, because she was not mentally ill. However, there was no basis for the first-degree murder charge either, because she killed her stepfather in a moment of rage. I told the prosecutor that I had good news and bad news. The good news for him was that I was of the opinion that the young woman had no basis for an insanity defense. The bad news was that I could not testify on behalf of the prosecution as long as she was charged with first-degree murder. It would have been unethical for me to testify against an insanity defense if the likely outcome was a first-degree murder conviction for someone who was obviously guilty of manslaughter. The charge was reduced to manslaughter, to which the young woman plead guilty.

34. Willis Spaulding, "Park Dietz: The Killing Expert Who Knows Too Much," *The Hook*, no. 0248, December 4, 2003.

35. Anastasia Touffexis, "A Conversation with Park Dietz: A Psychiatrist's-Eye View of Murder and Insanity," *The New York Times*, April 23, 2002.

36. Rich Daly, "Prison Mental Health Crisis Continues to Grow," *Psychiatric News* (October 20, 2006): 1.

37. Kaplan & Sadock's *Comprehensive Textbook of Psychiatry*, p. 1621.

38. Lisa Teachey, "Judge Will Formally Sentence Yates Today in Drownings of Her Children," *Houston Chronicle*, March 18, 2002.

39. On January 6, 2005, the Texas Court of Appeals reversed the convictions, because California psychiatrist and prosecution witness Dr. Park Dietz admitted he had given materially false testimony during the trial.

40. *Psychiatric News* 40, no. 30 (February 4, 2005).

41. Kenneth Dean, "Mother Sobs, Sings While in Jail," *Tyler Morning Telegraph*, May 11, 2003.

42. Casey Knaupp, "Prosecutors Touched by Emotional Trial," *Tyler Morning Telegraph*, April 10, 2004.

43. Transcribed from audio recording published under the auspices of AAPL.

44. Rick Casey, "Second Yates Expert Paid $242,966.74," *Houston Chronicle*, September 30, 2006.

45. Casey, "Second Yates Expert Paid $242,966.75."

EPILOGUE

As I write these words I am about to testify in the case of Harlan Drake in Owosso, Michigan. My testimony was scheduled tentatively for March 5, 2010, my eighty-second birthday. I testified in my first case of insanity defense in 1954 when I was a twenty-six-year-old psychiatry resident.

The cases of Harlan Drake and Andrea Yates expose the irrationality of the American criminal justice system in dealing with homicides perpetrated by psychotics. Harlan Drake was involved in an accident in 2004. A car with three teenagers drove in front of his eighteen-wheeler truck. Two of them died, one survived in a vegetative state. No one held Drake responsible for the accident. He was not issued a ticket by the police, who reassured him that he was not at fault. The families of the three youngsters did not blame him.

Drake became profoundly depressed and his depression continued for years until it reached psychotic proportions. His suicide attempts were unsuccessful. On September 11, 2009, Drake killed two people and attempted to kill a third. Drake shot one of his victims in broad daylight as the man carried a large sign depicting a dismembered fetus and the word abortion in front of a high school. Drake then proceeded to shoot a former employer of his mother seventeen times. When I examined Drake, he talked about the killings as if he had performed an ordinary daily chore. My opinion is that he attempted what is known as suicide-by-police, trying to provoke a deadly confrontation with the police.

Regardless of the outcome of his trial, Harlan Drake will spend the rest of his life in confinement in a psychiatric setting. The only issue of the protracted trial, which will consume considerable taxpayer funds, is the location of the psychiatric facility. If my testimony in support of an insanity defense fails, his confinement will be inside a prison system. In the unlikely event that the jury will find him insane, Drake will be confined to a psychiatric facility outside of prison. This was also the issue in the case of Andrea Yates. The injustice of the legal system and its irrationality is rooted in politics. Let me once again stress my opposition to the election of judges and prosecutors.

A second recurring theme in this book is the issue of the competence of lawyers and expert witnesses. The skill of professionals in the unique setting of a courtroom is rarely the focus of attention. Melvin Belli was known as the King of Torts, and there is no doubt that he was an outstanding personal injury lawyer; however, his defense of Jack Ruby was inadequate because he had no experience in criminal law. The law, like medicine, requires specialized knowledge. A trial lawyer differs from a legal advisor just as a surgeon differs from an internist. A criminal trial lawyer has different skills than an attorney whose trial practice involves personal injury litigation. In the hundreds of homicide cases in which I have testified, only a few defense lawyers had experience in defending homicide perpetrators. The fact that any licensed lawyer can take any case to trial ensures a high incidence of legal malpractice.

I participated in mandatory seminars for newly elected judges and was amazed by the variability of their professionalism. And many knowledgeable expert witnesses have limited or no testimonial skills, and the result is injustice. That was the case in the first trial of Andrea Yates. In a democratic society we cherish the pluralism of values, but we should not tolerate a high degree of variability of professional skills in licensed professionals.

This book focused on cases that showed the shortcomings of the American legal system. At the same time I am keenly aware of the fact that the law is the foundation of American society. The law has been evolving in America since colonial times. Every aspect of societal life is influenced by law. The injustice that I have described in these pages is only part of the story. This wonderful country has been, to a significant degree, shaped by law and lawyers. I hope that this book contributes to a better understanding of the legal system and to an improvement in the administration of justice.

INDEX

210; trial, 200–202, 205–7; verdict, appropriateness of, 207–9; verdict, reactions to, 209–12
Hinckley, John W., Sr., 202, 203
Hippocratic Oath, 259
Holbrook, John, 219
Holland, Judge, 225, 226
Hollywood, California, 204
Holmes, Sherlock, 178
Holocaust survivor, 3, 54, 56, 152
Holt, Diana, 163, 164, 165, 166, 167, 168
Holt, Rinehart, and Winston, 225
homicide, 1, 2, 4, 8, 32, 34, 60, 67, 71, 87, 97, 98, 101, 127, 133, 134, 138, 139, 141, 144, 147, 152, 173, 176, 195, 215, 219, 229, 233, 250, 255, 256, 257, 262, 268, 274; difference between murder and, 54; domestic, 191; egodystonic, 112, 113; egosyntonic, 112, 113; Europe, 39; impulsive, 21, 174; and insanity defense, 73, 196, 199; parental, 270n20; psychology of, 5, 38, 72, 111–14, 117, 123, 175, 177, 178, 188, 189, 190, 192, 216; by psychotics, 273; rational, 235; sexual, 163, 166, 271n34; spousal, 114–18, 122, 125, 174, 177, 180, 185, 189, 191; theories of, 178; and time, 113; type of weapon, 113–14; use of term, 270n20; varieties of, 109–26. *See also* murder; *specific individual cases*
The Hook, 261
Hopper, John, 203, 207, 208, 209, 213n13
Houk, Spencer, 172, 178
Houston, Texas, 231, 233, 235, 264, 268; Police Department, 238. *See also* University of Houston

Houston Chronicle, 240, 250, 260, 263, 267, 268
Hullett, William "Johnny," 40, 164, 165, 166, 167, 169
Hume, David, 34

Idaho, 200
Illinois, 3. *See also* Chicago; Elgin State Hospital
Illinois State Hospital, 199
Inbau, Fred E.: *Criminal Interrogation and Confessions*, 14
injustice: absolute, 13–16; relative, 17–18; roots of, 13–29
Inkster, Michigan, 84
inmate: concentration camp, 70; death of, 7; death row, 5, 27; disturbed, 33; fellow, 131, 166, 167; jail, 124, 199; mentally ill, 262; and sanity, 246; Starke Prison, 159
Innocence Project, 14, 15, 16, 27
innocent until proven guilty, 4
insanity, 8, 203; acquitted by reason of, 207, 209, 211; medieval England, 212n4; verdict, 45. *See also* insanity defense
insanity defense, 1, 3, 6, 8, 14, 18, 23, 34, 37, 39, 43, 45, 46, 48, 49, 63, 65, 67, 73, 87, 88, 89, 92, 93, 116, 128, 129, 168, 172, 196–200, 201, 206, 208, 210, 212, 273, 274; in Yates, 231–71, 274; in Ruby case, 215–29, 274; qualify, 133, 134, 150, 195;
Institute for Juvenile Research, 220
insults, 54, 57, 82, 90, 93
insurance companies, 9, 34, 40, 46, 48, 207, 232, 240, 268
Iowa, 35. *See also* Johnson County
Irving, Texas, 228

ABOUT THE AUTHOR

Emanuel Tanay, MD, is a highly regarded forensic psychiatrist who has served as an expert witness in the well-known cases of Jack Ruby, Ted Bundy, and Sam Sheppard. Dr. Tanay is a Distinguished Fellow of the American Academy of Forensic Sciences and of the American Psychiatric Association. A clinical professor of psychiatry at Wayne State University in Detroit, Dr. Tanay has taught widely in the United States and Europe and published numerous articles about forensic psychiatry, post-traumatic stress, and the Holocaust. He was a consultant to the German government regarding compensation to survivors of concentration camps. Dr. Tanay was Resident Scholar at the Department of Holocaust and Genocide Studies at Stockton College of New Jersey.

Dr. Tanay is the author of *Passport to Life: Reflections of a Holocaust Survivor*, an autobiography of his experiences in Europe during World War II and a series of essays about the roots of bigotry and genocide. He is a graduate of the University of Munich Medical School in Germany and completed an internship and residency in Illinois, as well as post-graduate work at the University of Michigan. Now retired from private practice, Dr. Tanay continues to write and lecture throughout the United States about forensic psychiatry and the Holocaust.

Breinigsville, PA USA
26 January 2011
254030BV00002BA/1/P

9 780765 707758